Foundational Learning
Insights from the Global South

Foundational Learning

Insights from the Global South

Edited by

Baela Raza Jamil, Felipe José Hevia de la Jara, Indrani Roy,
Ishmael Irungu Munene, Pauline Rose, Ricardo Sabates

Published by
Renu Kaul Verma
Vitasta Publishing Pvt Ltd
4348/4C, Ansari Road, Daryaganj
New Delhi-110 002
info@vitastapublishing.com

ISBN: 978-81-19670-53-6
© PAL Network
First Edition 2024

MRP ₹595

All Rights Reserved.
No part of this publication may be reproduced, stored in a retrieval system, or transmitted in any form, or by any means—electronic, mechanical, photocopying, recording or otherwise—without the prior permission of the publisher. Opinions expressed in this book are the contributors' own. The publisher is in no way responsible for these.

Coordinator: Rajarshi Singh
Vitasta Editor: Papri Sen Sri Raman
Layout and Cover by Somesh Kumar Mishra
Printed by Chaman Enterprises, New Delhi

TABLE OF CONTENTS

INTRODUCTION   **VII**
Felipe J Hevia de la Jara and Baela R Jamil

CHILDREN'S LEARNING AND WELL-BEING   1-119

In East and Southern Africa: Knowledge Adaptation Contextualising Teaching at the Right Level   **4**
Virginia Wanjiru Ngindiru, Zaida Mgalla,
Thato Letsomo, Mary Goretti Nakabugo and Amelia Ussene

In Times of Covid Pandemic: Innovations with a Play-based Approach for Foundational Learning   **30**
Anabel Velásquez-Durán, Samana Vergara-Lope Tristán,
and Felipe José Hevia de la Jara

Rebuilding with Mothers: How and Why do Mothers Engage with their Children's Education in Rural India?   **56**
Laura Cashman, Poorva Shekher, Ankita Jha and Preeti Manchanda

Evidence from Pakistan: Mitigating Learning and Development Losses for Children in Early Years   **82**
Hamza Sarfraz, Baela Raza Jamil and Saba Saeed

SYSTEMS, LEARNING AND TECHNOLOGY   121-217

Purpose-Driven Education Systems   **124**
Michelle Kaffenberger

Desired Code Vs Desirable Codes: Language Learning in a Multi-Cultural Context 136
Udaya Narayana Singh, Conchúr Ó Giollagáin, and Gordon Wells

PAL Network's ELTU Project: Foundational Learning Supported by Indigenous Resources Experiences 158
Adrián D Cetina Catzin, Winny Cherotich Ngeno, Indrani Roy, Rajarshi Singh, and Felipe Hevia de la Jara

A Scalable, Digital Learning Experiment: Analysing Children's Group Dynamics in Pratham's PraDigi Programme 185
Rajarshi Singh and Nishant Baghel

SCALING AND ROLE OF PARTNERSHIPS 219-293

An Education-Knowledge Bridge: Building Better by Advancing Evidence Use in Education 222
Suzanne Grant Lewis, Evangeline Nderu, Aleesha Taylor, and Randa Grob-Zakhary

Education Advocacy in Uganda: Capacity of Civil Society Organisations At Sub-national Level 244
Mary Goretti Nakabugo and James Urwick

The ALiVE Project in East Africa: Can Collaborative Action Drive Learning Outcomes? A Critical Examination 266
Florence Nansubuga, Purity Ngina, Mauro Giacomazzi, and John Mugo

REFERENCES 295

ABBREVIATIONS 335

ANNEXURES 339

EPILOGUE 347

BOOK EDITORS 351

ACKNOWLEDGEMENT 355

INTRODUCTION

Felipe J Hevia de la Jara and Baela R Jamil

This book brings together diverse yet practical perspectives to ensure that all children and adolescents, particularly those in the Global South,[1] are improving their foundational learning, especially after the COVID-19 pandemic around the world.

In recent decades, societies and their governments have made enormous efforts to ensure that all children and adolescents receive the education they need for life-long learning. However, in the twenty-first century, we have learned that it is not enough to go to school. Before the pandemic, we knew that a significant percentage of children were not attending school and that many of those who did attend school were not learning the minimum to at least continue their educational trajectories.[2] Therefore, 'schooling ain't learning', as said Pritchett in 2013.[3]

---

1. We use the concept of 'Global South' descriptively to refer to the countries and regions of Africa, Latin America and the Caribbean, and Asia, always with a view to promote south-south cooperation. Some discussions on these concepts can be found in (Dados & Connell, 2012; Gray & Gills, 2016).
2. In this regard, review the UNESCO's and World Bank reports, for example (UNESCO, 2018; World Bank et al., 2021) and the information that has been generated through the PAL network (Banerji, 2017; Banerji et al., 2013; Munene, 2021). Also the annual ASER Reports on the state of foundational learning in India.
3. (Pritchett, 2013).

School closures associated with the COVID-19 pandemic worsened the situation. In many African, Latin American, Caribbean and Asian countries, schools were closed for months or even years. As a result, it was estimated that decades of effort to get children into schools were lost. Moreover, these system-wide closures generated learning loss in practically the entire world. The losses were disproportionately higher in the Global South. Thus, the learning crisis in countries like India worsened after 2020.[4]

Due to this situation, the work being done by more than 17 organisations from Asia, Africa, and Latin America and those that form the People's Action for Learning Network (PAL Network) has become relevant. PAL's mission is 'To generate evidence through assessment and action to inform, influence and improve children's learning'. One of the actions to fulfil this mission is to systematise the experiences and generate evidence about PAL member organisations' actions to ensure fundamental learning.

This book incorporates the reflections and works of educational professionals, academics, and activists from the Global South into a discussion on education. The various chapters in this book pose some relevant questions: How to ensure fundamental learning? How to recover and accelerate it in a post-pandemic scenario? What were the emerging actions when schools closed their doors? How to promote learning in native languages? How to take advantage of not only new technologies but also of the 'old' methods? How to scale up the

---

4   UNESCO's institute of statistics shared a dashboard about school closures related with COVID-19 pandemic between 2020-2022 (UNESCO, 2022b).

existing systems? What roles do partnerships and collaborations play in education?

This introduction has two main objectives: 1) Identifying the significant reflections on education related to expanding the Right to Education and the learning crisis in the twenty-first century and 2) Analysing the relevance and pertinence of the texts that make up this book in these discussions.

Expansion of the right to education

Improving fundamental learning is part of expanding the Right to Education that has characterised the twenty-first century. Since its inception in the mid-twentieth century, the movement for the Right to Education has focused on the right to schooling, and ensuring that children attend school.[5]

This involved decades of effort by societies and their governments: building schools, providing teachers, printing educational materials, and, most importantly, enrolling millions of girls and boys in these new schools. This titanic

---

5   This process includes compulsory schooling in various countries in the eighteenth and nineteenth centuries. It also includes expanding educational systems linked with the generation of nation-states in the nineteenth and twentieth centuries in other regions of the world. See (Acosta, 2021; Maynes, 1985; Tröhler et al., 2011)"ISBN":"978-987-722-854-0","language":"spa","note":"OCLC: 1283852756","publisher":"CLACSO","publisher-place":"Buenos Aires","source":"Open WorldCat","title":"Derecho a la educación y escolarización en América Latina","editor":[{"family":"Acosta","given":"Felicitas"}],"issued":{"date-parts":[["2021"]]},"citation-key":"acostaDerechoEducacionEscolarizacion2021"}},{"id":20684,"uris":["http://zotero.org/users/474412/items/QM6ZIJIJ"],"itemData":{"id":20684,"type":"book","call-number":"LC191.8.E85 M39 1985","collection-title":"SUNY series on interdisciplinary perspectives in social history","event-place":"Albany","ISBN":"978-0-87395-976-6","language":"eng","note":"HOLLIS number: 990003820 130203941","number-of-pages":"ix+177","publisher":"State University of New York Press","publisher-place":"Albany","source":"hollis.harvard.edu","title":"Schooling in Western Europe: a social history","title-short":"Schooling in Western Europe","author":[{"family":"Maynes","given":"Mary Jo"}],"issued":{"date-parts":[["1985"]]},"citation-key":"maynesSchoolingWesternEurope1985"}},{"id":20671,"uris":["http://zotero.org/users/474412/items/S89VY2MU"],"itemData":{"id":20671,"type":"book","abstract":"This book is a comparative history that explores the social, cultural, and political formation of the modern nation through the construction of public schooling.

effort bore fruit in the second half of the twentieth century in the form of higher enrolment and improved access to schools. Additionally, this period also saw an increase in the number of years of schooling in various regions of the world.[6]

Despite these efforts, millions of children have not learned foundational skills such as reading and basic mathematics, even with multiple years of schooling. International literature refers to this phenomenon of schooling not translating into equivalent learning outcomes in many ways – educational crisis, learning gap and more recently, 'learning poverty'.[7] The definitions of these terms vary but share a central idea: There is a vast gap between what children are learning and what they should be learning, according to the school curricula of each country. This gap increases with each passing year and becomes more and more difficult to bridge as children grow older.

In some contexts, evidence of this learning gap sparked discussions and debates about the quality of education. Once the issue of access to schools had been more or less resolved, the quality of education had to be strengthened. This idea led to various educational reforms that focused on school autonomy and management, policies aimed at teacher training, and accountability.[8] Before 2020, it was believed that education systems could be improved by improving teacher recruitment and training processes, increasing societal pressure to achieve better results and establishing 'high consequence'

---

6   Ibid
7   On educational crisis, see (Banerji, 2014; Montoya, 2018; World Bank, 2018); on learning gap, see (Akmal & Pritchett, 2019; Vergara-Lope & Hevia, 2018; Writer, 2022) and Uwezo data from Kenya, Tanzania, and Uganda that test all children of given ages, whether in school or not, on simple measures of learning in math, reading (local language; on learning poverty, see (World Bank, 2019b, 2019a, 2021).
8   See, for intance (Honig & Rainey, 2012; Mayhew, 1990).

accountability systems.⁹ As a result, educational evaluation systems were created that sought to measure and compare progress in the quality of education. However, this perspective did not specifically address the fundamental learning gap. Instead, it incorporated this issue within broader proposals to 'improve the quality of education', seeking to increase scores on international standardised tests.¹⁰

In these discussions, the Right to Education expanded and broadened its goals to the Right to Schooling and the Right to Learn. This transition was evident in the most critical educational declarations at the turn of the century. Whereas in 1990, the Education for All by the Year 2000 declaration had focused on meeting basic learning needs through effective access to schools. The Dakar Framework for Action of 2000 specified that access to primary education should be free, compulsory, and of good quality. By 2015, the Education 2030: Incheon Framework for Action (SDG4) proposed to ensure inclusive and equitable quality education and promoting lifelong learning opportunities for all.¹¹

Sustainable Development Goal 4 (SDG4) and its targets and indicators are best understood against this background. Target 4.1 not only incorporates access to and graduation

---

9   See for example, (Anderson, 2005; Hanushek & Raymond, 2004). For a deep explanation about educative accountability, see (Hevia & Vergara-Lope, 2019).
10 See, for instance (Ball, 2015; Grek, 2009).
11 See (UNESCO, 2022a) Scientific and Cultural Organization. It seeks to build peace through international cooperation in education, the sciences, culture and communication. UNESCO's programmes contribute to the achievement of the Sustainable Development Goals defined in Agenda 2030, adopted by the UN General Assembly in 2015. Serving as a laboratory of ideas, UNESCO helps countries in adopting international standards and manages programmes that foster the free flow of ideas and knowledge sharing. In this spirit, it develops educational tools to help people live as global citizens free of hate and intolerance. UNESCO works so that each child and citizen has access to quality education.

from primary and secondary education but also states that this education should 'produce relevant and effective learning outcomes'. Thus, indicator 4.1.1 for this target defines the proportion of children and adolescents with minimum proficiency in reading and mathematics.[12]

Fundamental, lifelong learning for all

Guaranteeing an inclusive, equitable, quality and lifelong education requires, among many things, ensuring that all children, adolescents, young adults and adults secure fundamental skills. In general, foundational learning has focused on fundamental reading and mathematics because of their importance in building critical thinking, problem-solving and other fundamental skills both in and out of school. Thus, target 4.1.1 of the SDGs mentions that learning outcomes should be achieved at least in reading and mathematics. Nevertheless, there are other learnings that can be considered fundamental. Some of these are self-care, managing emotions, caring for the environment and digital skills.

Ensuring this range of fundamental learning requires, first of all, continuing coverage efforts and reducing school dropouts and exclusion. Secondly, it is necessary to ensure that all children, at an appropriate stage, acquire this fundamental learning that enables them to continue learning, both in and out of school. Here the role of the mother tongue in education comes into play. Literature points out the growing loss of languages or native tongues worldwide in recent decades, especially in the emerging countries in the Global South.

---

12   See (United Nations, 2022).

Therefore, talking about the wording of teaching and learning in the mother tongue also leads us to dwell on the importance of strengthening and revitalising the native languages.

Thirdly, specific actions are required to recover and accelerate learning that was not generated in the early stages or lost due to the pandemic and the closing of schools. Several organisations of the PAL Network have been pioneers in generating evidence-based, cost-effective, scalable and accessible practices that are being implemented in various parts of the world. Teaching at the Right Level (TaRL) and other Accelerated Learning Approaches based on TaRL philosophy, remote tutoring, learning camps, Citizen-led Assessments (such as ASER and Uwezo), and Large-scale Common Assessments (such as ICAN) are some key innovations conceived in the Global South by PAL Network and its members.

Finally, ensuring fundamental learning for all means educational inclusion, equity and social justice. Despite the increase in school enrollment, a disparity has remained between children who can read and those who cannot, even if they went to the same school, diminishing the function of the 'great social equaliser', so essential in achieving education for all.

As we shall see, these paths and implications are part of the questions this book aims to help resolve.

The organisation of the book

The chapters in this volume fall under three categories: Children's Learning and Well-being; Systems Learning and Technology; and, Scaling and the Role of Partnerships. Some of the writings deal with the period of the pandemic, others are about initiatives that were in place before the pandemic, and a few explore future pathways in education. The contributing authors come from policy, practice, and research domains. We have stitched their contributions together like a quilt to cover the essentials of how to build back stronger after the education crisis faced during COVID-19.

Even before the pandemic, several organisations that make up the PAL Network, as well as international organisations and academics from various universities, warned about an educational crisis. The research first generated by ASER, and later by Uwezo, Beekungo and Jadandoo in Asia and Africa was fundamental in understanding this problem and its intensity. Initiatives such as TaRL, first initiated in India, had already been successfully implemented in Africa to address the learning crisis. *In East and Southern Africa: Knowledge Adaptation Contextualising Teaching at the Right Level* describes the experiences in adapting TaRL by PAL Network members. The study describes how 'TaRL was adapted to improve foundational competencies in numeracy and literacy through programmes that applied school and/or community delivery models and were led by regular teachers at school and/or external facilitators'. Successful programmes like TaRL add to the evidence base that increases our understanding of the approaches that improve learning outcomes. This expanding evidence base is examined closely in the essay, *Purpose-Driven Education Systems*, which explores 'examples of education systems that have successfully shifted to being (more) coherent for learning, often resulting in large learning gains'.

One thing that makes education systems successful is collaboration among stakeholders such as civil society organisations, policymakers, teachers and parents. The role of civil society organisations and how this role can be better used for advocacy and raising educational awareness are issues looked at in *Education Advocacy in Uganda: Capacity of Civil Society*

Organisations At Sub-national Level. This work discusses how collaboration between Uwezo Uganda and its CSO partners work and the findings of a study on the usefulness and impact of such collaborations.

Another critical collaboration in the education sector is between partner organisations. Issues that cannot be handled individually can be addressed by using the shared resources and expertise of the partner organisations. *The ALiVE Project in East Africa: Can Collaborative Action Drive Learning Outcomes? A Critical Examination* studies and reflects on the 'collaboration process for developing contextualised assessment tools by the East African partner organisations'. The study also recommends best practices for collaborating partners to help them meet their goals successfully.

With the closure of schools, parents and caregivers became critical collaborators in implementing distance-learning programmes. As millions of children continued their studies outside of school, the learning environment at home became crucial. *Evidence from Pakistan: Mitigating Learning and Development Losses for Children in Early Years* presents an 'understanding of home-based learning' and identifies points that can be 'leveraged to ensure children's well-being and learning at a systems and household level'.

In Mexico, schooling was reinforced with educational innovations that were carried out by correspondents and teachers during the pandemic through a unique programme. The programme took a play-based approach to lessons in reading and mathematics. The implementation and the findings of these interventions are presented in *In times of Covid Pandemic: Innovations with a Play-based Approach for Foundational Learning*.

Some chapters in the volume are about interventions and innovations that were already in place when the pandemic struck. Analysing children's group dynamics and participation in Pratham's Pradigi Programme – a scalable, digitally-supported learning experiment in rural India – not just at a technology-based open learning programme but also explores the children's group dynamics, identity and learning. Pratham is one of the largest non-government organisations in India that is working in the education sector. These initiatives from Pratham and the schools showed us the role that technology can play in making education accessible for all.

Rebuilding with Mothers: How and Why do Mothers Engage with their Children's Education in Rural India? Takes a deep look at the dynamics between mothers of school-going children and the schools in rural India. As the lockdown forced children to be schooled at home, the role of mothers became critical. This study examines the reasons for the mother's engagement or non-engagement with their children's schooling. It hopes the 'findings can be used to devise efficient ways to better the mothers' engagements in improving their child's education in our post-COVID world'.

One of the reasons for the mother's lack of engagement with their children's education has been the medium of instruction. The difference between the medium of instruction and children's mother tongues is also believed to be the reason for significant school dropout rates. However, the difficulty lies in finding teaching-learning materials in the children's mother tongues. During the pandemic, PAL Network conducted a multi-language, multi-country project to create teaching-learning materials in the children's mother tongues, using language resources of these tongues. *PAL Network's ELTU*

Project: Foundational Learning supported by Indigenous Resources Experiences project talks about the motivation behind this exercise and how the project panned out.

The dissonance between children's language of learning and the language they need to use in their social context is discussed in *Desired Code Vs Desirable Codes: Language Learning in a Multi-Cultural Context*. The chapter advocates welcoming the children's home language into classrooms and explains how a 'mediating multilingual approach' in teaching could reduce the learning gap.

Like any crisis, COVID-19 also served as a learning exercise for the education sector. How could a similar crisis in learning be avoided in the future, and could the health sector, which was equally affected by the pandemic, provide answers? This is the question raised and discussed in *An Education-Knowledge Bridge: Building Better by Advancing Evidence Use in Education*. The study identifies 'what can be done to accelerate improvements in education by making more effective, the use of the evidence that should be driving education policy and practice….' It proposes an Education- Knowledge Bridge 'to lift experiences and voices into a sustainable evidence architecture'.

Aims, relevance and pertinence of the book

Coming at a time when the education sector has just entered the post-pandemic world, this book explores some critical issues that are related to children's foundational learning. These include the differences in foundational learning outcomes before and after the pandemic, proven processes of recovery and accelerating learning, and strategies to reduce learning gaps of children from marginalised communities.

As mentioned earlier, this volume brings together diverse

voices – academics, civil society leaders, activists, policy influencers and educational professionals. The writings in this volume add to a growing body of relevant knowledge on how to build back better after the pandemic. Furthermore, we have tried to create a Global South-North bridge to help us reflect on how to support the children's foundational learning outcomes, especially in developing societies.

Finally, we believe that we must take advantage of a very narrow 'window of opportunity' to position the backwardness of fundamental learning as a global and urgent problem that requires a wide range of alternative solutions. The pandemic, school closures and associated shocks to the education system and learners put a spotlight on the structural problems of many education systems. We present various interrelated strategies and processes to strengthen education and aid recovery from the learning loss resulting from closure of schools.

Through this volume, we wish to emphasise the importance and value of evidence-based policy and action, specifically how data from formative assessments can be used to improve learning and teaching practices, the importance of parental involvement in education, governments' willingness to prioritise the curriculum and establish recovery actions, and the position of international organisations such as the World Bank, UNESCO, and UNICEF regarding reduction of the 'learning poverty'. We hope the ideas and research shared in this volume will encourage fruitful discussions, debates, and, most importantly, effective action to help children learn better. We have consciously balanced academic rigour with experiences and learnings of practitioners to make this volume accessible to a broader audience-happy reading.

SECTION ONE

Children's Learning and Well-being

I. In East and Southern Africa: Knowledge Adaptation Contextualising Teaching at the Right Level
II. In times of Covid Pandemic: Innovations with a Play-based Approach for Foundational Learning
III. Rebuilding with Mothers: How and Why do Mothers Engage with their Children's Education in Rural India?
IV. Evidence from Pakistan: Mitigating Learning and Development Losses for Children in Early Years

THIS section brings voices from several countries in three continents, describing interventions and approaches for enhancing Foundational Literacy and Numeracy in children.

The first chapter in this section, *In East and Southern Africa: Knowledge Adaptation Contextualising Teaching at the Right Level*, presents systematic experiences from members of PAL Network. These members – Uwezo Tanzania, Uwezo Uganda, Youth Impact (Botswana), Facilidade (Mozambique) and Zizi Afrique (Kenya) – adapted and contextualised the Teaching at The Right Level (TaRL) approach pioneered by Pratham, India. The initiative aimed to improve children's basic literacy and numeracy skills in Grades 3 to 6 in their target geographies across Eastern and Southern Africa. This initiative reached over 41,000 students. The assessment tools used were aligned with the national basic curriculum expectations for the participating nations. The chapter also discusses the achievements of the programmes in light of improved literacy and numeracy skills, parental engagement, partnerships and teachers' professional development.

The second chapter, *In times of Covid Pandemic: Innovations with a Play-based Approach for Foundational Learning*, evaluates the impact of a series of educational innovations with a play-based approach based on the principles of CAMaL (Combined Activities for Maximised Learning) and TaRL. These interventions, built basic education and interest in reading and mathematics for young girls and boys from rural communities in Veracruz, Mexico. Correspondents and teachers implemented the innovations during the COVID-19 pandemic through the CIESAS-UV Special Programme, 'Independent Measurement of Learning (MIA)', under summer courses. The non-probabilistic sample included 301 participants between the ages of 6 and 12. An evaluation was done through questionnaires for facilitators, teachers, parents, children and adolescents. Results showed how the play-based approach and use of TaRL and CAMaL with the MIA project methodology had positive effects and helped in improving basic learning in reading and mathematics. The chapter also suggests that these interventions can be scaled through a co-construction model with communities and educational authorities.

The third chapter, *Rebuilding with Mothers: How and Why do Mothers Engage with their Children's Education in Rural India?*, considers why some parents do not – or cannot – offer learning support to their children. Findings indicated that while all mothers recognised the power of education, those with higher levels of education themselves were more likely to engage in school- and- home-based activities that supported their children's education. The qualitative element of this study attributes this finding to the various challenges that mothers with little or no education face, such as lower levels of self-efficacy and time and resource constraints. These barriers, alongside gender norms and a hierarchical school-community relationship, are also linked to the finding that all mothers, whether educated or not, were more likely to engage with home-based rather than school-based activities. The paper suggests that in the post-COVID scenario, when education systems are being rebuilt, mothers could continue to play a vital role in their children's education, as they had done during the school closures. However, to ensure this, stakeholders need to be aware of the obstacles that mothers, especially disadvantaged mothers, face.

Evidence from Pakistan: Mitigating Learning and Development Losses for Children in Early Years looks at the impact COVID-19 lockdown had on the early childhood (ages 3 to 7) education. This study investigates two questions related to children's learning and well-being. (1) What is the impact of COVID-19 on early years, and (2) What are the solutions to effectively fill the gaps in this area? MELQO (Measuring Early Learning Quality and Outcomes) tools for early years were used to collect evidence on home learning environments, socio-economic situations, child's well-being, teacher support, home learning practices, and distance learning. The evidence presented shows that during the school closures, parents engaged with children's academic and socio-emotional learning at home. There is also evidence of play-based learning emerging as a low-cost, low-tech sustainable solution for home learning and of such attempts made by teachers to ensure children's well-being during school closures. Yet, gaps remain in parents' capacity to support early years' pedagogy. The study identifies key nodes for further examination that can be leveraged to ensure children's well-being and learning at a systems and household level. It also presents systems-level and context-relevant policy suggestions.

In East and Southern Africa Knowledge Adaptation Contextualises Teaching at the Right Level

Virginia Wanjiru Ngindiru, Zaida Mgalla, Thato Letsomo, Mary Goretti Nakabugo, and Amelia Ussene

1. Introduction

The end of the Millennium Development Goals (MDGs) in 2015 was marked by notable improvements in access to education. The primary school net enrolment in developing countries stood at 91 per cent, up from 83 per cent. The period also saw the proportion of out-of-school children reduced by half, from 100 million in 2000 to 57 million in 2015. Sub-Saharan Africa reaped the greatest gains, recording a 20 per cent increase in net enrolment over 15 years (UN, 2015). Building on these gains, the Sustainable Development Goal (SDG) 4 shifted focus to ensuring inclusive, equitable and quality education and the promotion of lifelong learning opportunities for all children. Such a shift was necessary, given the evidence pointing to the gaps in learning, despite increased enrolment in the institutions of learning.

Children who fail to read by age ten are considered 'learning poor'. This inhibits their success in academics and later in their work life. Before COVID-19, 202 million children in Sub-Saharan Africa were experiencing learning poverty (UNESCO, 2017). Regional and country-level assessments, such as Uwezo assessments in East Africa, also showed that a significant proportion of children aged 6-16 years were not learning sufficiently.

Consistent with other assessments conducted in Kenya between 2011 and 2015, the Usawa Agenda learning assessment report showed that only 40% of learners in Grade 4 had met the reading expectations expected of them in Grade 3 (Uwezo, 2021). Reports from previous years showed that the proportion of children proficient in literacy and numeracy over the years stood at 40% in 2011, 37% in 2012, 41% in 2013 and 39% in 2014. There was significant inequality between children in marginalised and less-marginalised regions. For instance, compared to a child in the North-Eastern region, a child in Central Kenya was seven times more likely to excel in Grade 2 literacy and numeracy tasks (Uwezo, 2015).

A situational analysis report of basic literacy and numeracy levels at early grade levels in Botswana revealed a learning crisis even before COVID-19. A third of Grade 5 students in 2017 were unable to do basic subtraction, and a fifth of them were unable to read a simple paragraph. Although the children's literacy levels in Botswana are higher than in other African countries, with 60% of students able to read a simple story, it was found that only 10% of students were able to solve a simple division problem, revealing a greater need to address basic numeracy (Pansiri et al., 2017).

In Mozambique, a commitment to education has been made by abolishing school fees, giving direct support to schools and providing free textbooks at the primary level. Investments were also made in classroom construction, ensuring that the education sector receives over 15%, the highest share, of the state budget. As a result, there has been a significant rise in primary school enrolment over the past decade. Despite these efforts, the quality of education and improvements in learning continues to lag here. The 2013 national learning assessment found that only 6.3% of Grade 3 students had basic reading competencies. Further, a 2014 World Bank survey showed that only 1% of primary school teachers had the minimum expected knowledge, and only one in four teachers managed a two-digit subtraction. Absenteeism was high, 45% among teachers and 44% among directors, while about half of the enrolled students were absent on any given day (UNICEF Mozambique, 2017).

In Tanzania, Uwezo's citizen-led assessment report released in 2017 noted that literacy and numeracy skills among primary school children were still below the curriculum expectations across all grades. According to this report, 65% of those in Grade 3 and 28% of their counterparts in Grade 7 could not perform Grade 2 level tasks in literacy (English, Kiswahili) and numeracy. Notably, 52% of those in Grade 7 could not read a Grade 2 level story in English (Uwezo, 2017).

Uwezo Uganda's 2014 assessment report indicated that 9 out of 10 children assessed in Primary 3 could neither read nor comprehend a Primary 2 level story. Similarly, they could not solve Primary 2 level tasks up to division in numeracy (Uwezo, 2014).

The learning poverty, demonstrated by the data discussed above, needs to be reduced to strengthen the overall quality of the education systems in the countries under study. The 'Teaching at the Right Level' approach is one such initiative that is geared towards accelerating the acquisition of foundational competencies of literacy and numeracy. This paper presents systematic experiences from five countries and member organisations of the People's Action for Learning Network – Uwezo Tanzania, Youth Impact (Botswana), Facilidade - ICDS (Mozambique), Uwezo Uganda and Zizi Afrique (Kenya) – to show how Pratham's Teaching at the Right Level (TaRL) approach was adapted and contextualised to improve basic literacy and numeracy skills among primary school children in the ESA region.

The objectives of this paper are threefold: i) to demonstrate how different countries adapted TaRL for in-country implementation, ii) to discuss its impact on foundational literacy and numeracy learning outcomes and iii) to make recommendations for other organisations that were seeking to adapt the initiative to their contexts. Though TaRL has been adopted in various countries, there is a lack of documentation on how it works in Kenya, Uganda, Botswana, Mozambique and Tanzania. This paper hopes to address this aspect.

The paper is organised into five sections, with the first section introducing the status of learning in the focus countries. Section 2 presents a synthesis of literature and country-level adaptations of TaRL. Section 3 presents the methodology. Section 4 presents the discussion, and Section 5 presents conclusions and recommendations, respectively.

2. Background

The Millennium Development Goals (MDGs) promoted universal access to basic education – many countries acted to increase school enrolments. However, improvements in the quality of education outcomes have not kept pace. SDG 4 calls for a greater focus on inclusiveness, equity and quality in education. Learning outcomes feature prominently in SDG 4, with five targets and six indicators calling for data on learning outcomes and skills (UIS, 2018).

The gap between what children can do and what is expected of them often appears in the very first few years of school. The learning gap only increases with time. Children are expected to acquire foundational skills by Grade 2 or 3 so that they can negotiate more difficult content in higher grades. However, in most school systems, classroom teaching is guided by the need to cover an ambitious curriculum; thus, keeping pace with children's learning, especially struggling learners, is seldom prioritised (Banerji, 2017). Typically, children who lag fall farther behind.

2.1 Challenges and Status of Foundational Literacy and Numeracy Learning Outcomes in Kenya, Uganda, Tanzania, Mozambique and Botswana.

According to the World Development Report 2018 (WDR 2018), millions of students that year still lacked basic literacy and numeracy skills despite many years of schooling. The great schooling expansion had left some children behind, with gender, poverty, ethnicity, disability, and location cited as factors for disparities in learning. Pertinent to foundational learning, the report asserted that learning requires learners who are prepared and motivated. This can be achieved by investing in education in the early years as well as embedding remedial education programmes that assist those who need to catch up. The report also recommended providing effective teacher training programmes, which equip teachers to teach at the level of their learners, besides ongoing coaching and targeted professional development. In the following paragraphs, we discuss the challenges in the classrooms and the capabilities of the teachers in the five countries in focus.

Tanzania: An assessment done in 2017 showed that two-thirds (65%) of learners in Grade 3 and 3 out of 10 in Grade 7 had not acquired the literacy and numeracy competencies expected of them in Grade 2 (Uwezo, 2017). A follow-up report in 2019 pointed out similar gaps where only 15% and 47% of learners in Grade 3 and Grade 7, respectively, could read a Grade 2-level text in English. Mmasa & Anney (2016) commissioned a study which sought to interrogate the teachers' classroom practices in the teaching of literacy, examine the mastery of literacy skills in the Kiswahili language among learners in Grades 2 and 3, as well as document the challenges associated with literacy instruction in public schools in Tanzania. The study findings noted serious capacity gaps amongst teachers, hindering effective literacy instruction and resulting in 64% of learners in Grade 2 being unable to read, write or do simple numeracy. This was attributed to a delayed enrolment of learners in Grade 1; inadequate teaching and learning resources; low level of parents' education; shortage of literacy teachers while those available had adverse skill gaps in literacy instruction. The study recommended the need for professional learning for teachers teaching literacy as a measure to improve foundational literacy and numeracy learning outcomes.

Acknowledging the challenge of low learning outcomes, the Tanzanian government implemented a curriculum reform in 2015, focusing instruction on the 3Rs of reading, writing and arithmetic in Grades 1 and 2. This move saw increased time allocation for foundational literacy and numeracy instruction as a step towards improving the foundational learning outcomes during the early years of schooling. As a result, Rodriguez-Segura and Mbiti (2022) established that the policy increased learning by approximately 0.20 standard deviations in Kiswahili and numeracy test scores one year into the reform. The most significant changes were attributed to timely teacher training in the new curriculum.

Kenya: Following the introduction of the Free Primary Education (FPE) policy in Kenya in 2003, despite access, completion rates increased from 63% in 2002 to 81% in 2007, four years into the FPE policy (Chuck, 2009). Reflecting on universal access to education for all vis-à-vis this financial investment, Oketch et al. (2014) concluded that many learners were in schools but not learning, with most of the poor ones excluded from universal public access. Similarly, the Uwezo assessments showed that only 40% of children aged 7-13 years were proficient in Grade 2 literacy and numeracy tasks (Uwezo, 2015), with notable regional disparities. For instance, the North-Eastern region recorded dismal levels in performance, access, retention, adult literacy and school readiness (Uwezo, 2015) compared to the Central Kenya region.

A study by Wangia et al. (2011) highlighted key challenges in teacher preparation and ongoing support and showed how this impacted instruction and acquisition of foundational literacy outcomes. Among the gaps noted were: i) lack of effort to interrogate the quality of teachers and how the teacher education curriculum can be changed; ii) dissonance between the teacher education curriculum design and implementation, which compromises on moulding reflective teachers; iii) a teacher education curriculum that was heavy on theoretical content knowledge rather than skills for effective teaching of reading; and iv) little focus on early reading and mathematics in the continuous professional development programmes.

Uganda: The Uwezo report (2014) in Uganda noted the near triple increase in the number of children enrolling in primary schools, from 3.06 million in 1996 to 8.4 million by 2013. By 2014, the aspiration of the government in Uganda was that all those enrolling in Primary 1 complete the entire primary cycle on time with quality outcomes. Contrary to this objective, the system experienced longstanding bottlenecks in realising these aspirations. For instance, only 31% of those who enrolled in Primary 1 in 2008 completed the cycle in 2014. Among the few who completed the cycle and sat for the national primary examinations, 12% did not pass. The results of the Uwezo learning assessments conducted between 2011 and 2013 showed that only 1 out of 10 of those assessed in Primary 3 could read and comprehend a Primary 2 level story as well as solve a Primary 2 level numeracy task. Among the factors that had an impact on the learning outcomes were access to Early Childhood Development & Education (ECDE), parental involvement in learning and the literacy level of the mothers (Uwezo, 2014).

Mozambique: Inputs alone do not improve learning outcomes. In Mozambique, despite infrastructural investments in schools, and a 15% share of the budget invested in education, learning outcomes are still low. The 2013 national learning assessment found that only 6.3% of Grade 3 students had basic reading competencies. This situation was worsened by poorly-skilled teachers, where only 1% of primary school teachers demonstrated minimum expected knowledge, and only 1 out of 4 were proficient in 2-digit subtraction (World Bank, 2014). Absenteeism of teachers (45%), directors (44%) and learners impede quality learning (UNICEF Mozambique, 2017). Shockingly, the teachers' knowledge of Maths, language and pedagogy was only 29% (UNICEF Mozambique, 2020). Due to these inefficiencies in the system, only 45% of children completed primary education.

2.2 Teaching at the Right Level (TaRL) Approach

Like many other countries, such as the ones mentioned above, India too contends with the reality of low learning outcomes among school-going children. The 2015 ASER report (ASER Centre, 2005) showed that 39% of those in third grade could not read second grade-level text. On the other hand, there was evidence showing that interventions which target the teaching to the existing learning levels of learners have a large positive impact on learning levels (Banerjee et al., 2011, cited in Jukes, Sitabkhan, and Tibenda, 2021).

To address the issue of low learning outcomes, Pratham began designing and implementing programmes which focused on providing children with basic skills by tailoring the teaching to the children's learning levels (Banerji et al. 2016). In 2001 J-PAL (Abdul Latif Jameel Poverty Action Lab), a global research centre, and Pratham partnered to investigate the impact of Pratham's Balsakhi programme. Under this programme, children from Grades 2 to 4 who struggled with the curriculum, were taken out of their regular classes for two hours a day. During this time, the focus was on improving their basic reading and mathematics skills. Due to this intervention, their learning outcomes improved by 0.14 standard deviations in the first year and 0.28 standard deviations in the second year. This was the beginning of a long learning partnership between Pratham and J-PAL, and the start of what is now known as Teaching at the Right Level (TaRL). Since then, Pratham has partnered with J-PAL affiliated professors to rigorously evaluate, adapt, and improve TaRL models, which can be efficiently scaled (Banerjee et al., 2007).

The TaRL approach is designed primarily for learners who have completed second grade yet are lagging in their expected level of literacy achievements. The main aim of the intervention is to build basic reading and math skills among these children. The core elements of the TaRL approach include i) establishment of level-wise groups; ii) explicit learning goals for each group; iii) tailored teaching techniques, and iv) periodic tracking of progress (Banerji & Duflo, 2015, cited in Alcott et al., 2018). Instructors/implementers receive training to prepare them for implementation, onsite mentoring support and refresher training as need be. Furthermore, the project team does ongoing monitoring, including periodic reviews, conducts discussions and shares experiences (Banerjee et al., 2016).

2.3 Contextualising Teaching at the Right Level to Accelerate Learning Outcomes

Researchers such as Jukes et al. (2021) and Hoyle (1969, cited in Jukes et al.) have noted a mismatch between efforts to reform pedagogy and the culture of many low- and middle-income countries. This is attributed to the technical view of teaching that perceives the teacher as an implementer of proven teaching techniques, ignoring the reality that teachers have agency and the decisions they make while teaching are informed by the social and cultural context in which they operate.

Further, Jukes et al. (2021) recommended that any pedagogical approach should be analysed at the level of pedagogical principles and underlying learning theories. Therefore, it is imperative to subject pedagogical innovations that have been tried and tested from a different locale to a contextualisation process to determine the applicability of the principles that have been applied and which achieve contextual relevance.

Among the response actions adopted by different countries to address the challenge of low learning outcomes, compounded by the increased student enrolments, were different adaptations of the Teaching at the Right Level approach. This followed the success of TaRL in India, where the initial pilots improved student test scores by 0.28 standard deviations by the second year of implementation, with incremental impact over the years (TaRL Africa, 2023). The TaRL approach was contextualised for each country to address the low foundational literacy and numeracy outcomes in a manner that was relevant to the particular country.

While retaining the four core elements of TaRL, Ghana adapted TaRL, opting for a teacher-led implementation model, in which teachers apply principles of assessment and level-wise grouping in classrooms rather than deploying extra personnel to deliver the remediation sessions. This approach had modest results on the learning outcomes while positively contributing to increased teacher attendance (Davidson et al., 2022).

In Zambia, the government piloted a TaRL intervention with three model variations, including 20-hour lessons per term, 20-hour sessions during school holidays and a staggered model in which learners were met daily for an hour over two school terms. In line with the principle of aligning pedagogical principles to the realities of the context, Zambia scaled up the third approach in which intervention was spread over two school terms. This followed the prevalent challenge of finding time within the school schedule to conduct remediation sessions. However, the overall principles of assessment, level-wise grouping, targeted instruction and reskilling of implementers were retained (Davidson et al., 2022).

Table 1 provides a summary of how different countries adapted TaRL to their contexts.

Though the available literature summarised in the table lacks specific details on how the countries adapted the four

Table 1: Summary of TaRL Models by Country in Africa

Country	Details of the Intervention	Duration of Intervention	Impact
Ghana	• The two models adopted include Teacher Community Assistant Initiative (TCAI) and the STARS. Implementation of the former was led by high school graduates (teacher community assistants) while STARS was led by teachers. • Whereas the TCAI duration wasn't clear, in the STARS model, children were taken out of regular classes for 4-hours per week to study English and 1-hour per day to study mathematics.	• The in-school and after-school durations of the TCAI variation are unclear. However, for STARS, the intervention lasted for 12 weeks.	• The impact varied across the various models of the TCAI. Overall, the different variations yielded an 18% increase in the local language and a 10% increase in English scores. • The model that applied only targeted instruction resulted in improved English and math scores by 0.07 standard deviations. • The model, which combined targeted instruction plus management coaching, increased the outcomes by 0.13 standard deviations.
Zambia	• The programme targeted learners in Grades 3 to 5 in literacy and numeracy and was implemented by teachers in the focus schools.	• The three variations were 20-hours over a school term, 20-hours during school holidays and 1-hour daily after school over two terms.	• The proportion of children who could read a basic story increased from 34% to 52% in literacy. • The proportion of those proficient in two-digit subtraction increased from 32% to 50%.
	• The three variations implemented were i) 1-hour daily of targeted instruction for 20 days during the school term, ii) a 20-day intensive model during the holiday break and iii) daily 1-hour lessons after school over two school terms.		

Cote D'Ivoire	• Though the specific details of the model are unclear, the programme targeted learners in Grades 3 to 6, exposing them to 1.5-hours of daily combined sessions in French and Mathematics. • Trained government mentors and teachers facilitated the sessions.	• The intervention involved 1.5-hours of French and Mathematics every day (combined)	• The proportion of learners proficient in reading a paragraph increased from 14% to 51%. • The proportion proficient in simple subtraction increased from 12% to 63%.

TaRL components, they all applied assessment-informed targeted instruction, ability-wise grouping and periodic tracking of progress to determine the impact. The literature also demonstrated that despite the varied models of implementation, there was a notable improvement in basic literacy and numeracy outcomes. For instance, the Ghana implementation resulted in an 18% increase in literacy proficiency, an increment similar to that of Zambia, where proficiency of story readers increased from 34% to 52% (+18%).

3. Methodology

This paper is a systematic synthesis of efforts by five members of the PAL Network (Botswana, Kenya, Uganda, Tanzania and Mozambique) to customise the TaRL approach to the context of East and Southern Africa, while also outlining the impact on foundational learning outcomes in literacy and numeracy. The paper applies a descriptive study design. This type of design is useful for describing the desired characteristics of a sample being studied and allows generalisation of the findings for a larger target population (Omair, 2015).

Regarding the different interventions, the organisations submitted write-ups detailing how they tweaked their programmes in light of the four core elements of the TaRL approach. This information was then summarised and presented in section 4.1. Furthermore, each organisation provided data on the programme's reach and impact on the children's foundational learning outcomes. To determine progress, the learning outcomes data was presented as a comparison between baseline and endline, and the proportion of learners in each level was compared. These statistical summaries were then presented in the form of graphs and tables.

The illustration is a model of how progression was incrementally tracked across the two subjects:

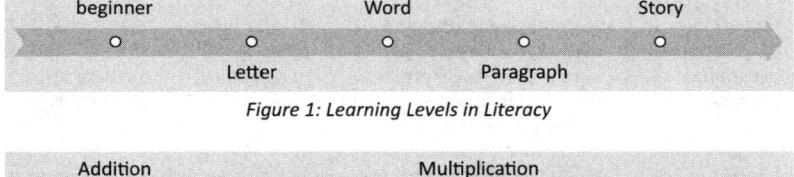

Figure 1: Learning Levels in Literacy

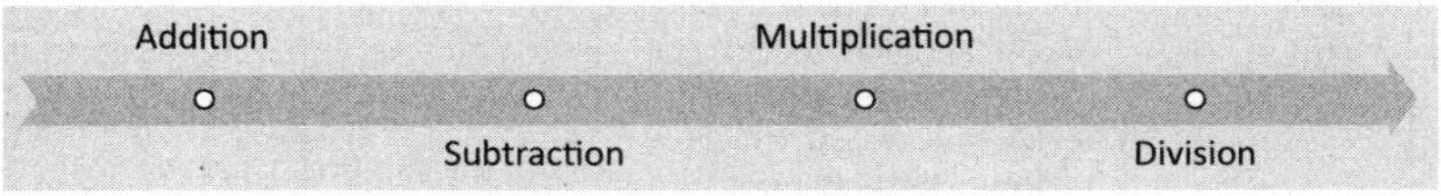

Figure 2: Learning Levels in Numeracy

4. Discussion

4.1 Contextualising TaRL in Kenya, Uganda, Botswana, Mozambique and Tanzania.

The journey of contextualising TaRL in Africa began with an experiential workshop in India in 2017, followed by a material development workshop in Nairobi, Kenya, in 2018. The latter was attended by over 50 participants from seven countries, who, over ten days, immersed themselves into the TaRL approach in terms of steps for implementation and material development processes, coupled with practice sessions at schools. Post the workshop, many countries launched TaRL-like initiatives. Organisations such as TEP (The Education Partnership) centre in Nigeria and Building Tomorrow are among those not covered in this paper but whose inspiration came from the Nairobi workshop (TaRL Africa, 2018).

In discussing the contextualisation process, below is a summary of how the various countries designed their interventions, keeping in mind the core elements of the TaRL approach:

Table 2: Summary Intervention Models by Country

Country	Details of the Intervention	Duration of Intervention	Impact
Kenya (Accelerated Learning Programme). **Grades** 3 to 5	• Implemented in schools by Teacher Assistants. These were trained teachers who were directly engaged by the programme to support the partner schools. Before implementation, teacher assistants were retooled for six days on assessment-informed instruction. • The learning intervention lasted two hours daily - one hour each for literacy and numeracy sessions. In literacy, the programme intervention was conducted in Kiswahili and English. • Learning took place within school hours. • At the County level, trained programme officers provided mentoring support and ongoing monitoring during implementation. • Periodic assessments were conducted using Uwezo Kenya assessment tools.	30 – 50 days for each subject (literacy and numeracy).	Over 25,000 learners in 150 schools in 3 sub-counties.

Uganda (Action for Learning Initiative). **Grades** 3 to 6	• Adopted a hybrid of a community-school approach, which was volunteer-led and implemented at the school level. • Volunteers were trained for five days ahead of implementation. • Sessions lasted 1 to 2 hours during the school day, after school hours or over the weekend. The focus was on English reading. • Trained officials provided onsite monitoring and mentoring to the volunteers, supported data collection and evaluation as well as helped strengthen the connections between various district offices, schools and communities.	25-40 days for literacy intervention.	675 learners. Five schools (2 of these in refugee settlements and 3 in the host communities).
Botswana (TaRL) **Grades** 3 to 5	• Botswana implemented a direct delivery model by engaging young unemployed youths, mostly graduates, to deliver the TaRL numeracy sessions. • Through the government model, Youth Impact (formerly Young love) engaged teachers or national programme	30 days for numeracy.	10.074 learners in 4 districts.
	Service participants and government interns in schools as teacher assistants. • Facilitators were trained for 5-days in numeracy, followed by 2-days refresher training after every block of implementation. • Each school had an assigned mentor supported by a regional coordinator in charge of 10 schools.		

Mozambique (Wiixuutta Nithweelaka – learning while playing). **Grades** 3 to 5	• In Mozambique, TaRL was implemented in public primary schools in partnership with the provincial department of education. • TaRL sessions were integrated into the language and mathematics lessons for 2-to 3-hours per day. • The sessions were conducted by Grade 3 to 5 teachers and facilitators recruited by Facilidade, the implementing entity. • The target was in literacy (reading in Portuguese) and Mathematics. • Implementing teachers participated in a 5-day training.	50 days	690 learners in 1 district.
Tanzania (Jifunze) **Grades**	• Uwezo Tanzania implemented a school model in public schools in partnership with government officials in 6 districts. • The focus was on children in Grades 3 to 6, lagging in Kiswahili (literacy) and numeracy competencies. • Sessions ran for 1-to 2-hours daily, with a facilitator: pupil ratio of 1:45. However, in any given school there were two facilitators – a government teacher and a volunteer engaged by the programme. • Teachers received 6-days of training, 3 in each subject (literacy/numeracy).	30 days for each subject	10,000 learners in 30 schools in six districts.

Reflecting on the four core elements of the TaRL approach, it is evident that the interventions are inspired by TaRL. Notably, even when these main aspects were retained, country-level decisions were made regarding each of them as described below:

i. **Establishment of level-wise groups:** The standard Pratham approach in literacy was to group learners into either beginner, letter, paragraph, or story levels. While these learning levels were retained in the literacy interventions, the ESA intervention (Engage, Study, Activate) did not include children at story levels. They were considered to have acquired the basic minimum reading skills and would attain higher-order skills with practice. Also, the grouping in numeracy was different from Pratham. Whereas at Pratham, grouping in numeracy was done by number recognition, the numeracy interventions in Kenya, Botswana, Tanzania and Mozambique were done based on the ability in mathematical operations.

ii. **Explicit learning goals and tailored teaching techniques:** Consistent with the TaRL in India, all programmes adopted goal-setting and targeted-reskilling of teachers, ensuring that learning experiences matched the individual learning levels of the targeted children.

iii. **Periodic tracking of progress:** Progress was tracked through assessments conducted at the end of every camp cycle. For instance, in Mozambique, there were two assessments within 50 days (at the end of each 25-day phase), whereas, in Kenya and Tanzania, the assessment was conducted after every ten days. Though Botswana used the ASER assessment tools, Kenya, Uganda, Mozambique, and Tanzania each used adapted versions of ASER in their countries. These tools were developed in line with country-level curriculum expectations for Grade 2.

iv. **(Re)skilling of implementers was critical prior to implementation:** Implementers across the countries varied in number, minimum academic qualification and duration of their training. There was also a variation in the number deployed per institution and mentorship support structure during implementation. The next table highlights how various countries organised their training programmes for volunteers/teacher assistants:

Table 3: Summary of Training Approaches by Country

Country	Description of the training and mentoring support structure for implementers.
India	• Instructors trained for ten days in literacy and ten days in numeracy.
Botswana	• Five days in numeracy only. • Two days' refresher after every round of assessment (usually 15 days). • One mentor assigned per school, and a regional coordinator oversees ten schools.
Tanzania	• Six days of training for both literacy and numeracy. • Mentoring conducted by ward and district officials.
Kenya	• Six days of initial induction (3 days each for literacy and numeracy modules). • 2-day refresher training at the end of the first three months. • Mentoring support provided by trained programme officers.
Uganda	• Volunteers trained for five days total in literacy and numeracy. • Government officials, including head teachers and class teachers, provided mentorship support.
Mozambique	• Five days of training for both literacy and numeracy.

It is evident that the focus, duration and structure for providing ongoing support to implementers varied by country. The number of days dedicated to inducting the implementers into the TaRL approach was shorter across all countries compared to what was originally done in TaRL in India. Even with much shorter training, the programmes delivered significant impact, as demonstrated in the later sections of this paper.

4.2 Impact on Literacy and Numeracy Learning Outcomes
4.2.1 Overall Programme Reach by Country

Table 4 summarises the reach of the various programmes. The five interventions impacted 41,739 learners in Grades 3 through Grade 6 in 15 districts. Kenya reached the highest number of learners, followed by Tanzania and Botswana. Mozambique and Uganda had the least reach, respectively. This varied reach shows the various stages of different interventions, which limits the comparison of data across countries. Impact on learning is therefore discussed per country.

Table 4: Programme Reach by Country

Country	District(s)	Children reached
Botswana	North East; South East; Khatleng; Chobe	10,074
Mozambique	Larde	690
Tanzania	Ludewa, Mbarali, Kilolo, Chamwino, Mvomero and Kisarawe	12,000
Uganda	Yumbe	675
Kenya	Bungoma, Turkana and Tana River	18,360
	Total	41,739

4.2.2 Literacy Outcomes by Country

Four out of the five countries (Kenya, Mozambique, Tanzania and Uganda) conducted literacy interventions to equip learners to read with comprehension. At baseline, learners who were at beginner (hawezi), letter (silabi), word (maneno) and paragraph (aya) levels were targeted for remedial sessions, with the goal of moving them to story (hadithi) level, the highest level in the assessment tool, and which marked that a learner had achieved basic proficiency in literacy that was expected of them in the intervention.

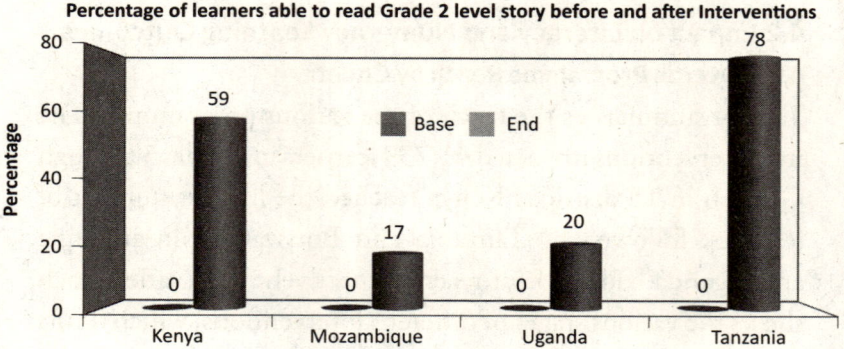

Figure 3: Literacy Proficiency Levels by Country

Figure 3 shows the proportion of learners who attained story-level proficiency during the various interventions. The baseline (BL) percentages are at zero because learners at the story level, at baseline did not participate in the learning intervention. However, in the endline (EL), a sizeable proportion had progressed to the story level, with Tanzania recording the highest achievement at 78%. The intervention in Tanzania was in Kiswahili, which is also the national language, and this may partly explain the higher scores compared to the other countries. Kenya recorded the second highest proportion of learners reading at the story level, in Kiswahili at 59% within 30 days. In Uganda, 20% of those in the intervention could read at story level after 30 days, whereas in Mozambique, after 45 days of intervention, 17% of learners involved could read a story.

Table 5 depicts the distribution of learners across various literacy levels at baseline and endline. The beginner level is the lowest (denoting learners who cannot identify letters/letter sounds or syllables). The letter, word, paragraph and story levels denote learners who were proficient readers in these levels at baseline and end line.

Table 5: Progression in Literacy Learning Levels by Country and Timeline

	Beginner/ hawezi		Letter/silabi		Word/ maneno		Paragraph/ aya		Story/ hadithi	
	BL	EL	BL	EL	BL	EL	BL	EL	BL	EL
Kenya	27%	2%	21%	6%	25%	14%	28%	18%	0%	59%
Mozambique	42%	11%	27%	32%	15%	29%	8%	9%	9%	19%
Uganda					22%	61%	8%	41%	5%	20%
Tanzania*	Missing data									

In Kenya, the 27% of learners in the beginner category reduced to only 2%, implying that the majority had progressed to higher reading levels by the endline. The scenario was similar at letter/syllable, word and paragraph levels. Since there were no learners at the story level in the intervention at baseline, data in the table shows that 59% of those reached attained proficiency in story reading.

Similar trends were observed in Mozambique, where the beginner category reduced from 42% at baseline to only 11% at endline. Those who could read words increased from only 15% at baseline to 29% at endline, whereas at the story level, the proportion of proficient readers increased from 9% to 19%.

On the other hand, Uganda recorded higher increases in the proportion of learners who could read words, a 39 percentage points increase from 22% to 61%. At paragraph levels, whereas only 8% were proficient at baseline, it increased to 41% at the endline. There was a 15-percentage points margin of increase in the proportion of those who could read a simple story, from 5% at baseline to 20% at endline.

This paper does not seek to compare the margin of progress across countries. However, from the foregoing discussion, it is evident that despite the varied modifications applied to the design of the programmes, improvement in learning is possible within a relatively short time.

4.2.3 Numeracy Outcomes by Country

As with literacy, numeracy results were also obtained and are summarised in Figure 4. The focus of all numeracy interventions was to ensure that enrolled learners acquired proficiency in the four basic operations – addition, subtraction, multiplication, and division. The addition and subtraction concepts involved regrouping.

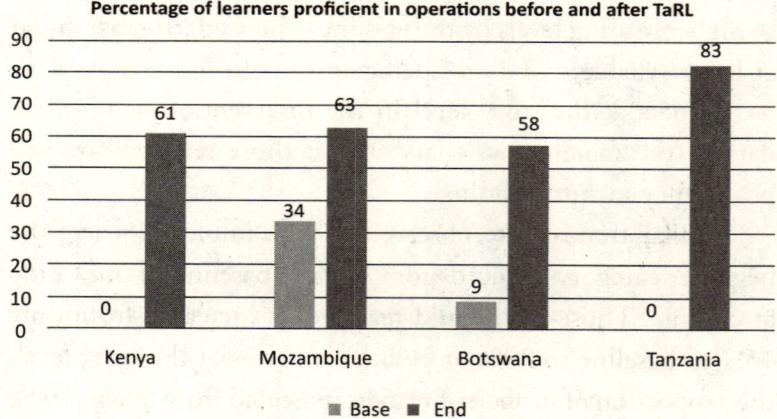

Figure 4: Comparison of Numeracy Learning Levels at Baseline and Endline

As seen in Figure 4, Tanzania recorded the greatest gains in numeracy, with 83% of those in the intervention reaching the division level within 30 days. Kenya followed closely with 61% of learners proficient in the four operations by the end of 30 days. In Mozambique, the proportion of learners who could multiply increased from 34% at baseline to 63% at the endline, whereas in Botswana, the number increased from 9% at baseline to 58% at the endline.

As with literacy, this paper notes that despite the differences in the duration of facilitator training, duration of numeracy learning interventions, the language used during interventions and structure of implementation, there was commendable progress made in reducing the proportion of innumerate learners.

Though this paper does not seek to demonstrate attribution and contribution, it is worth noting that the numeracy intervention in Tanzania was also conducted in Kiswahili, the national language and a language familiar to most learners, even at home. This may explain the high levels of achievement; though further research may be needed to ascertain this.

5. Conclusion and Recommendations

Research evidence posits that many pedagogical reforms fail to achieve effectiveness when applied in different contexts due to the failure in considering the cultural context. In their paper, Jukes et al. (2021) noted that the process of adapting pedagogy should consider the contextual realities, including the behaviour of teachers and students while adhering to fundamental principles of effective learning that is proposed in any pedagogical approach.

It is on this basis that this paper sought to profile the various models of implementing TaRL in Botswana, Kenya, Uganda, Tanzania and Mozambique and reflect on the gains made in foundational learning outcomes. The adaptations and modifications ranged from a shortened duration of facilitator training (a decision made in light of available resources), the duration of intervention as expressed through the number of days, languages adopted, the facilitator-learner ratio as well as the range of resources assembled for the intervention.

Consistent with the research recommendations of retaining the pedagogical principles while adapting any approach to the local context, the five programmes yielded the same goal – improved learning outcomes. The interventions retained the core elements of TaRL while also tweaking the implementation structure as per the different country contexts. Though the paper does not go into the details of each core element's contribution level or in any way attempts to compare the gains across programmes, the data shows some promise in the feasibility of adapted TaRL in reducing learning poverty.

Experiences from the programmes demonstrated that by equipping teachers with the skills necessary for assessment-informed instruction and level-based pedagogies, adapting resources and learning activities to the local context as well as dedicating time for remediation, learners lagging in their foundational competencies can be supported so that they can level up to the average student within a relatively short period. As the data from the countries show, most programmes were designed to last between 30 and 60 days, during which over half the learners involved acquired the desired competencies.

The literature reviewed cited teacher capacity as a key barrier to effective foundational learning. Studies in Kenya and Uganda highlighted teacher capacity as an area of improvement for the countries to achieve the desired levels of learning during the early years. From Table 3, it can be seen that reskilling teachers in assessment and level-based instruction was a key consideration and one of the factors in the programmes that resulted in improved outcomes. This shows that when given due attention, reskilling teachers and setting aside time for remediation could work towards alleviating learning poverty.

The paper recommends further research to establish the

level of contribution and attribution of the various elements in the results shared. Particularly, the language of instruction vis a vis the language used during remediation as well as the language of the content, duration of facilitator reskilling/ training and onsite support and the contribution each of these had in the posted results.

In Times of Covid Pandemic Innovations with a Play-based Approach for Foundational Learning

Anabel Velásquez-Durán, Samana Vergara-Lope Tristán and Felipe José Hevia de la Jara

1. Introduction

In its plan Nacional de Desarrollo 2019-2024 (National Development Plan), the Mexican government committed to ensuring access to education and improving infrastructure and conditions in schools (Presidency of the Republic of Mexico, 2019). Likewise, through the Secretaría de Educación Pública (Ministry of Public Education), it aimed to provide excellent education with equity, universality and completeness, with the goal that by 2030 all Mexicans receive a modern, quality education that allows them to acquire knowledge, skills and also values (Secretariat of Public Education [SEP], 2021). The government sought to promote education for life under the approach of learning to learn, continuous updating, adaptation to changes and lifelong learning.

In addition, the Nueva Escuela Mexicana - NEM (New Mexican School) aimed to reverse the historical backwardness and improve students' knowledge acquisition and develop skills and abilities in basic areas such as communication, mathematics and science. It focussed especially on 0 to 23 years of age, promoting inclusive, multicultural, cooperative and equitable learning in the school career of children, adolescents and youth, that is, from birth to the completion of their education, taking into account the regional context (SEP, 2019). To ensure equal learning opportunities for all, the NEM involved the community in the teaching and learning process and prioritised children and youth in vulnerable contexts. However, Mexico has historically seen low student performance on various international, regional, and national tests.

The OECD's Programme for International Student Assessment (PISA) is a triennial survey of 15-year-old students (secondary school) that assesses the extent to which they have acquired the knowledge and skills necessary for full participation in society. In 2018, Mexican students performed below the OECD average in reading, mathematics, and science: (a) only 1% achieved the highest levels of performance in at least one area (while the OECD average is 16%), and (b) 35% did not achieve even a minimum level in the three areas mentioned (while the OECD average is 13%). In reading, 55% scored at least Level 2, i.e., they could identify the main idea in a medium-length text, find information using clear criteria, and think about the purpose and form of texts when explicitly asked to do so.

In mathematics, 44% scored at Level 2 or higher, meaning they could interpret and recognise how to represent a simple situation mathematically without direct instruction (Organisation for Economic Cooperation and Development [OECD], 2019). In addition to this, learning poverty, which tracks the percentage of 10-year-old children who are unable to read a simple sentence, was 48% in Latin America (Azevedo, 2020; Azevedo et al., 2020), and 43.2% in Mexico, before the pandemic (World Bank, 2019).

The Third Regional Comparative and Explanatory Study (TERCE) found that 39.5% of third graders and 18.4% of sixth graders scored only at Level 1 in reading (see Table 6); in mathematics, 47.2% of third graders and 46.9% of sixth graders scored at this level (see Table 7) (Flotts et al. 2016).

Table 6: Level 1 in reading (Source: National Institute for the Evaluation of Education [INEE] (2016))

Grade	Students can:
3rd	In literary narratives, especially fables, short lyrical texts, letters, and posters, students can: find explicit information repeated literally or synonymously in prominent places in the text (at the beginning or end) and distinguish it clearly from other information; draw inferences from connections between obvious ideas; infer the meaning of known words from the text's clues; recognise the types of short texts with a familiar and close structure.
6th	In literary narratives (predominantly), letters, notes, messages, and stories, students can: locate explicit information repeated literally or synonymously (paraphrased) at various points in the text and distinguish it from other information; establish causal relationships among explicit information in the text; interpret expressions in figurative language; recognize text types by their familiar and close structure; recognize the sender of a text; recognize elements that establish co-reference relationships in the text that are close or proximate to each other and clearly distinguishable.

Table 7: Level 1 in mathematics (Source: INEE (2016).

Grade	Students can:
3rd	Order natural numbers and compare quantities, recognize basic geometric figures, identify missing elements in simple sequences (graphs and numbers), and read explicit data in tables and graphs.
6th	Estimate weights (masses) and lengths of objects, recognise relative positions on maps, recognise and continue rules or patterns for forming simple number sequences, order natural numbers and decimals, use the structure of the decimal system and monetary systems, solve simple problems involving proportional variations, and read explicit data in tables and graphs.

National Plan for Learning Assessment in Mexico (PLANEA) 2018, evaluated learning of language and communication, as well as mathematics because it saw them as relevant to the acquisition of knowledge in other areas. Thus, it was found that in language and communication, 49% of sixth-grade students reached Level 1 or unsatisfactory (they could only find explicit information in narrative and explanatory texts), 33% reached Level 2 or basic (they could relate segments of explicit information and determine the meaning of non-explicit elements in narrative and explanatory texts), 15% reached Level 3 or satisfactory (the connection between explicit and implicit information in narrative, expository and argumentative texts) and only 3% reached Level 4 or excellent (comparison and evaluation of information in narrative, expository, argumentative and dialogic texts).

On the other hand, in mathematics, 59% achieved Level 1 or unsatisfactory (solving only basic arithmetic operations such as addition, subtraction, multiplication and division with natural numbers), 18% achieved Level 2 or basic arithmetic operations (solving problems requiring basic arithmetic operations with natural numbers; solving basic arithmetic operations of decimal numbers with natural numbers), 15% reached Level 2 or satisfactory (solving problems requiring basic operations with decimals and multiplying a fraction by a natural number) and only 8% were at Level 4 or excellent (solving problems requiring basic operations with decimals and fractions involving conversions) (INEE, 2018).

In recent decades, a learning gap has also emerged in Mexico. This refers to the lack of expected learning in relation to students' age and grade level (Vergara-Lope & Hevia, 2018), especially in cognitive areas such as basic reading and arithmetic, and in non-cognitive areas such as social-emotional and citizenship skills, among others.

Adding to this historical problem is the loss of learning that occurred after a prolonged absence from school because of the COVID-19-related school closures. During this time children and adolescents were confined to their homes, and emergency teaching happened remotely (Galindo et al. 2020; Hodges et al., 2020; Portillo et al, 2020). This led to major challenges for the Mexican education system, such as increase in the probability of dropping out of school and the widening of the learning gap (UNESCO Institute for Statistics [UIS], 2019).

In Mexico, the National Journey of Healthy Distance[1] and the Learning at Home[2] strategies were implemented. One of the points in the first strategy announced the suspension of classes as an action to fight the spread of COVID-19. Due to this measure, students had to face great obstacles to receive educational services and exercise their right to education. For the students, there was lack of computer equipment, televisions, internet connection, insufficient digital literacy and economic problems in their households, among other things (Institute of University and Education Research [ISSUE], 2020; Kuhfeld, 2019; Portillo, Reynoso & Castellanos, 2020; Sabates & Carter, 2020), which widened the existing educational gaps (United Nations [UN], 2020).

---

1 Mexican government´s strategy that included confinement policies and basic prevention actions for the COVID-19 pandemic. https://www.gob.mx/cms/uploads/attachment/file/541687/Jornada_Nacional_de_Sana_Distancia.pdf
2 Mexican government's national distance learning strategy, which provided basic education services through television, internet, radio and free textbooks to children and adolescents to guarantee their right to education. https://aprendeencasa.sep.gob.mx/

For the 2020-2021 school year, the Secretariat of Public Education (Ministry of Public Education) developed the Learning at Home II programme, which focused on distance education via television (SEP, 2020). Despite all these strategies, estimates of the pandemic's impact on education are alarming: at least 10% of elementary school students and 8% of high school students dropped out this school year (Arellano, 2020).

In this discouraging context, it became necessary to implement effective distance learning innovations with a play-based approach (Caballero, 2021; Reimers & Schleicher, 2020) to improve basic learning, especially in reading and mathematics, and reach as many children as possible through a scaling up process. This study reported on the research conducted at Independent Measurement of Learning (MIA), to evaluate the impact of a series of educational innovations with a play-based approach to basic learning and interest in reading and mathematics among children and adolescents. Based on the principles of CAMaL (Combined Activities for Maximized Learning) and TaRL, the research studied children and adolescents from rural communities in the State of Veracruz, Mexico.

2. Literature Review

2.1 Educational Innovations

Educational innovation is a means of creating social change through education by developing and implementing teaching-learning and assessment processes with social consequences. A key challenge is to create processes in favour of students, which means changes in attitudes, skills, actions, and the paradigm of the knowledge society in which students and teachers learn together (Prince, Tenorio & Ramírez, 2016). Moreover, it means integrating novelty into the educational reality such as articulating new strategies or creating resources, so that actors change their nature and positively affect the learning experience and outcomes (Hidalgo, Tenorio & Ramírez, 2016).

According to UNESCO, educational innovations are deliberate and planned acts of problem-solving that seek a higher quality of student learning and move beyond the traditional paradigm, i.e., they involve moving from passive student learning to an approach in which learning occurs among all participants and the learner naturally becomes an active entity (United Nations Educational, Scientific and Cultural Organization [UNESCO, 2014]).

> For Fidalgo (2014), an educational innovation 'consists of the introduction of changes that enable the improvement of training and learning processes, and that these changes are sustainable, transferable, effective, and efficient' (p. 1). Some of these changes are achieved by incorporating information technologies, new trends, new processes, or new approaches. Likewise, Cárdenas, Farías and Méndez (2017) emphasised that the goal of educational innovation is 'to achieve quality education at all levels and in all areas of the organisation' (p. 22).

From this perspective, since 2016, the MIA special programme has developed, implemented and evaluated the effectiveness of interventions to develop basic reading and mathematics skills in children and adolescents. The programme terms these as educational innovations which have different modalities, including in-school, out-of-school, curriculum autonomy and summer courses. These innovations, especially the summer courses, have a global approach that incorporates play-based learning, elements of the cognitive, social and community paradigm, and elements of the TaRL principle[3] and CAMaL[4] (Banerjee 2012, Banerjee et. al 2016; Pratham Education Foundation [Pratham] & Abdul Latif Jameel Poverty Action Lab [J-PAL], 2019; Pratham, 2016, 2017, 2018).

In terms of play-based approach, the innovations allow for the formation of groups or levels in which short activities and games are carried out, facilitating the acquisition of new knowledge and skills that can be applied to specific circumstances or events. Thus, in innovations in reading, the emphasis is on playful activities such as the elaboration of stories, narratives, drawings and different games as a means of nonverbal transmission of a message related to the environment of each participant and part of their personalities, which allows them to develop different skills such as abstraction, decoding and skills and awareness according to the type of intelligence that each child possesses, which determines the way it relates to others (Suárez, Maiz & Meza, 2010; Mujica, 2012). Mathematical innovations integrate games and playful activities as a strategy for children to help them understand different concepts that allow them to assimilate mathematics as

---

3   Teaching at the Right Level aims to improve NNA basic education through activities carried out by teachers or facilitators working in coordination with the organisation, the education system, and the government.

4   Combined Activities for Maximised Learning, to develop children's basic skills in literacy and numeracy, facilitating learning through structured activities that contribute to the development of multiple competencies and where activities are introduced in a way that ensures learning by helping the participants to move from the simple to the complex and from the concrete to the abstract.

a tool for daily life, count, stimulate memory, develop creativity, know dimensions of things, spaces, objects and manipulate objects. In the activities proposed by MIA, strategies are used to train visual memory and to work with numbers through playful activities, also, creativity and reflection are stimulated to solve mathematical problems and exercises (Giganti, 2014).

In general, the proposed interventions were developed for different face-to-face contexts and had yielded good results (Hevia, Vergara-Lope & Velásquez-Durán, 2021; Velásquez-Durán, Hevia & Vergara-Lope, 2021; Vergara-Lope, 2018), and during the COVID-19 related school closures, these strategies were adapted to distance learning contexts.

2.2 Scaling Educational Innovations

There are several lines of evidence on how short courses focused on accelerated learning as community interventions, such as summer courses, help to reduce the learning gap (Cooper et al., 2000; Hevia, Vergara-Lope & Velásquez-Durán, 2019). Similarly, different activities developed under the TaRL and CAMaL principles have shown to reduce learning losses and lag substantially and significantly in a variety of contexts in developing countries (Banerjee, 2012; Banerjee et al., 2016).

The focus on basic learning, the direct and horizontal collaboration with educational and governmental authorities and the application of rigorous tools for formative evaluation and pedagogical interventions (Hevia, Vergara-Lope & Velásquez-Durán, 2020) allow the creation of close links with schools, communities and municipalities in the country. Therefore, the implementation of these interventions must be done through a scaling process that involves expanding, replicating, adapting and sustaining educational programmes or projects in geographic spaces and times to reach a greater number of people; all the while considering five key components: Innovation, Vision of Scaling, Presenters, Spaces and Monitoring, Follow-up and Evaluation (Cooley & Linn, 2014).

As Velásquez-Durán, Hevia, and Lope-Tristán (2021) mention, the scaling process enables educational interventions that consider the context and reach the largest number of children in and out of school in a sustainable and cost-effective way, ensuring basic education (Velásquez-Durán, Hevia & Vergara-Lope, 2020).

2.3 Play-based Approach to Teaching and Learning and Innovations from MIA

For the NEM, children and adolescents are active subjects, so depending on the school level, the goals of education are set considering their maturity and abilities. In this way, the aim is to achieve sustainable progress in education, in acquisition of knowledge and in the development of skills relevant to the student's life, that is, to adapt the content to achieve the premise of learning for life. All this aims to provide a comprehensive education in which activities are approached from a humanistic, scientific, artistic, play-based and critical perspective, depending on the level, type and educational modality (SEP, 2019).

Given the nature of the activities that NEM seeks to implement, this document emphasises the play-based approach, which consists of applying the elements of play in a teaching-learning environment to improve cognitive, affective and social relationships and socialising mediation of knowledge (Nunes, 1994). Play allows students to develop different skills from collaboration networks, promote active participation, and make sense of the natural and social world around them, and therefore, it becomes a learning resource and research strategy for understanding the complex world (Córdoba, Lara & García, 2017; Naik, 2014; Park, 2014).

Resuming playful activities not only promotes the development of key competencies (United Nations Children's Fund [UNICEF], 2018), but also the formation of personality, self-confidence and autonomy. As part of this approach, MIA developed the summer MIAventura 'distant play' strategy to serve children and adolescents in the Mexican Southeast during the period of health disruption caused by COVID-19. Its goal was to help strengthen basic learning skills in reading, writing and mathematics, in addition to promoting the development of socio-emotional skills during the 2020 academic break.

To develop this innovation, it was necessary to strengthen multidisciplinary approaches in which knowledge of the processes and dynamics of the relationship between family, school and community was required. This knowledge was required to understand how and under what processes these educational innovations could be replicated over time in multiple locations (McDonald, Keesler, Kauffman & Schneider, 2006; Robinson and Winthrop, 2016) with a cost-effective scheme (Velásquez-Durán, Hevia & Vergara-Lope, 2020).

This educational intervention emerged in response to the unfavourable educational conditions that were becoming increasingly evident among students from rural and marginalised areas. The goal was to narrow the learning gap (Kuhfeld & Tarasawa, 2020; United Nations [UN], 2020) by working collaboratively, directly and horizontally with rural communities. This strategy was based on a play-based approach, as it integrated 'instructive, entertaining, and enjoyable activities developed in a recreational environment, whose pedagogical impact promotes meaningful learning planned through play' (Alcedo & Chacón, 2011, p. 72); these were dynamic agents of the educational process that let go of the monotony of traditional teaching and allowed for play-based learning and development of creativity (Stefani, Andrés & Oanes, 2014; Ramírez-Sánchez, Díaz-Murillo & Cuenca-González, 2011). Similarly, the principles of TaRL and CAMaL were incorporated into the strategy (Banerjee 2012, 2016; Pratham Education Foundation [Pratham] & Abdul Latif Jameel Poverty Action Lab [J-PAL], 2019; Pratham, 2016, 2017, 2018).

3. Methodology

3.1 Paradigm, Approach and Design
The paradigm of this research was positive and focused on deductive and logical reasoning along with the use of statistical techniques to know the outcomes of the population under study (Hueso & Cascant, 2012). In addition, a quantitative approach was considered, maintaining a pre-established control and a working scheme based on scientific methods (Creswell, 2018; Creswell & Plano-Clark 2017; Martínez, 2018); and a non-experimental cross-sectional design (Ato, López & Benavente, 2013).

3.2 General Objective
The objective of this study was to evaluate the impact of using a series of educational innovations with a play-based approach, developed according to the principles of CAMaL and TaRL, in basic learning and interest in reading and mathematics, among NNA from rural communities in the State of Veracruz, Mexico.

Also, the goal of the intervention was to help NNAs master the ability to read and comprehend text in their language and do basic math problems.

3.3 Sampling

Sampling was non-probabilistic in that the study participants were not selected at random, but rather by considering the conditions on the ground for feasibility of implementing educational innovations in the above-mentioned communities. In other words, intentional or convenience sampling was used, characterised by a deliberate effort to obtain representative samples by including typical groups in the sample (Arias-Gómez, Villasís-Keever & Miranda-Novales, 2016; Blaxter, Hughes, & Tight, 2011; Walpole & Myers, 1996). For this study, there were 301 participants with an average age of 8.5 years (from 6-to 12-years-old) from rural areas of Veracruz, Mexico, who were served by correspondents and teachers during the health emergency due to COVID-19, through the MIA special programme.

3.4 Data Collection and Analysis

Data collection was conducted by using survey techniques (Casas, Repullo & Campos, 2002; Cea, 1998), with two valid and reliable instruments: (a) a questionnaire for correspondents, teachers and parents with an index Cronbach's alpha of $\alpha=0.90$; and (b) questionnaire for children with $\alpha=0.82$. Both were utilised virtually through online forms developed through GoogleForms©. Likewise, in this study, descriptive statistical analyses were performed to present the data collected in the form of charts or tables, graphs or figures, so that the evidence found in the research could be summarised simply and clearly for interpretation. (Miranda-Novales et al., 2016). This was done in SPSS© software, with each area included in the two questionnaires.

3.5 Research Procedure

The general procedure carried out for implementation of the educational innovation of the summer MIAventura was: (a) planning, defining the sections, content, format (radio capsules[5]), programming and schedule; (b) didactic design of scripts for the radio capsules, the scripts per section, recording and production; (c) output of the radio programmes, production of 15 programmes of 30 minutes each was elaborated; (d) management and linkage, radio programmes were promoted, in addition to management with communities, teachers, schools, and with state radio stations; (e) transmission and dissemination, through the MIA website, social networks, WhatsApp, radio stations and communities; (f) follow-up and monitoring, remotely through synchronous and asynchronous channels by correspondents (local facilitators who were not teachers but were interested in implementing the innovations in their communities to support children and adolescents, and who were trained by the MIA team) and teachers (education professionals who worked as teachers, who were trained by MIA but already had experience in the teaching-learning process); and (g) evaluation, through the questionnaires mentioned above.

---

5 Short radio programmes on local stations with didactic and fun activities developed in a recreational environment to promote meaningful learning that allowed children and adolescents to learn through play and develop their creativity (Alcedo & Chacón, 2011; Ramírez-Sánchez et al., 2011; Stefani, Andrés & Oanes, 2014).

3.6 Limitations

Limitations of the study included the fact that correspondents and teachers could not interact personally with the children, i.e., all development was conducted remotely considering the COVID-19 pandemic. Similarly, it was not possible to conduct a probabilistic sample because the participating children had individually agreed to participate in the summer course and their fathers, mothers, guardians, or caregivers who provided the necessary permissions. In addition, the data reported was of the children and the fathers or mothers, who sent in their questionnaires, i.e., it was not possible to obtain the opinions of the participants who were unable to send them or who had difficulty in completing the intervention.

3.7 Ethical Criteria

This study can be considered risk-free because as per Title Two, Chapter I of Ethical Aspects of Research Involving Human Beings, no interventions were made that compromised the integrity and privacy of the children. In addition, informed consent regarding the procedures used in the study was sought from participants as well as their fathers and mothers, teachers and correspondents.

4. Results

4.1 Implementation of Radio Summer Courses

The radio summer courses had the following thematic axes or sections: reading (By hearsay) and mathematics (1, 2, 3 Radio count) mainly, but also other areas such as socio-emotional learning (Exciting), caring for the environment (MIAction transforms), science (Exper-science) and cooking (Radio with flavor) (Independent Measurement of Learning [MIA], 2020). A total of 1062 NNA from 26 localities in 13 municipalities of the State of Veracruz, with 37 correspondents and 44 teachers participated. However, the questionnaires were completed only by a total of 301 children who were considered participants in the study. Summer classes were conducted in three periods: July 20 to August 7, July 27 to August 14, and August 3 to 21 of the year 2020.

An important achievement of the project was collaboration with students from the Faculty of Pedagogy of the Universidad Veracruzana, who acted as correspondents and encouraged the children to listen to the broadcasts and talked to them about the revised content, especially in the areas of reading and mathematics.

Fathers and mothers, as well as members of school groups, joined this initiative to broadcast the audios to children who did not have access to the Internet or who, due to the broadcast schedule of the programmes on the radio stations, were unable to listen to them.

4.2 Reach on Social Networks

On Facebook, this educational innovation was promoted through regional segmentation in the municipalities managed for implementation, resulting in significant reach (see Table 8).

Through WhatsApp, a network was established in which constant communication was maintained with correspondents to share the audios in areas where it was not possible to download them from the internet. This was useful to clarify the doubts of students and the public. Additionally, it was also used to obtain evidence from elsewhere in the country, from fathers, mothers and children and comprised a daily interaction with 40 to 50 radio listeners.

Table 8: Scope of educational innovation of summer courses on Facebook

Template	Scope	Interactions with post	People reached	I like it	No. of times shared
1a.	42,047	2,354	35,004	667	193
2a.	24,608	1,322	26,568	621	62
3a.	10,177	785	10,610	479	24
4a.	1,478	80	1,400	44	2
Total	53,702	4,541	12,010	1,811	281

Source: Own elaboration.

4.3 Reach of Radio Stations

Collaboration with various radio stations in the State of Veracruz allowed the radio programmes to be broadcast (in Mexico Time) in four of them, which are listed below:

1) Radio la Voz de la Sierra de Zongolica, a member of the Indigenous Cultural Broadcasting System, is in the Sierra Oriental of the States of Veracruz in the municipality of Zongolica and broadcasts to 155 municipalities in the State of Veracruz, Oaxaca, Puebla and Tlaxcala. The station broadcasts its signal in Nahuatl and Spanish at XEZON-AM 1360 kHz and via the Internet. The summer MIAventura was broadcast from 20 July to 7 August 2020, from Monday to Friday from 8:00 to 8:30 am.

2) Radio Teocelo, a community radio station based in the municipality of Teocelo in the State of Veracruz, with a reach of just over 400 locations in 12 municipalities in the area, with broadcasts in Spanish on XEYTM-AM 1490 kHz and online, with a potential audience of 500,000 people. The summer MIAventura aired from 20 July to 7 August 2020, from 4:30 to 5:00 pm, Monday through Friday.

3) Radio Universidad Veracruzana is a radio station that broadcasts programmes for cultural dissemination and extension of university services and promotes citizen participation by performing functions of communication, outreach, education, extension of university services and social bonding. It is broadcast on 90.5 MHz and through the Internet. The programme summer MIAventura was broadcast from 27 July to 14 August 2020, from Monday to Friday, from 9:00 to 9:30 am.

4) Radio Ciudadana of the Ayuntamiento de Xalapa, with broadcasting hours from 4:00 to 4:30 pm, broadcast the programmes during the period 27 July to 14 August 2020, from Monday to Friday, covering 600 neighbourhoods that make up the municipal territory.

4.4 Questionnaire for Correspondents, Teachers and Parents

In general terms and by using this questionnaire, the figures show that the reading section has an excellent acceptance rate among NNAs at 92% and the math section at 82%. Although it is not the aim of this work to go into other areas, it was estimated that the social-emotional learning had an acceptance rate of 91%, caring for the environment 90%, science 81%, and cooking 93% (see Figure 5). Regarding the ease of the topics, the reading section was rated as easier with 89% than the mathematics section with 78%; and considering their usefulness, both sections were considered basic learning of great benefit to the participants' school career with 91% acceptance rate.

4.5 Questionnaire for NNA

Of the NNA attended by correspondents and teachers, 85% reported that they felt comfortable and very comfortable during each radio programme, 80% enjoyed listening, and 91% liked the content that was covered as they learned, and did exercises and activities that included games. Similarly, 66% increased their interest in reading and 79% increased their liking for mathematics; and 99% were satisfied with the content, dynamics, and presentation of the programmes they listened to.

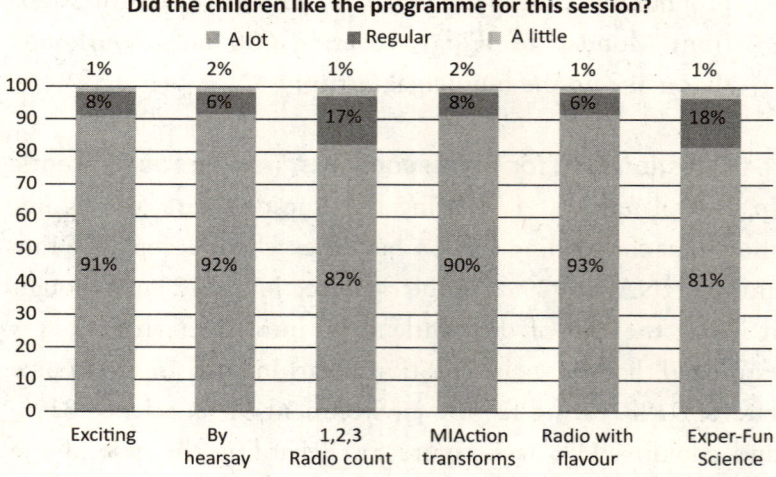

Figure 5: *Percentage of acceptance of educational innovations by thematic axes or sections*

4.6 Evaluation of Educational Innovation

In terms of monitoring and evaluation of educational innovation, a continuous process has been implemented that includes observation, feedback and in some cases discussion, as well as critical reflective analysis of the performance of the teacher or the correspondent (depending on which of these two figures implemented the intervention), the sessions or modules and the impact of their actions on NNA learning (Guach & Peña, 2001).

4.6.1 Play-based Approach

Regarding the play-based approach, the results of the questionnaire for NNA showed that 88% of those who were supervised by correspondents and 69% by teachers enjoyed listening to each programme, acquired knowledge, and developed skills while playing; 94% of those who were supervised by correspondents and 73% by teachers felt very comfortable during each programme; 94% correspondents and 73% teachers enjoyed being with each other while listening to the programmes; 91% correspondents and 71% teachers said they liked the content of the programmes very much because it allowed them to learn and play at the same time; 100% correspondents and 97% teachers were satisfied with the methodology and content of the programmes (see Figure 6).

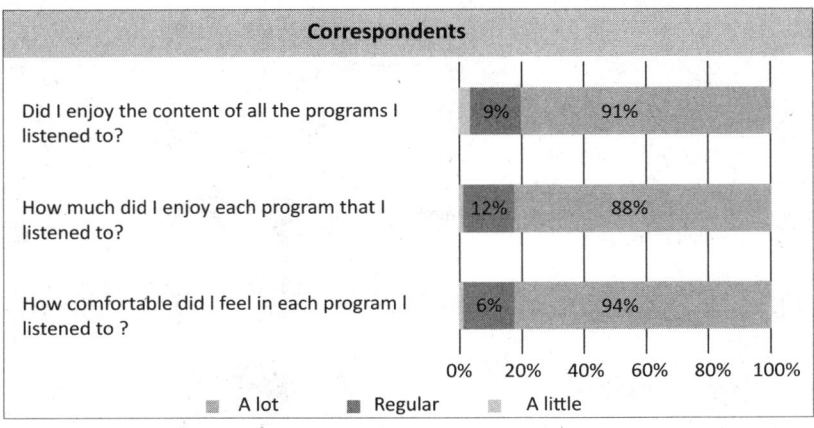

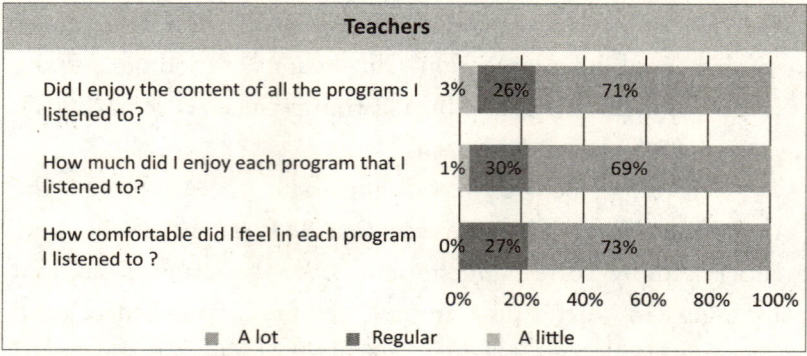

Figure 6: Main results of the intervention of summer courses in relation to the play-based approach. (Source: Own elaboration)

4.6.2 Basic Learning and Interest in Reading and Mathematics

The results of the questionnaire for children showed that 78% of those served by correspondents and 49% by teachers increased their interest in reading after listening to the radio programmes and by receiving the appropriate reinforcement, and 77% served by correspondents and 59% by teachers increased their interest in mathematics (see Figure 7).

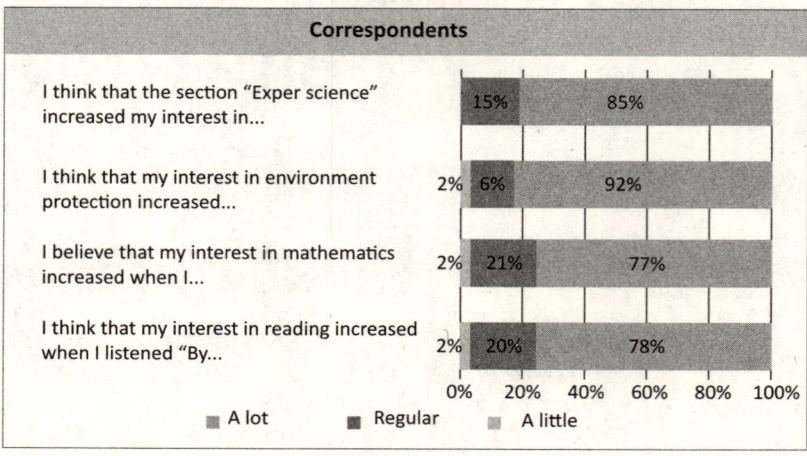

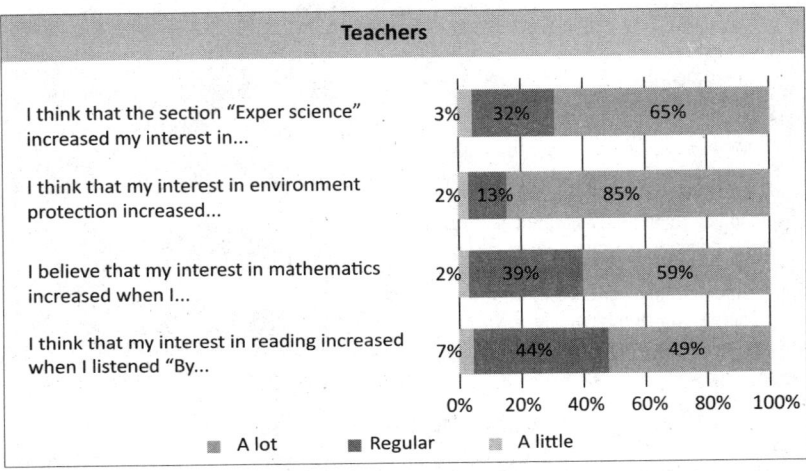

Figure 7: Main results of summer school intervention on basic learning and interest in reading and mathematics. (Source: Own elaboration)

On the other hand, 50% parents of children attended to by correspondents and 68% attended to by teachers considered that their child's interest in reading increased when listening to the radio programmes; and 72% parents of children attended by to correspondents and 70% attended to by teachers considered that the programme motivated their child to learn mathematics (see Figure 8).

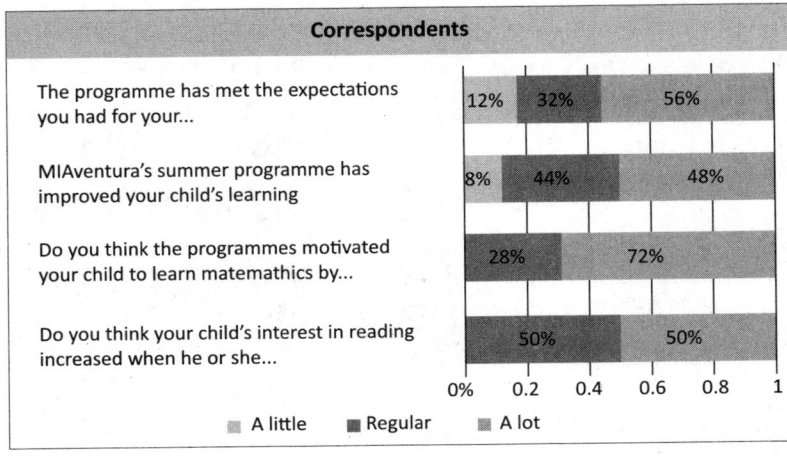

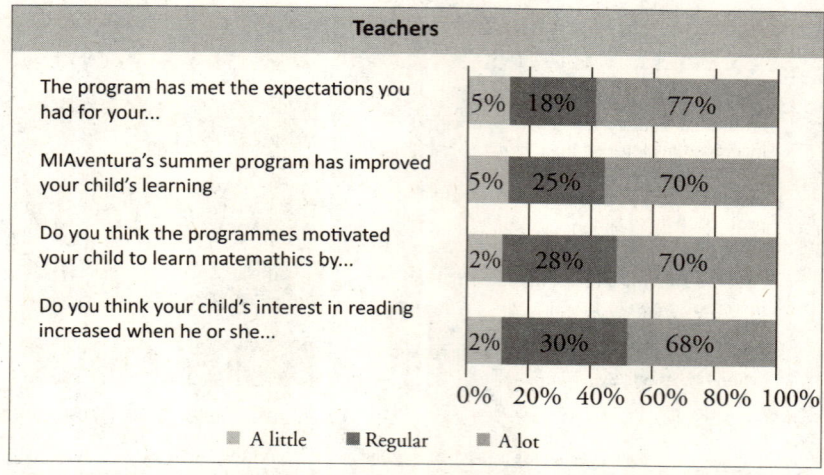

Figure 8: Main results of the intervention La Radio es MIA from the satisfaction survey of fathers, mothers, guardians, or caregivers.
(Source: own elaboration)

The general opinion of fathers, mothers, guardians, or caregivers was as follows: 56% of NNA parents visited by correspondents and 53% visited by teachers felt that the material for the sessions was very good, and 72% correspondents and 61% teachers felt that the activities conducted were very good (see Figure 9).

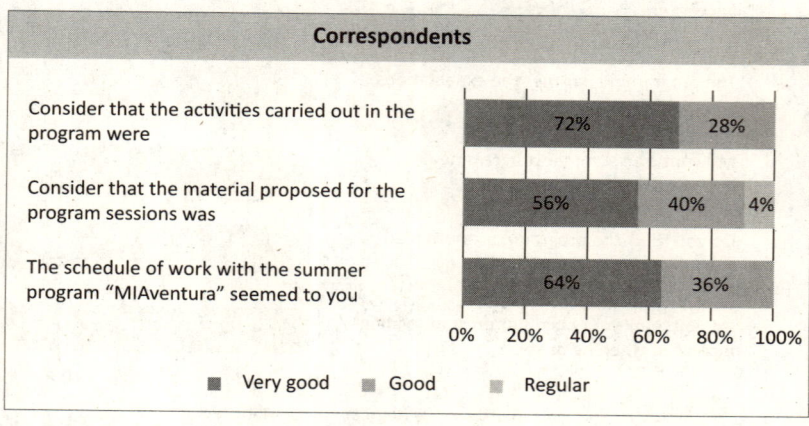

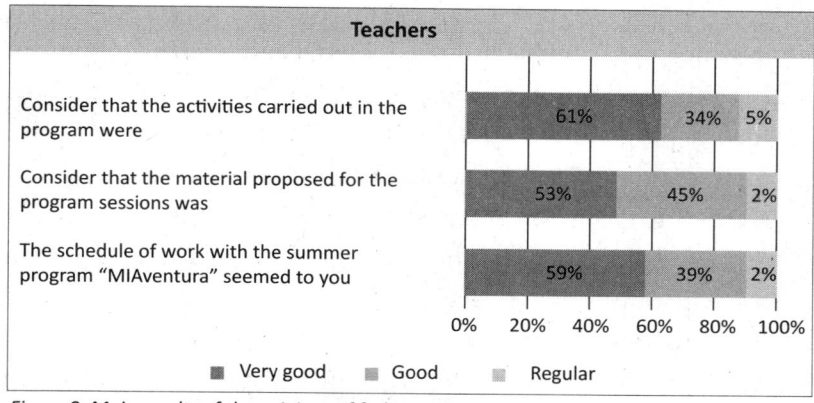

Figure 9: Main results of the opinions of fathers, mothers, guardians, or caregivers of the educational intervention La Radio es MIA.
(Source: Own elaboration)

5. Discussion and Conclusions

It can be concluded that the effect of play-based approach (Córdoba, Lara & García, 2017; McDonald, Keesler, Kauffman & Schneider, 2006; Naik, 2014; Park, 2014; Robinson & Winthrop, 2016) in the use of TaRL and CAMaL (Banerjee 2012, Banerjee et al. 2016; Pratham Education Foundation [Pratham] & Abdul Latif Jameel Poverty Action Lab [J-PAL], 2019; Pratham, 2016, 2017, 2018) among children aged 6 to 12 from rural communities in Mexico, particularly in educational innovations of summer courses using the MIA special programme methodology, is effective in helping to improve basic learning and interest in reading and mathematics, which in turn helps in reducing the learning gap (Hevia, Vergara-Lope & Velásquez-Durán, 2019; Velásquez-Durán, Hevia & Vergara-Lope, 2020).

The implementation of this play-based strategy (McDonald, Keesler, Kauffman & Schneider, 2006) has shown positive effects, so it can be claimed that these educational interventions can be scaled through a co-creation model with communities, in which they provide human, material and financial resources. For implementation of these educational innovations, and the special programme MIA transfers the technical capacity for intervention, follow-up, and monitoring to correspondents or teachers to ensure the effectiveness of innovations in the scaling process. MIA considers this a mechanism with intense citizen participation since it achieves the management and direct participation of municipal authorities in improving education. To this model of co-creation with municipalities can be added the development of a second model of collaboration with educational authorities.

It is important to note that educational interventions cannot be standardised, as 'context strongly shapes innovative processes' (Benedetto, 2013, p. 15). Therefore, for future approaches, it is suggested to consider scaling not as a replication, but as an adaptation of educational innovations that bring about significant changes. (See the chapter *Knowledge Adaptation in the Global South; Contextualising Teaching at the Right Level (TaRL) in East and Southern Africa (ESA) Regions* to see how such adaptations can work.) Based on these experiences, it was also possible to identify some factors that would allow the replication of the educational interventions presented in other contexts: (a) networks with government agencies, educational authorities, public and private institutions, and society in general (strategic partners); (b) recruitment and selection of facilitators with skills, attitudes, and values to work with children and have basic knowledge of reading and mathematics, to subsequently train them in the methodology of educational innovations; (c) support for parents, guardians, or caregivers to implement the innovations; (d) cost-effective methodology (play-based approach and TaRL and CAMaL principles); and

(e) monitoring and follow-up (educational and operational support for the process). It is worth noting that this type of intervention can be implemented as a strategy to help children and adolescents to further improve their basic learning skills during the summer months and can even be a complementary strategy to personal innovations during school breaks.

Finally, the main lessons learned from the special programme MIA are: emphasis on the planning process for educational activities, negotiations with the government and educational institutions; the use of monitoring and follow-up tools that act as a control mechanism allowing decisions to be made; strengthening operational coordination between all roles involved and promoting remote accompaniment of correspondents and NNA to obtain information on the implementation and development of innovations.

Rebuilding with Mothers
How and Why Do Mothers Engage with Their Children's Education in Rural India?

Laura Cashman, Poorva Shekher, Ankita Jha, Preeti Manchanda

1. Introduction

The COVID-19 pandemic led to – or elevated – numerous challenges in providing equitable and quality education globally. At the peak of school closures, over 94% students worldwide, i.e. 1.6 billion children and young people were unable to access educational institutes in person (UNESCO, 2020). This disruption in learning is estimated to have led to disadvantaged children in the Global South losing up to a year of progress (Sabates et al., 2021).

To examine the effects of the pandemic on children's foundational learning outcomes in India, the Annual Status of Education Report (ASER) conducted field surveys across the States of Karnataka, Chhattisgarh and West Bengal in March 2021.[1] This report informed that children's reading levels in all primary grades (Grades 2 to 5) dropped across all three States during the 2018–2021 period (ASER, 2021). Yet, despite

---

[1] Any fieldwork undertaken by ASER during this time received the necessary approvals, with the necessary precautions adopted.

these issues, the pandemic also brought a remarkable period of innovation, as practitioners and stakeholders began to introduce effective solutions to complex problems in education. One such solution was the effort to include and engage parents and caregivers in children's schooling and learning throughout the closures on a global scale. This initiative was successful across many contexts, with evidence from rural India demonstrating that 75% children in rural areas received familial support for their learning during the pandemic (ASER, 2020).

Parental engagement with children's learning has been linked with various positive educational outcomes over the decades (Epstein, 1990; Epstein & Becker, 1982; Fan & Chen, 2001; Fan & Williams, 2010; Finn, 1998; Hoover-Dempsey & Sandler, 1997; Jeynes, 2007; Sui-Chu & Willms, 1996; Tan et al., 2020). While there is demonstrable benefit in engaging parents, it is also widely recognised that increasing the quantum and type of parental engagement can be a complex undertaking. Increasing engagement is further complicated by the fact that the area around the potential motivators and enablers of parental engagement is relatively under-researched in educational literature. However, many existing studies highlight potentially compelling starting points.

One such example includes a recent research from the community within which this study is situated. It demonstrated that higher levels of household wealth, disproportionately and exponentially, lead to higher involvement levels among parents (Cashman et al., 2021). Similarly, further research from rural India demonstrated that the more educated the parents, the more help their children received during the pandemic (ASER, 2020). On the other hand, one also has to consider the arguments about studies which make associations between low parental involvement and low socio-economic status (SES) families, without exploring the potential reason(s) for these differences, are responsible for the 'deficit view that fails to recognise the wide variability among low-income families' (Machida et al., 2002, p.176). Therefore, these findings need to be expanded to include an exploration of the potential reasons for these associations.

In response to the above, this study explores how and why mothers of varying educational backgrounds become engaged in their children's schooling and learning in rural India. Mothers are often the primary caregivers for children in India. Therefore, by narrowing the focus to mothers in this study, it is hoped that more light will be shed on the link between the educational background of the primary caregiver and their engagement in their children's schooling and learning. Contrary to other studies in this area, the analysis here expands from parental involvement to engagement. Carreón, Drake and Barton's (p.467, 2005) definitions of the terms involvement and engagement have been adopted, whereby 'involvement' is the description of the specific things parents do, while 'engagement' also includes 'parents' orientations to the world and how those orientations frame the things they do' (Carreón et al., 2005, p. 467). Using the term 'engagement' goes beyond describing what mothers do to consider how their worldview influences their beliefs and practices while educating children.

The study uses cross-sectional, mixed methods data from the PAHAL project (PAHAL means 'initiative' in Hindi, but it also stands for Pratham Activity in Home and Learning) that aims to evaluate whether schools' accountability for learning can be strengthened from the grassroots in rural Uttar Pradesh, India (Accountability: Faculty of Education, Cambridge University, UK 2018). The PAHAL project is implemented by Pratham Education Foundation, a non-governmental organisation based in India; the ASER Centre, the assessment, survey, evaluation and research unit within the Pratham network; and the Research for Equitable Access and Learning (REAL) Centre at the University of Cambridge.[2]

The key research questions that guided this study were, 1) Through what activities and to what extent do mothers become involved in their child(ren)'s education? And 2) Why do engagement levels in this community differ based on the mother's educational background? A mixed methods approach was adopted where first the how question was quantitatively explored (i.e. activities by mothers and the level of their involvement). After this, data from in-depth interviews and focus group discussions with mothers was used to answer the why question regarding the educational background of the mothers and their engagement levels.

It is hoped that by considering both how and why, mothers of different educational statuses become engaged in their children's education. This study can inform the targeted policies and practices that aim to increase maternal engagement in rural India, post-COVID. The following section presents the methodology employed to explore these questions, the resultant findings, and their implications. However, first, we introduce the theoretical and conceptual underpinnings of this study.

2. Theoretical and conceptual underpinnings

The conceptual underpinnings of this research are based on PAHAL's theory of change, which focuses on three sub-

---

[2] https://www.educ.cam.ac.uk/centres/real/researchprojects/ongoing/accountability-in-india/

outcomes: (1) Improving parental and teacher-level awareness about children's learning levels, (2) Enhancing parental desire and actual participation in children's education, and (3) Improving parental and school-level ownership of educational support and actions. This study focuses on the second and third sub-outcomes. The main variables of interest, maternal engagement and maternal education levels, are directly linked to the project's areas of interest. Beyond the influence of the PAHAL theory of change and study design, findings from existing literature have also driven the development of the frameworks that guide this study.

Parental support for children's schooling and learning garnered significant attention in light of the disruptions to education due to the COVID-19 pandemic. Much of this attention focused on how educationists can continue to harness and encourage this engagement post-pandemic. According to educational research, this requires understanding wherein groups of parents become more engaged in their children's schooling and learning and why (Park and Holloway, 2013). Existing studies demonstrate that parents from lower socio-economic backgrounds are less engaged in their children's education than affluent parents (Camacho-Thompson et al., 2016). Considering that this has subsequently been linked to poor academic performance among children from low-income backgrounds (Jeynes, 2007), one needs to ask why is this the case.

Low-income parents report lower expectations from their children's educational achievement than their affluent counterparts (Benner & Mistry, 2007). Could this less-optimistic view of children's educational attainment, in turn, predict parents' low engagement in educational activities with their children at home and school? At a practical level, low educational involvement or engagement may reflect such parents' perception of 'barriers related to their economic status'. For example, low-income parents tend to experience time and energy constraints associated with work (Waanders et al., 2007), low social support, and increased stress associated with a lack of financial resources (Reynolds, 1992).

While these studies provide potential starting points for this exploration, they broadly focus on the influence of socio-economic status. Interestingly, Duncan and Magnuson state that studying the individual components of SES is essential as these may influence children's developmental outcomes through particular mechanisms (Duncan & Magnuson, 2003). Empirical research from rural India demonstrates a specific link between involvement levels and a parent's educational background (ASER, 2020). Another study in rural India indicates that this could be attributed to the fact that when parents lack formal schooling experience, it may be difficult for them to support their children's journey through the system (Banerji et al., 2015).

This study will focus mainly on mothers' engagement with their children's education. The literature demonstrates that maternal education may be a significant factor because it is mostly the mothers who are the primary caregivers for children, particularly in low-income families. The vital role that mothers play has been examined in Banerji et al.(2015) study, which demonstrated that community intervention programmes designed to increase maternal literacy levels improved not only the numeracy skills of young children but also the home learning environment. This finding is echoed by Carneiro et al. (2013), who also finds that maternal education improves the learning environment at home. They demonstrated that more educated mothers invest more quality time with their children by reading books to them and engaging them in additional outdoor recreational activities.

However, research demonstrates that disadvantaged mothers could engage in different practices (or different contexts) to support their children's education. For example, Reininger & Santana López (2017) demonstrated that parents in Chile with more time and energy – often linked to their employment status - were more likely to partake in school-based involvement activities. This finding is also supported by a study in the USA (Green et al., 2007). Therefore, context will be a key focus of this study, alongside employment considerations which have also been linked to parental involvement through mediating variables of time and energy in literature. This research demonstrates that both mothers' and fathers' hours of employment reduced their time spent with children (Sayer et al., 2004).

Lastly, existing research also suggests that disadvantaged parents are less likely to be invited by school actors to become involved in their children's education, which could be why these parents have lower involvement levels (Crozier, 1999). Building on this assertion, the quantitative element of this study considers the relationship between maternal education background and involvement through a home-based and school-based scale. This relationship is also studied on an activity-by-activity basis, as Reininger and Santana Lopez state that some of the findings in their study may be related to the type of activities and how these were used to define parental involvement. For instance, a parent may not necessarily need specific skill sets or knowledge to visit the child's school or to encourage the child to read. Perhaps they would have gained more nuanced findings if they had considered each activity separately, as in this study, rather than examining them as a single combined set of activities. The following section outlines the practical, methodologically-focused considerations that have been developed in line with the theoretical and conceptual underpinnings of this study.

3. Methodology

3.1 Sampling

Data collection for this project was carried out using an explanatory or sequential design-quantitative data that was collected first, followed by qualitative data. The two rounds had a nested relationship; the qualitative sample was a subsample of the quantitative respondents.

For the quantitative stage, 400 villages in rural Sitapur, Uttar Pradesh, with at least two government schools, were randomly selected from the 2016-2017 District Information System for Education (DISE) frame. A baseline study was carried out in each government school (853 schools in total) in these villages. Twenty children from Grades 2, 3 and 4 were randomly selected per school enrollment register at the school level. These children were then tested using the ASER tool for measuring foundational reading and arithmetic skills. Of the 20 tested children in each grade, the first ten children who were unable to read a text at a Grade 2 level of difficulty were selected for inclusion in the study sample. These children were to be tracked throughout the project.

For the qualitative stage, multistage purposeful sampling was carried out to select four villages in rural Sitapur, UP. These villages were used as samples for qualitative case studies using the baseline quantitative data and inputs from the programme teams. Thirty-four in-depth interviews and focus group discussions were conducted with 40 mothers in the four selected sites. Within each site, mothers were selected from different hamlets and socio-economic sections. Out of the total sample, 26 mothers were classified as uneducated (having no exposure to formal education), while 5 had less than five years of education. The majority belonged to Hindu Scheduled Castes (20) and Other Backward Classes (20) social categories that are the marginalised sections of the population in India.

3.2 Data Collection Tools

Both quantitative and qualitative instruments were designed to understand the mothers' attitudes, perceptions and actions towards their children's education. The quantitative data was collected through the caregiver's questionnaire, which consisted of six main sections: general information; family engagement with the sample child's school; perceptions, attitudes and actions related to the sample child's learning and education; general perceptions and attitudes towards learning and education; a household roster and, lastly, a section on household indicators.

Before rolling out the questionnaires to the entire sample, each tool was extensively tested through a pilot carried out with a different set of respondents in the villages adjoining the sample area. The study team adapted each of these tools, including the caregiver's survey, based on this piloting which increased the reliability, validity and practicability of the main study tools (Cohen et al., 2007). The caregiver's survey was then administered at the household level during the main study for all the children in the sample.

The qualitative interviews, which were conducted using a semi-structured interview protocol, explored themes like mothers' background and education experience, views about their community, household education environment, perceptions towards education, awareness about learning levels and their overall awareness and involvement in the ongoing intervention. Interviews were first translated and transcribed from Hindi to English and were coded in NVivo. To ensure data credibility, the qualitative data collection was conducted by four primary researchers (including two co-authors of this paper) who were also a part of developing and piloting the quantitative research for the project. The interview protocols were created after visiting the region multiple times. Different variations of the interview protocols were tested in the communities to ensure that the respondents could comprehend the questions and engage in the discussion.

Final interviews took approximately a month. The team conducted the interviews by visiting each village for 5-7 days. A prolonged engagement ensured that the researchers were familiar with the site and that the respondents were comfortable in interacting with the team. At least two researchers were present during each interview for quality assurance and recording observations regarding the interview and/or the respondent. A research diary was maintained by the team to document insights and reflections. In addition to the interviews, detailed background information was collected from each site. Investigator triangulation was also done during the analysis process, and each theme and sub-theme was discussed in detail before reaching a final consensus. The analysis was also shared with the project's principal investigators and other research team members.

3.3 Measures (Quantitative element)

Maternal education was measured in the quantitative element through a categorical variable with three groups: those with no formal education, those with up to five years of formal education and those with five or more years of formal education. Maternal involvement was measured using two different approaches. Firstly, by using a home-based and a school-based scale (as presented in Table 9). Secondly, by looking at these indicators individually.

Table 9: School-based and home-based activities

School-based activities	% HHs who said yes	Home-based activities	% HHs who said yes
Did a household member visit the school this session?	34	Do you look at the sample child's textbooks or notebooks?	67
Do you know the name of at least one of the sample child's teachers?	27	Does a member of the household read or tell stories to the sample child?	21
Do you know about the School Management Committee (SMC)?	4	Do you ask [sample child] what s/he does in school every day?	77
		Do you tell [sample child] to work hard in school?	93
		Do you encourage [sample child] to read books other than school textbooks?	35

Eleven other factors were controlled for in the quantitative analysis. Maternal employment status was measured using the formal employment groupings: unwaged, waged, and other/doesn't apply/don't know. Household religion and caste were used as control variables. Religion categories that were used were Hindu and Non-Hindu, and standard caste categories

(Scheduled Tribes and Scheduled Castes, Other Backwards Castes and General Castes). The sex of the child was also included as a control variable. A village fixed effect was used in each of the models.

To account for intra-village differences across schools, we also controlled school and teacher characteristics –additionally, the study controlled whether the school had a road leading to it. Teacher level controls comprised the number of years they had taught at the school, whether they had grown up in the locality, their caste, religion and whether they lived in the village where the school was located.

3.4 Analytical Approach

Nine OLS (a linear least square) regressions were carried out as part of the quantitative analysis. The first considered the relationship between maternal education and school-based and home-based involvement, without accounting for other factors. The other eight regression analyses considered the influence of maternal education on involvement in individual school and home-based activities, conditional on a set of control factors. We assumed that the probability that mothers become involved in learning activities with their children is a function of the parent, child, household, school, teacher and village-level factors. Among the parent-level factors, we included demographic characteristics that could influence the likelihood of mothers becoming involved with their children's learning. The following linear equation outlines the model estimated:

$$Pr(PI_j \mid X) = \beta_0 + \beta_{n1}Parent_j + \beta_{n2}Child_i + \beta_{n3}Household_j + \beta_4 MaternalEdu_j + \beta_{n5}Schools + \beta_{n6}Teachers + \beta_{n7}Village_v + \varepsilon_j \quad (1)$$

Where j denotes parents, i denotes child, s denotes school and v denotes village. PI represents each of the eight parental involvement activities (visited school, knows teachers' names, knows SMC, tells stories, asks about the day, asks to read, checks books, tells to study hard) and MaternalEdu represents the mother's education level. The equation captures other explanatory variables in terms of the parent, child, household, school, teacher and village characteristics. The error term εj is assumed to be random, normally distributed, and uncorrelated with the regressors.

The analytical approach for the qualitative element of the study consisted of three main steps. Firstly, provisional coding was carried out based on the interview protocol and preliminary reading of the transcripts (Saldaña, 2009). Secondly, it was sub-coded to understand the relationships and different arguments within the main code. Lastly, the emergent themes were analysed to unpack the mothers' views, perceptions and actions towards their children's education. The resultant findings of these analyses are outlined in the following section.

4. Findings

Broadly speaking, our study indicates that mothers with higher levels of education are significantly more likely to become involved in activities that support their children's schooling and learning. For example, Figure 10 demonstrates that both mothers with up to and beyond five years of education are more likely to become involved in these activities than those mothers in the reference group, with no formal education. This graph also demonstrates that mothers are more likely to engage with their children's learning at home rather than in school, no matter their education level.

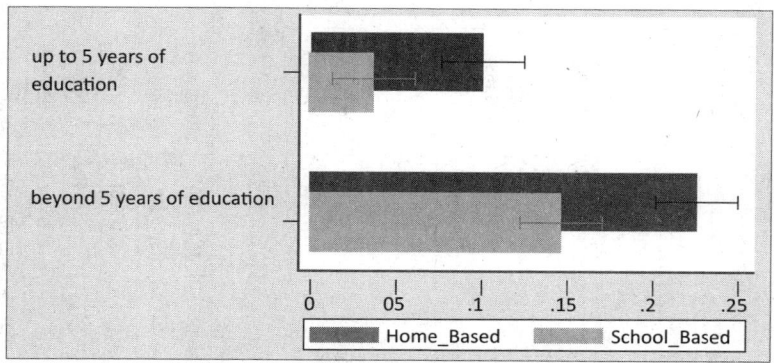

Figure 10: Relationship between maternal education levels and home- and school-based parental involvement levels

Building on this, Table 10 presents the results of OLS regression analyses that explores the relationship between maternal education levels and involvement in these eight activities individually while also accounting for other contributing factors. There is a pattern across all home-based and school-based activities, where involvement levels increase disproportionately and exponentially with the mother's education level. For instance, those with up to five years of education are nine percentage points more likely than those without education to indicate that they check their child's notebook/textbook at home. Those with more than five years of formal education are 20 percentage points more likely than those with no education to check the child's books. Similarly, those with up to five years of education are two percentage points more likely than those without education to indicate that they visit the child's school. Those with more than five years of formal education are nine percentage points more likely than those with no education to indicate that they visit the school.

Table 10: Regression results of maternal education level on eight school-based and home-based involvement indicators

	School-based				Home-based				
	Visited School	Knows Teacher(s) Name	Knows SMC	Tells Stories	Asks About Day	Asks to Read	Checks Book	Tell to Study Hard
Maternal education (ref: No formal education)									
up to 5 years of education	0.0234**	0.0200**	0.00192	0.0347***	0.0344***	0.0447***	0.0862***	0.0125**
	(0.00956)	(0.00862)	(0.00300)	(0.00762)	(0.00933)	(0.00963)	(0.0106)	(0.00593)
beyond 5 years of education	0.0910***	0.0696***	0.00743***	0.0856***	0.0652***	0.0906***	0.198***	0.0281***
	(0.00872)	(0.00791)	(0.00283)	(0.00706)	(0.00819)	(0.00868)	(0.00916)	(0.00503)
Maternal employment status (ref: Waged)									
Unwaged	0.0288	0.157***	0.0268*	0.0101	-0.00673	0.0596*	-0.0437	0.0578***
	(0.0311)	(0.0344)	(0.0155)	(0.0266)	(0.0293)	(0.0316)	(0.0363)	(0.0151)
Other/don't know	-0.00110	0.0411***	0.0242***	0.0323**	0.00525	0.0358**	0.0428***	-0.00358
	(0.0158)	(0.0151)	(0.00667)	(0.0137)	(0.0142)	(0.0158)	(0.0154)	(0.00878)
Household religion (ref: Hindu)									
Non-Hindu	-0.0401***	-0.0453***	-0.000666	-0.0385***	-0.00496	0.180***	-0.0199	-0.00453
	(0.0129)	(0.0119)	(0.00413)	(0.0104)	(0.0123)	(0.0137)	(0.0139)	(0.00778)
Household caste (ref: ST/SC)									
OBC	0.00567	0.0410***	0.000911	0.00460	0.0121	0.0133	0.00331	0.00239
	(0.00880)	(0.00806)	(0.00274)	(0.00716)	(0.00846)	(0.00880)	(0.00947)	(0.00538)
General	0.0672***	0.104***	0.0109*	0.101***	0.0779***	0.0624***	0.142***	0.0245***
	(0.0156)	(0.0155)	(0.00569)	(0.0138)	(0.0135)	(0.0160)	(0.0146)	(0.00796)
Child's gender (ref: Boy)									
Girl	-0.00689	-0.0154**	0.00401*	0.00856	-0.00656	-0.0119	-0.000244	-0.0182***
	(0.00728)	(0.00669)	(0.00232)	(0.00591)	(0.00695)	(0.00736)	(0.00773)	(0.00435)
Teacher no. of years at school	-0.000306	0.00435***	3.14e-05	-0.00116	-0.000545	-0.00147	0.000152	-0.00103**
	(0.000929)	(0.000828)	(0.000263)	(0.000711)	(0.000929)	(0.000911)	(0.000917)	(0.000515)

Mostly in another village	0.0278**	-0.00217	0.00335	0.00367	0.0460***	-0.0499***	0.0625***	-0.00232
	(0.0131)	(0.0120)	(0.00418)	(0.0111)	(0.0125)	(0.0133)	(0.0137)	(0.00752)
Mostly in a city	0.0203	0.0138	0.00939**	-0.00413	0.0448***	-0.0421***	0.0559***	0.0109
	(0.0139)	(0.0127)	(0.00451)	(0.0114)	(0.0132)	(0.0140)	(0.0146)	(0.00792)
Teacher current address (ref: This village)								
Other village	-0.00465	-0.00213	0.00300	-0.00615	-0.0668***	0.0222	-0.0191	-0.0209**
	(0.0156)	(0.0142)	(0.00474)	(0.0129)	(0.0147)	(0.0156)	(0.0162)	(0.00867)
City	-0.0257	0.00547	-0.00110	-0.00523	-0.0628***	0.0252	-0.0356**	-0.0176**
	(0.0158)	(0.0141)	(0.00497)	(0.0130)	(0.0146)	(0.0159)	(0.0165)	(0.00880)
Teacher religion (ref: Hindu)								
Other	0.0231	-0.0242	0.00666	0.0345**	-0.0370**	-0.0178	0.00830	-0.0256**
	(0.0188)	(0.0169)	(0.00602)	(0.0159)	(0.0173)	(0.0180)	(0.0193)	(0.0111)
Teacher caste (ref: General)								
SC/ST	-0.0178	-0.00252	0.00835**	-0.00543	-0.0150	0.0191*	-0.0155	-0.00235
	(0.0110)	(0.0101)	(0.00354)	(0.00902)	(0.0108)	(0.0112)	(0.0119)	(0.00685)
OBC	-0.00425	0.00342	0.000968	-0.0118	0.000922	-0.000510	-0.0147	0.00528
	(0.00987)	(0.00912)	(0.00320)	(0.00792)	(0.00952)	(0.0100)	(0.0106)	(0.00596)
Road leading to school (ref: No)	-0.0179	0.0270	0.00188	0.000582	-0.0170	-0.00753	-0.0392**	-0.0353***
	(0.0174)	(0.0170)	(0.00622)	(0.0154)	(0.0174)	(0.0187)	(0.0193)	(0.0110)
Village fixed effects: Yes (432 villages)								
Constant	0.309**	-0.0369	-0.0323***	0.156	0.748***	-0.00500	0.535***	1.030***
	(0.126)	(0.0866)	(0.0103)	(0.103)	(0.0974)	(0.0695)	(0.102)	(0.0172)
Observations	14,644	14,072	14,834	14,858	14,720	14,604	14,814	14,740
R-squared	0.149	0.169	0.084	0.119	0.121	0.172	0.139	0.108

The symbols (*) in a regression table show how statistically significant a regression coefficient is. In this case, one asterisk (*) means "p < .1". Two asterisks (**) means "p < .05"; and three asterisks (***) mean "p < .01"

Considering these associations, the qualitative analysis asked: why do educated mothers appear to have higher levels of involvement in activities that support their children's education? As outlined above, a definition of engagement was employed that included how the parent's orientations to the world or their perceptions frame their involvement (the specific things they do) in activities that support their children's education. The question asked in the qualitative analysis was examined by focussing on how mothers in the qualitative sample - with no education and some education – perceived their children's education. For example, one mother said:

> If she studies, she can at least tell what is good or bad for her. If she is not educated, then if, for example, someone asks you to sign something in return for something. Later you come to know that rather than giving you anything, they have taken from you instead. What will you do then? So at least she should be able to read and know better.

Echoing this thought, all mothers in our sample, irrespective of their education level, cite the benefits of education when asked if they think education is essential. Mothers report that education is vital in today's world for many reasons, such as employment opportunities, other livelihood options and better marriage prospects. Mothers feel that these advantages often lead to comparatively better lives for their children. Others mention that education equips their children with the knowledge and understanding that they need to better comprehend the world around them. Therefore, considering this broad appreciation of education and the findings of our quantitative analyses, we need to question what prohibits some mothers from engaging more than others.

Our analyses demonstrate that mothers with little or no education are hesitant to engage in their child's studies because of their own lack of education. One mother sums this up by declaring, 'what do we know? We are not educated'. We also found that mothers with some experience with schooling and education tend to be more aware and involved with their child's education prospects and plans. Mothers with more education engage more with children in various ways; one of the main ways is asking direct questions to the child, such as asking them to demonstrate what they have learnt by reading something, counting or reciting multiplication tables.

Additionally, it was found that mothers in rural regions face many barriers in their day-to-day life. Such barriers limit the engagement levels of all mothers, whether educated or not. However, this is sometimes amplified for mothers with no education as educational background often intersects with other difficulties, such as the double burden of household chores and farm work, which can hinder them from engaging with their children's education and learning. For example, one mother explained:

> Most of these women are busy at work all day. They don't know if their children can read or not or what they do all day. They have to believe what the children say. If they say they went to school, it might be true and might not be true; the reason is poverty.

Similarly, mothers said the financial burden was a barrier to their engagement with their children's schooling and learning. For example, one mother discussed the financial implications of her husband's inability to work. She explained that due to this reason, she and her daughter had to work to provide for the family. Such situations have been linked to absenteeism at school, which might lead to an increased lack of interest in studies and poor learning outcomes. However, while these constraints might limit the mothers' engagement in their child's education, the findings also indicate that most mothers aspire to educate their children and try to understand their child's learning level through various mechanisms, irrespective of their education levels.

While the analyses show that mothers with higher education levels are more likely to engage in activities that support their children's schooling and learning than mothers with little or no education, they also show that all mothers are less likely to be involved in school-related activities compared to home-based activities. For example, as shown in Table 10, those with five or more years of education were five percentage points more likely to have visited the school than those with no education. Based on these findings, we asked mothers if there is any interaction between mothers and teachers, and if so, who initiates it? We found that mothers often equate children's learning with their schooling, but irrespective of their own education level, the majority do not initiate interactions with teachers. They either do not go to school or go only if the teacher directly extends an invitation to them. For instance, we asked a mother whose house was close to the school if she visited it for meetings. She responded:

> *I didn't go. I only go if there is some work; Madam calls me... if there is any work. Otherwise, if there is 26 January (Republic Day) or something, I look from here (my house) only, but if they do not call, I don't go.*

Most mothers mentioned that teachers come to their

hamlet for roll calls. However, they do not have any interaction with the mothers. One mother said:

> No, they (teachers) don't talk; they just come and walk around the village. So I know that they have come. I am telling the truth. If they come and say that, 'I want to talk to Ashish's mother', then I will say that they have talked to me. That doesn't happen. I only got information that they had come to the village.

Mothers in our sample also named household responsibilities as a reason they couldn't engage with the school. Many mothers juggled multiple works such as household chores like cleaning and childcare, farm work, or paid labour. School visits, as a result, were often seen as a secondary priority. For instance, when the mothers in a group discussion were asked if they had ever been called to the school? A mother replied.

> Yes, they had called us, but we didn't go. There is so much work, goats and all; we go to work, so we have never been to school.

Additionally, many women did not venture outside their house (apart from household and farm work) due to existing gender norms in the household. Generally, either the men or older women (like their mother-in-law) oversaw outside work or talked to outsiders, which may be why mothers were reluctant to visit schools despite receiving invitations. When asked about having a conversation with teachers, a mother mentioned,

> 'See, I do not go to talk about anything. There are other family members, so I don't go. There are older men like my brother-in-law in the family, so he goes and talks to them.

Otherwise, women in our house do not go out like that.'

In such cases, we found that mothers often did not learn the purpose of the meeting.

Several respondents also said that teachers sometimes don't welcome parents or respond well to their questions. For example, a mother, while explaining why she does not go to school, said:

'I don't go there (to school) or speak to anybody until called for... The teachers got angry with one man in the village; they told him, "if your son is doing something wrong and fighting, then we will deal with it. Why have you come here?" After that, I fear them, and I don't go to school if there is a fight.'

Another mentioned that when she inquired about her child's learning level, the teacher replied, 'What can we do? We teach, but your children are not able to learn.' Following this exchange, she enrolled her children in a nearby private school. Such incidents discourage mothers from visiting schools and enquiring about their child's well-being and learning.

Mothers' lack of participation could also be attributed to the impact of social norms and the perception of teachers in the community. There seems to be an established hierarchy between schools and communities, because of which mothers hesitate to visit schools or talk to teachers. When asked, who is responsible for speaking to teachers about low learning levels? A mother said that:

'It's the parents who should go and speak up if their children are unable to study. But nobody from the village goes to school to talk to teachers. It's not my child only who

goes to school, so why would I go alone to talk to teachers?'

There were some exceptions where mothers mentioned visiting the school to ask about their child's progress, complain about attendance or collect uniforms, among other reasons. However, overall, there seems to be minimal engagement between mothers and teachers. As demonstrated in Figure 10, this is particularly pronounced for mothers with little or no education. However, this figure also shows that no matter the mother's education level, all mothers are more likely to become involved in home-based activities, compared to school-based activities.

Discussion

This study asked why and how mothers of varied educational backgrounds engage with their children's schooling and learning in rural India. In doing so, a significant association between maternal education and maternal involvement in activities at home and school was found. Essentially, this study demonstrated that the higher the mother's level of education, the more likely she is to be engaged in her child's schooling and learning through these activities. However, while maternal engagement is directly proportional to the mother's education level, this in no way suggests the absence of engagement or desire to engage among mothers with no or low educational experience. The analyses presented here demonstrated that all mothers – no matter their level of education – believe that their children's education is essential. This belief appears to drive their desire to secure education for their child, despite their own lack of education. This led to the question: what challenges and barriers do these mothers face that impede their engagement in their children's schooling and learning?

Through in-depth interviews and focus group discussions, it was found that mothers with little or no education appeared to have low levels of self-efficacy. They believe they are not in a position to support their child's education, which translates into a feeling of helplessness. This finding is supported by a broad strand of parental self-efficacy literature which highlights its importance in determining parenting behaviour (Giallo et al., 2013; Jones & Prinz, 2005; Shumow & Lomax, 2002). More specifically, recent research in France demonstrates that maternal self-efficacy positively influences involvement and, in turn, children's academic achievement (Tazouti & Jarlégan, 2019).

Furthermore, our study demonstrated a link between an inability to engage in children's education and financial constraints. Many mothers expressed difficulty in engaging when they or their children had to work to support the household financially. These mothers are also often faced with significant time constraints that appear to hinder their ability to engage with their children's education. For instance, mothers talked about having to dedicate time to house and farm work, which took away from the time and energy they could spend engaging with their child's schooling and learning. A 2007 study in the USA, which sought to find a link between parental time, energy and involvement, recommends that schools account for parental time resources in their planning (Green et al., 2007). The authors suggested that this could include offering flexible teacher-parent conference times or providing parents with specific time-limited suggestions on participating in the child's homework. In light of the present study's findings, these recommendations could also be helpful for school actors, policymakers and researchers in rural India.

The analyses from this study also show that all mothers,

educated or not, are more likely to engage in home-based activities rather than school-based activities. This supports existing literature which demonstrates that home-based involvement activities are often more accessible than school-based activities due to transport, childcare and employment considerations (Green et al., 2007; Reininger & Santana López, 2017). Considering the findings outlined above regarding mothers with little or no education facing challenges of time and energy, this is unsurprising. Moreover, many mothers attest that they only visit the school when the teacher extends an invitation. As outlined in our literature review, existing research suggests that parents from lower SES backgrounds are less likely to be invited by school actors to become involved in their children's education (Crozier, 1999). This situation would put certain groups of mothers, including those with lower levels of education, at a disadvantage and warrants further investigation.

Lower levels of engagement with the school may also be attributed to societal gender and social norms and the pressures they bring. The measures put in place to account for these issues (e.g. teachers visiting the village) may also need to be reconsidered. This study shows that while mothers who were part of the sample said that teachers visit the village, they also indicated that these visits do not necessarily lead to teacher-mother interactions. However, it is important to note that teacher-mother interactions in this community may have changed post-COVID. Teachers were encouraged or required to send learning material to households and visit them to enquire about children's learning at home during the school closures. However, whether this happened and if this is still the case following school reopening, will require further enquiry.

This study presents some of the limitations and challenges all mothers, especially those with low or no education, face daily in this community in rural Sitapur, Uttar Pradesh. Yet, despite these barriers, this study also demonstrates that all mothers are strongly inclined to support their children's education in whichever way possible. This provides ample opportunity for future programmes to cater to the desire of the mothers to become engaged and remain involved in their child's education. The PAHAL intervention (from which this study received its data) attempts to build mechanisms where mothers from each hamlet meet at least once a month to discuss their children's education and well-being. Before the recent school closures, meetings and other activities were held in the school premises to allow mothers to become familiar with teachers and other school actors and feel comfortable engaging with them.

Preliminary findings from the project have brought out certain insights that traditional forms of analysis may not capture. One of these is that the level of involvement of mothers with little or no education could be higher through informal, indirect means. For instance, parents may not necessarily read with a child, but they may observe a child reading to check for fluency. This is demonstrated by one of the mothers from the sample group, who noted,

> *He (her son) reads at home. I have noticed, if he doesn't know how to read, how does he read at home?*

Another mother noted that her daughter had some reading and writing fluency, as she could write the names of family members and read her schoolbooks.

> *She (her daughter) can write the names of everyone in the*

family and can read whatever is written in her schoolbooks, I have noticed.

This postulation warrants further exploration. Nevertheless, it is crucial that school systems learn from and adapt the findings of studies such as this. The findings reported that mothers find it challenging to fit parent-teacher meetings into their busy schedules and are unable to engage with their children's education due to lack of financial resources and time constraints. They might also feel unwelcome in schools due to their limited education. Therefore, building trust between caregivers and school stakeholders through engagement-based activities, including open conversations and home visits by teachers, is vital.

Establishing smoother communication mechanisms between families, especially mothers and schools, such as creating digital mother-teacher chat groups, is equally important. This could also help in identifying new ways to address the learning crisis and prevent school dropouts, particularly in marginalised communities. It is essential that policymakers, researchers, teachers, and other school actors continue to have conversations around these and other findings as the education systems are strengthened to better cope with future crises and the post-COVID education system is rebuilt with mothers as partners and stakeholders in their children's schooling and learning.

Evidence from Pakistan
Mitigating Learning and Development Losses for Children in Early Years

Hamza Sarfraz, Baela Raza Jamil and Saba Saeed

1. Introduction

In many global South settings, such as Pakistan, schools serve as spaces for childcare and enabling environments for early development and growth. As the global education community continues to investigate the ramifications of COVID-19-related closures and disruptions, this paper assesses its impact on early-years schooling in Pakistan.

Two questions related to children's learning and well-being are investigated in this paper. These are (1) What is the impact of COVID-19 on early years, and (2) What are the solutions to effectively fill the gaps in this area? The paper presents an understanding of home-based learning to address learning losses and children's socio-emotional well-being. MELQO tools for early years were used to collect evidence on home learning environments, socio-economic situations, child's well-being, teacher's support, home learning practices and distance learning for children aged 3-7.

As the global education systems forge ahead into the final decade to meet the Sustainable Development Goals (SDGs) 2030, the case for investing in Early Childhood Education

(ECE) as a critical foundational pillar is stronger than ever. The Sustainable Development Goals highlight pre-primary education for all as a key global target (4.2) to address learning, equity and inclusion. Early childhood (ages 0-8) is a critical period for cognitive, social, emotional and physical development. The economic case for support of education in early years is also strong – children who experience sub-optimal development have a 26% reduction in potential earnings as adults (Richter et al., 2019).

Recent estimates suggest that as many as 250 million or 43% children in low- and middle-income countries (LMICs) are at risk of not reaching their developmental potential (Gil et al.,2020). Poverty, nutritional deficiencies, poor health care, and insufficient learning opportunities are cited as key factors underpinning these failings that worsened during the COVID-19 pandemic due to school closures and uprooted the basic pedagogical structures central to early years' learning. The pandemic-induced lockdowns made ECE inaccessible to a significant number of children. According to UNESCO estimates, in 2020, as many as 155 million children at the preschool level were affected by COVID-19. There has been an observable trend of pre-primary education being relatively neglected, compared to other levels of education during school closures (ARNEC, 2020).

This neglect is particularly pronounced in Global South settings where young children from marginalised families and communities bear a heavy 'pandemic burden' in terms of both psychological well-being and resilience to crisis, the consequences of which are yet to be fully measured. In a regional survey of organisations serving young children conducted by the Asia Pacific Regional Network for Early Childhood (ARNEC), more than 50% respondents in the Asia-Pacific region assessed said that their families were under pandemic-induced stress (stressed and very much stressed). Respondents from Pakistan, Bangladesh, India and the Philippines said that they and their families faced some of the worst situations ever, medically and socio-economically, with over 70% of the respondent's from these four countries saying they were under significant stress.

School closures had a long-term impact, as many young children who remained at home did not get the early learning support they needed for healthy development (UNICEF, 2020). With lack of evidence on the prevalence of disability and the resulting learning challenges among children with disabilities, the effect of school closures may be even more pronounced for such children. Within this context, this study assesses and documents the short- and medium-term impacts of COVID-19 on early learning systems. More specifically, the research hopes to help in identifying and understanding the extent to which parents and caregivers could support the development of their children at home – the kind of resources they had access to and the level of preparedness of the schools and teachers to respond to the pandemic. The survey, done telephonically, was carried out in the Punjab province of Pakistan in partnership with the World Bank under the umbrella of Early Learning Partnership (ELP) Systems Research.

1.1 Literature Review and the Background of the Study

The developmental period from 0-5 years lays the foundations of an individual's life, setting the trajectory for their long-term outcomes in health, education, employment and well-being (Ramey et al., 2004). Interventions targeted at this stage have a far-reaching impact than those targeted later in life.

As Heckman (2008) observes, 'skill begets skill', suggesting that positive later development is dependent on robust early development, not only in cognition but also factors such as social and emotional development, which influences a child's ability to learn. It is well-recognised that Early Childhood Education (ECE) is crucial for attaining the education targets of the UN Sustainable Development Goals (SDGs), with evidence suggesting that: (1) ECE equips children with good language, literacy and numeracy skills in the early years, which are vital for success in school (Fricke et al., 2013) (2) it prevents subsequent costs associated with grade repetition and 'churning' (Fricke et al., 2013) and (3) it leads to considerable economic and social returns, offsetting equity gaps due to gender, disability and poverty, resulting in transformative gains through child development (Walker & Baboo, 2019; Rose & Zuberi, 2019).

Despite many tools and instruments, challenges exist in assessing and measuring children's developmental status within and across countries. Policymakers, practitioners and delivery agents often do not have the tools and data to identify the children and communities at risk, track the progress of State and district standards and evaluate service effectiveness. Research gaps are thus apparent in the extent to which children in preschool years are learning and 'ready' for primary school and the extent to which the school is, in turn, ready to receive these children into the primary setting. Improved measurement of child development status will thus enable policymakers and programme managers to make informed decisions regarding policies and resource allocation and help in accelerating progress towards the Sustainable Development Goals related to early childhood development (Raikes et al., 2015). There are also significant gaps in the understanding of disability in the general population. Identifying and assessing children with disabilities is imperative to target those at a greater risk of marginalisation.

In Pakistan, especially in Punjab and Sindh provinces, ECE has gained an increased system-level attention and relevance in recent years. In three out of the five Right to Education Acts for Article 25 A (a fundamental constitutional right of all children aged 5-16 years), ECE has been included by provincial governments as a target area of support for children aged 3-5 years. Sindh was the first province to develop a holistic ECCE (Early Childhood Care and Education) policy in 2015. The Sindh ECCE Policy was focused towards establishing developmentally appropriate pre-primary ECCE that would support the learning preparedness of primary schools to improve outcomes in the province. The Sindh government has also developed its official provincial ECE curriculum and initiated workforce reforms with a designated cadre for the subsector.

Balochistan also created an ECE policy framework in 2015 that addressed the main challenges facing the subsector in the province. However, there are severe challenges in ECE implementation in the province.

Soon after Sindh, the Punjab government finalised its first ECE Policy in 2017, which clearly incorporated a systems-based approach for the subsector. Subsequently, provisions and plans for ECE were laid out in New Deal 2018-23, which has a dedicated section on improving and scaling high-quality pre-primary education across Punjab (SED, 2019). Moreover, the discourse revolving around the latest iteration of the National/Pakistan Education Policy (PEP) 2021 also places ECE as a foundational pillar for school education in the country.

As of 2022, all the provinces have made ECE a key priority in the education sector. Sindh's most recent provincial education sector plans had specific objectives and improvement areas for early learning. Similarly, Punjab's latest five-year Education Sector Plan 2019-23 also pinpoints the specific gaps in ECE throughout the province, including 1) low enrollment in multiple ECE grades, with significant variation in the age of children as well as intra-regional and rural-urban differences, 2) low parental engagement which serves as a significant impediment to child learning outcomes, and 3) service-delivery and institutional challenges, particularly with workforce recruitment and ECE financing.

Evidence from the ASER Pakistan survey shows that the case for investing in early childhood is strong, with enrolment increasing to 39% in 2019, before the pandemic, and school readiness of children improving as a result of ECE classrooms (ASER, 2021).

2. Methodology

The key objective of this research was to collect data on home learning environments and teacher support. This was done by deploying a set of tools that were developed by a global consortium that has been used extensively.

The Measuring Early Learning Quality Outcomes (MELQO) tools are part of an initiative undertaken from 2012–2016 to provide high-quality, free, global tools for measuring children's development and early learning and the quality of early learning environments. Led by UNESCO, UNICEF, the World Bank and the Center for Universal Education at the Brookings Institution, MELQO's measurement modules provide a core set of items that are relevant across countries, with the goal of devising items that are globally comparable but locally adaptable. These tools were administered along with background questionnaires to capture details of the early learning situation during the pandemic. In order to chart a better situational analysis, qualitative data was collected through key informant interviews (KIIs) with key stakeholders. The data collection focused on the political and economic situation as well as government efforts made in the area during the early years of the pandemic.

The study was designed by keeping in view the COVID-19 health requirements and limitations. Therefore, the data collection exercise was undertaken exclusively on telephones/mobile phones, instead of face-to-face interviews to ensure the safety of both enumerators and respondents. Evidence from previous studies on early years in Punjab well demonstrates well the efficacy of phone-based quantitative surveys (Bulsari et al., 2020), as they allow flexibility in collecting data in otherwise infeasible settings. The responses collected from caregivers and ECE staff were then recorded on a dedicated Android application.

2.1 Ethical Considerations

Apart from health considerations, ethical considerations were also kept in mind. An instruction manual was developed and provided to each enumerator. The manual explained how to implement each instrument and the various data collection techniques that enumerators had to use throughout the exercise. Parts of the manual also laid out steps about critical matters on the ethics of data collection, such as introducing the study and gaining informed consent, building rapport, maintaining participant confidentiality and maximising the ease of data collection and validity of data. The study participants were explicitly informed about their right to refuse. Moreover, the data collection exercise was based on collecting anonymous data and the final dataset did not include any direct identification of the participants.

2.2 Data Collection Process

The data collection exercise comprised two arms. A household survey deploying a core set of items that were developed by the World Bank, and adapted to the context of the country, was administered to parents/caregivers. The survey questionnaire was based on the MODEL caregiver module and captured detailed information on the following:
- the child's home learning environment during the pandemic
- parental practices about play-based learning and health/hygiene
- socio-economic characteristics of the households and the extent to which they were impacted by the pandemic
- nature of parent-child interaction, especially within the context of resilience and coping with stress
- access to health and social safety schemes that were launched by the government etc.

In addition, another tool incorporating a shorter version of the Washington Group on Disability Statistics Child Functioning Module was deployed to capture the incidence of disability among young children. The responses obtained from this tool were then matched with the responses from the main caregiver survey to assess the scale and type of parental involvement in the education of children with disabilities during COVID-19.

The ECE school staff (teachers and head teachers) were interviewed using some items from MELE (Measure of Early Learning Environments), and additional items that were developed specifically for teachers of young children during the COVID-19 pandemic. This survey covers professional and financial support that was to the ECE workforce (if any); communications with children/caregivers; how teachers supported learning and development through distance learning during the school closures; and how teachers were involved in the operations of their schools.

The research was conducted in eight districts of Punjab (Bahawalnagar, Chakwal, Chiniot, Faisalabad, Kasur, Lodhran, Multan and Sargodha), ensuring representation of North, South and Central Regions of the province. These districts were randomly sampled from a sampling frame derived from the 2017 Population Census of Pakistan.

Approximately 20 villages were randomly selected from the sampling frame of the provisional village directory of the 2017 Population Census of Pakistan, using the probability proportional to size (PPS) method. A list of 10 additional villages was selected from each district as a replacement sample in case data from one of the sampled districts was unavailable. It was expected that one ECE school from each village would be covered. Once the villages were sampled, the study team engaged with the District Education Authorities (DEA). The teams shared the list of villages and obtained the contact number of the head teachers, responsible for government ECE classrooms in each village.

Following the listing exercise and obtaining contact details, 20 children from each ECE classroom were randomly selected. The household contact information of these children was shared by the head teacher. The households were then contacted via phone to administer the caregiver and CFM survey modules. Meanwhile, both the head teacher and the class teacher were interviewed for each school.

Table 11 summarises the overall sample across all eight districts:

Table 11: Overall summary of sample across all eight districts:

District	Caregiver Interview	Child Functioning Module	Teacher Interview	Head teacher Interview
Bahawalnagar	193	193	15	15
Chakwal	186	184	17	17
Chiniot	324	324	22	22
Faisalabad	321	317	24	24
Kasur	310	306	18	18
Multan	246	246	18	18
Lodhran	201	194	22	22
Sargodha	223	209	20	20
Total	**2007**	**1989**	**156**	**156**

Qualitative data for the research was collected via structured interviews with system-level informants (actors who are part of the policy process and implementation system). The aim was to identify their role in the overall system and the institutional factors that guided the structural response to early years learning during the pandemic. Some of the key themes investigated by the qualitative research were distance learning for early years, aspects of governance and accountability (including financing), particularly during the pandemic, data on learning losses, future plans to mitigate lthe losses that were incurred during lockdown, parental engagement, teacher support, communication across districts, development of feedback loops and intersectoral coordination for the early years during the pandemic. Informants were sampled from subnational levels, e.g., officials from School Education Department Punjab, Programme Monitoring and Implementation Unit (PMIU) and Quaid-e-Azam Academy for Educational Development (QAED), officials from the integrated sector such as Health and Nutrition and others. District-level informants included officials from the District Education Authority, including Chief Executive Officer (CEO) Education and Assistant Education Officers (AEOs).

As part of the primary data collection efforts, it was decided to supplement the quantitative surveys with open-ended and detailed data collected from parents. This took the form of focus group discussions (FGDs). These discussions aimed to garner parental views, particularly their involvement in early learning efforts during the pandemic. Ten in-person FGDs were conducted across three of the sampled districts (Chiniot, Multan, Lodhran).

The FGDs were based on the specific aspects of parental engagement, client-provider relationship, information barriers, child learning at home, stress management and contact with the official education system. Some open-ended questions were slightly modified and developed/adapted from MELQO questionnaires used globally.

A total of 103 parents, nearly 5% of the survey sample size, participated in the FGDs. On average, there were about 9-11 participants from each school. An overwhelming majority of these were mothers. The selection criteria for participation in the FGD comprised the following:

1) Parents who had been surveyed in the quantitative study
2) Parents whose children had attended school in the past six months

As the aim was to cover a variety of parents, no explicit exclusion criteria was applied on socio-economic conditions, digital connectivity and/or engagement with the school.

The sessions lasted 30-45 minutes each, where ECE parents were invited to a group discussion within the school premises while following the required social distancing measures.

Table 12: Distribution of Focus Group Discussion samples

FGD Sample		
District	No. of Schools	No. of parents
Chiniot	2	23
Lodhran	4	41
Multan	4	39
Total	10	103

3. Findings

This section looks at the survey results on three dimensions –the situation of teachers, the situation of children and their families and the situation regarding resources and prioritisation of ECE. First, the professional development support provided to teachers is examined, followed by the financial support they received during the school closures. Next, the situation of the children is looked at, first the participation levels of ECE students in distance learning activities and then the learning activities that children experienced at home, their learning outcomes and outcomes of the child functioning module. For the purpose of this study, distance learning includes children's regular and sustained engagement with relevant educational content through various mediums such as television, radio, internet and materials provided by the school (such as books/brochures). Finally, the situation regarding the ECE budget and prioritisation in the eight districts is described.

3.1 Professional Development and Support to Teachers

With the onset of the COVID-19 pandemic in Pakistan, both the federal and provincial governments took on a proactive approach towards education. However, the ECE subsector was neglected at the beginning of the pandemic. The first resilience plan, developed by the federal government to continue educational activities, did not identify early years as an action area. But, as the lockdown situation unfolded across the province, actors of the provincial systems adopted a leading role in the response strategy, thus increasing ownership of ECE in the province during the pandemic. It remains unclear if any substantial training to improve ECE-specific learning outcomes was provided. Officials noted that ECE pedagogy involves play-based learning instead of specific formative/summative assessments, which made it difficult to track the academic progress of these students during the lockdown.

Field interviews with head teachers in Multan and Chiniot also suggested that while a few school staff members had received training relevant to ECE, others did not. Besides this, they also noted that they were a part of WhatsApp groups and were in regular contact with their DEAs and thus were constantly informed about the school reopening situation. However, they were not invited to share their input on the question of school reopening. Similarly, the DEA officials themselves did not receive any ECE-specific training. At the district level, the provision of relevant training remained fragmented, as summarised in Figure 11. Some districts, such as Sargodha and Kasur, show increased training compared to others, such as Bahawalnagar, which emerged as a low-priority district.

Data from the teacher surveys sheds some light on the kind of support available to teachers during the pandemic-induced

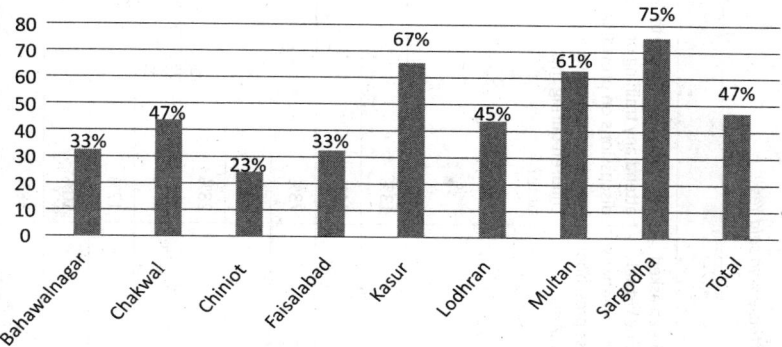

Figure 11: Teachers who received any kind of professional development/other support during school closures (n = 156)

lockdown and is summarised in Table 13. A significant majority of the teachers in all the districts were able to get up-to-date information on the operating status of the school, had regularly scheduled meetings with their principal/ head teacher and were able to contact their supervisor for guidance. However, the situation is less encouraging when it comes to professional development, teachers' feedback on preschool reopening plans and training on providing learning support to children.

Similarly, data from the head teacher survey indicates that an overwhelming majority of them had some way to get updated information and were in contact with their supervisors (AEOs) across all districts. Still, as supported by findings from the KIIs, the proportion of head teachers who received professional development training is low. In some districts, such as Faisalabad, only one-third of the head teachers reportedly received this form of support.

Table 13: Teachers provided support during lockdown (Teacher Survey). Percentage of those who said Yes.

	Teacher Support during lockdown (n = 156)					
	Do you have a way of getting up-to-date information on the school's operating status?	Do you have regularly scheduled meetings with your Principal or Head Teacher?	Are you able to contact your supervisor (Head teacher/ Principal/ Equivalent) as needed for guidance?	Have you received any professional development or other forms of support during the school closures?	Have you been asked to attend any virtual or in-person meetings that discuss preschool reopening plans?	Have you been asked to attend any training or discussions on providing learning support to children during this time?
Bahawalnagar	100%	100%	100%	33%	40%	13%
Chakwal	100%	100%	100%	47%	65%	24%
Chiniot	100%	95%	95%	23%	55%	73%
Faisalabad	96%	100%	100%	33%	63%	92%
Kasur	100%	100%	100%	67%	28%	28%
Lodhran	95%	100%	100%	45%	32%	27%
Multan	100%	100%	100%	61%	28%	17%
Sargodha	100%	95%	95%	75%	20%	10%
Total	99%	99%	99%	47%	42%	38%

Table 14: Support provided to the Head Teachers during lockdown (Head Teacher Survey). Percentage of those who said Yes.

Head Teacher Interview: Head Teacher Support during lockdown (n = 156)

	Do you have a way of getting up-to-date information on the school's operating status?	Have you been in contact with the Assistant Education Officer (AEO) of your area or anyone else in a supervisory role?	Are you able to contact your supervisor (AEO/Equivalent) as needed for guidance?	Have you received any professional development or other forms of support during the school closures?	Have you been asked to attend any virtual or in-person meetings that discuss preschool reopening plans?
Bahawalnagar	93%	100%	87%	40%	53%
Chakwal	100%	100%	76%	35%	71%
Chiniot	95%	100%	73%	50%	77%
Faisalabad	92%	100%	92%	33%	67%
Kasur	100%	100%	83%	44%	72%
Lodhran	95%	100%	91%	59%	68%
Multan	100%	100%	67%	22%	56%
Sargodha	90%	100%	80%	50%	70%
Total	96%	100%	81%	42%	67%

Another aspect of ECE staff's engagement was their involvement with the parents and how they transferred the information and training provided by the government to the parents. Therefore, support and training for ECE staff is further

Table 15: Support provided to teachers and teachers' support for children (Teacher Survey). Percentage of those who said Yes.

Support provided to Teachers & Teacher's Support for Children (n = 156)							
	Have you received training to support preschool children's well-being?	Have you received training to support preschool children's protection from abuse and neglect?	Did you use strategies to help you get in contact with hard-to-reach preschool children and their families?	Were there any preschool children or families you targeted more than others with your support?	Did you take measures to support preschool children's psychosocial well-being?	Did you take measures to support preschool children's protection from abuse and neglect while they are not in school?	Did you take any extra measures to support preschool children with disabilities while they are not in school during the COVID-19 times?
Bahawalnagar	40%	47%	7%	33%	80%	60%	7%
Chakwal	29%	35%	29%	29%	71%	71%	24%
Chiniot	14%	18%	9%	18%	32%	14%	14%
Faisalabad	38%	46%	21%	17%	67%	63%	29%
Kasur	33%	50%	17%	39%	89%	56%	17%
Lodhran	23%	45%	23%	23%	68%	55%	9%
Multan	33%	44%	11%	28%	78%	67%	6%
Sargodha	25%	35%	10%	20%	75%	50%	15%
Total	29%	40%	16%	25%	69%	53%	15%

Table 16: Financial support for ECE Staff during the lockdown. Percentage of those who said yes.

	Financial Support for ECE Staff During lockdown (n = 156)	
	When schools were closed, did you receive a salary?	Did you receive any special support from the government or your school during this time?
Bahawalnagar	100%	0%
Chakwal	100%	0%
Chiniot	95%	0%
Faisalabad	100%	4%
Kasur	94%	6%
Lodhran	91%	5%
Multan	100%	0%
Sargodha	100%	0%
Total	97%	2%

reflected in how they engaged with parents and children. There are, however, major lags concerning inclusivity and equity in teacher support for children. In three districts, fewer than 1 in 10 teachers reported taking extra measures for preschool children with disabilities. Similarly, across all districts, only a small proportion of teachers reported using any strategies to engage with hard-to-reach children and their families. A similar insight emerged from FGDs with parents who highlighted the challenges faced in staying in contact with the school during the lockdown. Thus, there is a significant number of students with whom teachers did not regularly engage during the lockdown.

3.2 Experience of Children and Families
Participation in Distance Learning for ECE during COVID-19
While children in primary grades were offered some form of distance learning opportunities in addition to regular contact

with teachers for assignments/homework, a similar approach was lacking for children in ECE during the early days of the pandemic. However, this changed, and some improvements were seen during the pandemic as more initiatives aimed at ECE children were introduced at the provincial level (discussed in the section above).

Although a majority of the teachers in the sample reported assigning home learning activities to ECE students during the lockdown period (86%), there was some ambiguity on the uptake of distance learning activities. More than half of the surveyed teachers estimated that less than 50% of the children in their ECE classrooms participated in distance learning activities (Figure 12). Thus, according to these teachers, less than half of the school-going ECE population was utilising the distance learning facilities through digital mediums such as TV/smartphones/computers etc. Nonetheless, 19% of the teachers thought that over 75% of their students had participated in the distance learning activities.

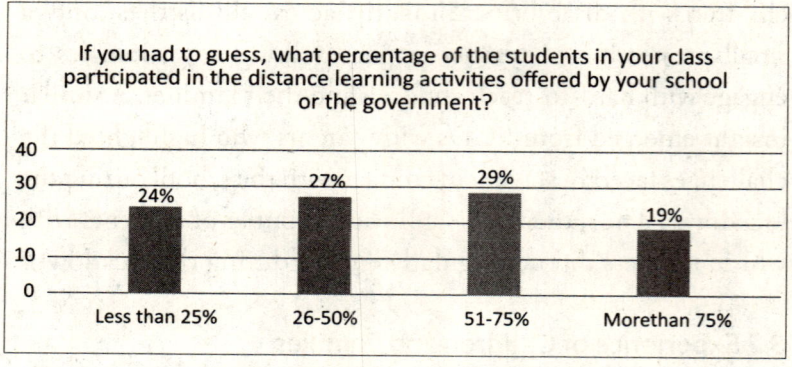

Figure 12: Percentage of Students in a Class who participated in Distance-learning Activities

3.3 Learning Activities at Home

As play-based learning is increasingly being recognised as a major component of learning in the early years and a crucial factor in child development, its presence in official ECE pedagogy is slowly emerging. In this regard, parental engagement has an essential role. Play-based learning is a process that continues in both official ECE classroom settings and at home. This was particularly the case in lockdown situations where young children did not and do not have access to ECE classroom settings which encourages learning and discovery. Thus, play-based learning at home with parental engagement became and becomes a substitute learning outlet and a much-desired one where the parents' bond with their children is strengthened.

Evidence from the study indicates a high uptake of play-based learning, with 87% of caregivers reporting to have played with their child during the past 15 days (Figure 13). Similarly, 91% of caregivers claimed to have read books and 87% said they had told stories to their child during the 15 days prior to the survey.

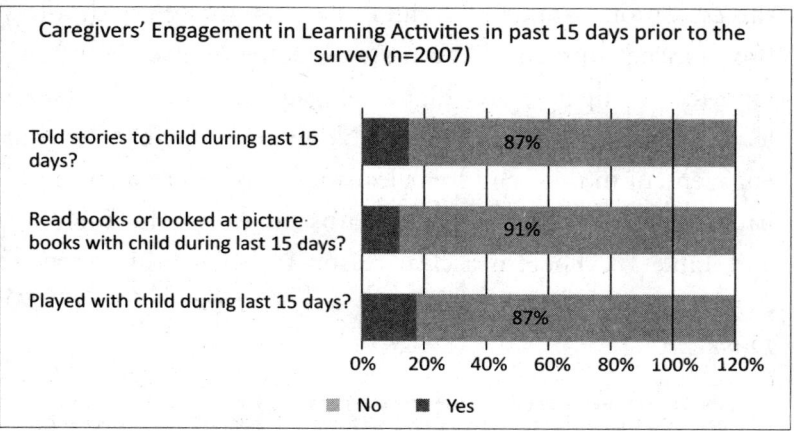

Figure 13: Caregiver's Engagement in Learning Activities

When divided across gender, the same consistency was on display except for reading books/looking at picture books with children, where the percentage was 95% for boys compared to 88% for girls. Apart from this, there were no significant differences in caregivers' engagement in learning activities across genders which is an encouraging sign.

Table 17: Gender-wise Caregivers' Engagement in Learning Activities in the 15 days before Caregiver Survey. Percentage of those who said yes.

Caregivers' Engagement in Learning Activities in the 15 days before survey (n = 2007)			
Child's Gender	Played with the child during the last 15 days	Read books or looked at picture books with the child during the last 15 days	Told stories to child during last 15 days
Boy	87%	95%	87%
Girl	86%	88%	86%
Total	87%	91%	87%
T-Test Significance (p-value)*	0.2647	0.0000	0.5784

There is also a link between play-based activities and the educational status of a child's parents, though with a less pronounced difference. Parents with some level of schooling reported comparatively higher engagement in play-based learning activities with children. Nonetheless, parents' overall engagement in their children's learning activities remains high, irrespective of their schooling status, as shown in Table 17 and Table 18. There is a clear reason to believe that *parental engagement in play-based learning can be termed the COVID Dividend.*

---

* The t-test answers whether the differences in percentage are statistically significant or no. P > 0.05 is the probability that the null hypothesis is true. For significance, the p-value has to be < 0.05. Free Learning Materials include all those materials which are available for public access and do not incur a direct cost.

On the other hand, access to distance learning was limited. As data from the qualitative interviews and FGDs also illustrate, children's access to distance learning depends on their socio-economic background, among other things. Therefore, the overall uptake for distance learning options was limited, as shown in Figure 14. The highest uptake for learning materials was the printed materials from school (73%). Distance-learning initiatives through computers with internet connection were accessed by a mere 4% of children, and only 12% accessed distance learning on a mobile phone or tablet. The lack of universal internet coverage was a major hindrance, as 93% of households reportedly did not have an internet or Wi-Fi connection. Outside of printed materials provided by schools, the second largest source of free learning material accessed by children was the television, with as many as 35% of children accessing it. Extrapolating these trends to the school-going ECE population in these districts, hundreds of thousands of ECE students accessed free learning materials[1] through printed materials[2] provided by schools and TV. This is positively encouraging and shows the huge impact and potential of these interventions and provides lessons for similar interventions in the future.[3] However, access to free learning materials also comprises a gendered dimension, as the following table demonstrates. This is especially true for printed materials from school, with 68% of parents of girls reporting access to these free learning resources, compared to 79% for boys.

---

1 Free Learning Materials include all those materials which are available for public access and do not incur a direct cost.
2 These printed materials include picture books and images shared by ECE teachers for children.
3 It is possible for a child to have used more than one option for accessing free learning materials.

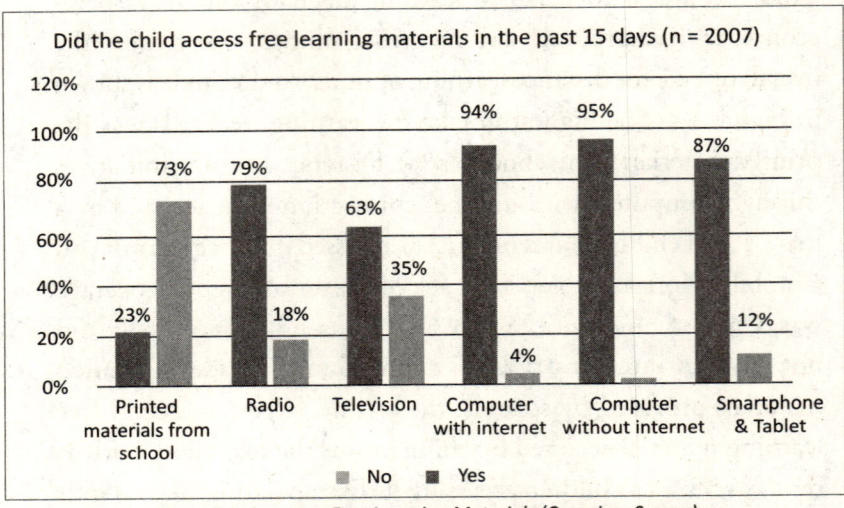

Figure 14: Access to Free Learning Materials (Caregiver Survey)

Table 18: Gender-wise children's access to Free Learning Material (Caregiver Survey). Percentage of those who said yes.

Did the child access free learning materials in the 15 days before survey (n = 2007)?						
Child's Gender	Radio	Television	Computer with internet	Computer without internet	Smart-phone/ Tablet	Printed materials from school
Boy	20%	37%	5%	2%	13%	79%
Girl	18%	34%	4%	3%	11%	68%
Total	18%	35%	4%	2%	12%	73%
t-Test Significance (p-value)*	0.7098	0.1097	0.2009	0.2009	0.9825	0.0000

* For significance, the p-value has to be < 0.05

3.4 Learning Outcomes

As schools closed and access to classrooms and teachers became limited, one of the major concerns for service providers and policy planners across the province was the learning losses incurred as children continued to stay at home. This concern was even more for children in the early years, where the lengthened suspension of schooling was likely to have ramifications in the long term.

As part of the Caregiver Survey, children's learning outcomes reported by their parents/caregivers were also recorded to acquire a sense of the learning levels of the children after an extended lockdown. Spread across three domains –literacy, numeracy and socio-emotional –the data provided insights into how the above-mentioned learning activities affected the child's development and learning.

Within the literacy domain, there were variations in both genders and across various competencies. For instance, while more than 82% of parents reported that their child could name at least three Urdu letters, and 75% reported the same for English letters, the proportion decreased significantly for reading and writing words. Only 57% parents said their children were able to write a simple 3-letter word in English. There was no consistent trend seen across genders. For instance, in some cases, boys outperformed girls in reading and writing simple English words, while girls had relatively better-reported outcomes in naming, reading and writing simple Urdu letters and words.

Compared to the literacy domain, the data for numeracy noted better learning outcomes. Except for one competency (identification of shapes), girls outperformed boys across all other numeracy competencies. Both genders reportedly performed well across the domain.

Along with literacy and numeracy, the caregiver survey also examined the socio-emotional state of the children, as reported by parents/caregivers. As Table 20 shows, the proportion of children from both genders with a stable socio-emotional state is unexpectedly high, as 79% children reported adjusting easily to transitions, and as many as 94% got along with their peers.

Table 19: Gender-wise reported learning outcomes of children at home (Caregiver Survey). Percentage of those who could read.

Reported Learning Outcomes at home – Literacy (n = 2007)						
Child's Gender	Is able to name at least three alphabets/letters in Urdu	Is able to name at least three alphabets/letters in English	Able to read four simple three-letter words in Urdu	Able to read four simple three-letter words in English	Able to write a simple three-letter word in Urdu	Able to write a simple three-letter word in English
Boy	80%	75%	69%	61%	66%	61%
Girl	84%	76%	71%	54%	68%	54%
Total	82%	75%	70%	58%	67%	57%
T-Test Significance (p-value)*	0.6263	0.0849	0.5959	0.0002	0.2771	0.0004

Table 20: Gender-wise reported learning outcomes of children at home (Caregiver Survey). Percentage of those enabled.

Reported Learning Outcomes at Home – Numeracy (n = 2007)					
Child's Gender	Identifies (says the name or points to) at least three shapes	Knows that a giraffe is taller than a cat	Accurately tells if it is yesterday, today and tomorrow	Knows that an elephant is heavier than a sheep	Knows that 8 is more than 2
Boy	76%	87%	74%	89%	78%
Girl	69%	89%	78%	91%	87%
Total	73%	88%	76%	90%	83%
t-Test Significance (p-value)	0.6034	0.9634	0.6646	0.8555	1.0000

* For significance, the p-value has to be < 0.05

Table 21: Gender-wise reported socio-emotional outcomes of children at home (Caregiver Survey). Percentage of those enabled.

	Reported Socio-emotional Outcomes (n = 2007)				
	Has good concentration	Remembers all the instructions when asked to do several things	Plans in advance before doing things	Gets along with other children	Adjusts easily to transitions (for example, a new teacher or classroom)
Boy	91%	88%	84%	92%	78%
Girl	88%	88%	85%	95%	81%
Total	**89%**	**88%**	**85%**	**94%**	**79%**
T-Test Significance (p-value)	**0.0039**	**0.8444**	**0.2088**	**0.9672**	**0.9858**

As highlighted by the data, the learning and development outcomes sketched a more encouraging picture of children staying at home. Nonetheless, these outcomes were reported by parents and are not necessarily indicative of the exact learning levels that children may possess. This gap between parental perception of the child's learning and the actual learning level is substantiated by FGDs and KIIs at the school level. During interviews with DEAs and head teachers, another significant set of problems emerged once the children returned to school. According to the informants, while parents may have engaged with children during the lockdown, the learning losses were immense. For instance, an AEO pointed out that in some schools under his jurisdiction, the proportion of children retained in ECE class and not promoted to the next grade was as high as 80%.

Moreover, according to the FGDs, gaps had emerged in the non-academic aspects of ECE, such as hygiene, social skills and etiquette. FGDs with parents and teachers indicated that being away from school and the absence of discipline that was enforced in the classrooms had resulted in behavioural changes for children. According to them, children weree less likely to behave as they would have before the lockdown, particularly in how they greeted, spoke, engaged, and played, engage and play with their teachers and peers. As respondent teachers indicated, this was also reflected in the language children used, which, according to them, no longer matched the tone set by the teachers in the ECE classrooms. The absence of teacher supervision during school closures, resulting in non-enforcement of discipline, affected child learning and socio-emotional growth. Although, this particular use of language, i.e. 'non-enforcement of discipline' is not ideal for ECE and is again a cause for caution and concern where 'enforcement of discipline' takes precedence over 'establishment of routine'.

3.5 Resources and Prioritisation of the ECE Sub-Sector

Evidence from the study suggests that ECE was not a high-priority area for the government at the start of the pandemic. However, the situation started improving, and more stakeholders took ownership of the ECE sector with time. ECE students were provided printed learning materials, while ECE staff members were provided with training on psycho-social development and general COVID-19 SOPs (Standard Operating Procedures).

4. Funding

On the financial side, qualitative fieldwork highlighted that the pandemic did not prompt any significant shifts in the overall funding for ECE from the government's side. Previously, the

---

* Planning and Development Department Punjab, 2020

funding for ECE in the province was less than 5% of the total funding for the education sector.* The overall budget allocation for school education during the fiscal year (2020-21) amounted to PKR 350.1 billion, out of which 27.1 billion was dedicated to development funding. While none of the allocations in the development budget were directly related to the early years, there were a few allocations which were expected to directly influence ECE service provision, such as teachers' training (800 million) and free textbooks (2.97 billion). The allocated budget for primary and pre-primary education was 2.089 billion (Ministry of Finance, 2021-22).

Along with government funding, several donor-funded interventions for the ECE sector were also introduced.[4] Moreover, during the interviews, multiple departmental, district and school actors agreed that ECE funding needed adjustments, particularly the Non-Salary budget.

Education funding, including funding for early years, is divided into two broad categories in Punjab: Current and Development Budgets. Salary Budget (SB) falls under current budget, while Non-Salary Budget (NSB) is a recurrent development grant that is provided directly to the schools for non-salary expenses. Due to a large number of ECE staff members across the province, most of the ECE funding was allocated to SB, which left lesser funds for the development of ECE rooms and provisions for other relevant facilities through the NSB grants. Quantitative data from the study indicated that most schools in the sampled districts did not face significant cash flow problems.

---

4   Schools had reopened partially at the time that the qualitative fieldwork was conducted.

4.1 ECE Policy and Implementation

One of the critical elements identified during all KIIs in ECE service provision, particularly in a pandemic-like situation, were the challenges associated with the learning assessment of younger children. Currently, there is no assessment measure–formative or summative–that can accurately capture the learning and development outcomes for children in ECE. As a result, the teachers could only gather data on each child's learning outcomes after the schools resumed. Post-COVID, various government units such as PMIU, PEC (Punjab Examination Commission) and QAED have now begun to define a framework for assessment in the ECE sector, as highlighted by QAED officials. The exact modalities of this new assessment mechanism and its efficacies are still under discussion and are likely to take shape soon.

Contrary to this, as noted by ECE teachers and the DEA staff, measuring learning outcomes for children in Katchi classes (pre-primary/often unofficial) is relatively feasible. The Katchi class has a defined syllabus and involves more direct learning than indirect play-based learning, which is a key feature of ECE classrooms. However, this classification between ECE and Katchi classes is itself rife with implementation issues. Most schools in Punjab have the same classrooms for children in both ECE and Katchi, making it difficult to ascertain the precise boundaries between the two and develop assessment measures accordingly. Thus, the process of learning assessments was further curtailed during the pandemic as children remained unassessed and untracked in their learning trajectories.

5. Discussion and the Way Forward

The key questions guiding this research are related to ECE in COVID-19 in terms of response, prioritisation, learning at home, staff support and eventual return to school. The study deployed a mixed-methods approach with quantitative data which was complemented by qualitative key informant interviews and focus-group discussions spread across eight districts, 2000+ households and more than 150 schools in Punjab. The findings of the study provide some critical insights into the early learning situation in Punjab.

- **A positive trend of play-based learning in ECE:** There is inherent potential in play-based learning. The high prevalence of play-based learning at home with parents, with teacher guidance is an important positive aspect, particularly due to the increasing recognition that play is gaining within ECE pedagogy worldwide. Thus, there is an opportunity to further engage parents to ensure that the learning environments for children are well-developed at both the classroom and household levels.

- **Potential space for distance learning:** Findings show that there is scope for distance learning in ECE. It is abundantly clear that various government and non-government actors have taken different steps to incorporate early learning into the larger distance learning response strategy. There is evidence that households are also eager for the same. Thus, this fulfils the basic necessary conditions on both the supply and demand sides. However, demand-side issues – such as access to the internet or television –and supply-side issues, such as budgetary and implementation constraints, continue to affect distance learning in ECE.

- **ECE Prioritisation in emergency response settings:** While government actors worked well over the past few years to transform and bring ECE up to modern standards, the findings show that there are still many milestones to achieve. The limited prioritisation of ECE during the pandemic and the learning losses demonstrated in the findings highlights the need to develop more coherent, entrenched and formalised ECE-specific strategies at a systems level that can mitigate the negative impact of emergency situations and ensure high outcomes at other times.
- **Improved Assessment Measures:** ECE in Punjab has come a long way in terms of formalisation and establishment of classrooms, monitoring and quality control. However, as noted by KIIs, there is potential to develop further processes and undertake reform actions in data collection, monitoring, child assessment and parental engagement. These processes must ensure a continuous feedback loop from the school level to the highest policy platforms – including SDG 4.2 and SDG 4.1.1 (lower primary learning) reporting –and vice-versa, eventually resulting in better learning outcomes
- **Progressive ECE financing:** The funding and budgetary allocations for ECE needs progressive and mainstream commitments. There is a need to provide increased recurrent and development budgets to ensure system-wide improvements in ECE. These include effective recruitment of a dedicated ECE cadre and professional development of ECE staff (teachers, head teachers, assistant teachers/ caregivers and monitors), establishment and upgrading of ECE classrooms, investment in play-based learning with

parental engagement, capacity for making localised learning materials and a more robust planning and implementation budgetary cycle.

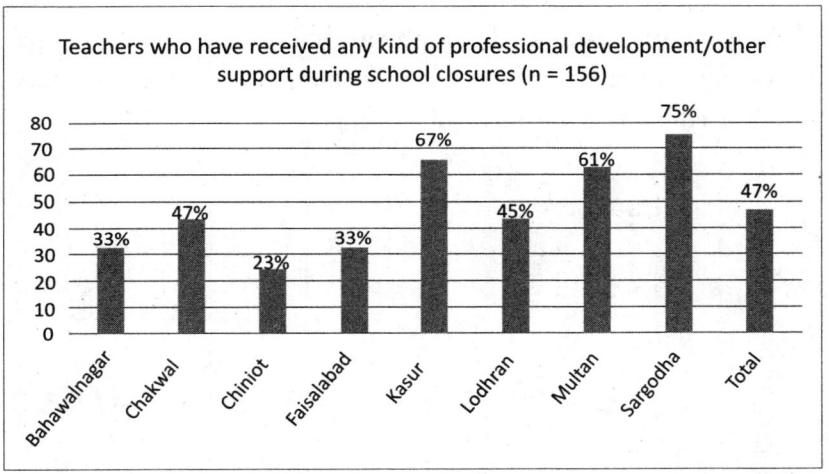

Figure 15: Teachers who have received any kind of professional development/other support during school closures (Teacher Survey)

Data from the teacher survey sheds some light on the kind of support available to teachers during the pandemic-induced lockdown and is summarised in Table 22. A significant majority of the teachers in all the districts had been able to get up-to-date information on the operating status of the school, had regularly scheduled meetings with their principal/ head teacher and had been able to contact their supervisor for guidance even during the pandemic (Figure 15). However, the situation is less encouraging when it comes to professional development, teachers' feedback on preschool reopening plans and training on providing learning support to children.

Similarly, data from the head teacher survey indicates that an overwhelming majority of head teachers had some way to get updated information and were in contact with their supervisors (AEOs) across all districts. Still, as supported by findings from the KIIs, the proportion of head teachers who received professional development training is low. In some districts, such as Faisalabad, only one-third of head teachers reportedly received this form of support.

Table 23: Support provided to the Head Teachers during lockdown (Head Teacher Survey). Percentage of those enabled.

Head Teacher Interview: Head Teacher Support During Lockdown (n = 156)					
	Do you have a way of getting up-to-date information on the school's operating status?	Have you been in contact with the Assistant Education Officer (AEO) of your area or anyone else in a supervisory role?	Are you able to contact your supervisor (AEO/ Equivalent) as needed for guidance?	Have you received any professional development or other forms of support during the school closures?	Have you been asked to attend any virtual or in-person meetings that discuss preschool reopening plans?
Bahawalnagar	93%	100%	87%	40%	53%
Chakwal	100%	100%	76%	35%	71%
Chiniot	95%	100%	73%	50%	77%
Faisalabad	92%	100%	92%	33%	67%
Kasur	100%	100%	83%	44%	72%
Lodhran	95%	100%	91%	59%	68%
Multan	100%	100%	67%	22%	56%
Sargodha	90%	100%	80%	50%	70%
Total	**96%**	**100%**	**81%**	**42%**	**67%**

Another aspect of ECE staff's engagement was their involvement with the parents and how they transferred the information and training provided by the government to the parents. Therefore, support and training for ECE staff was further reflected in how they engaged with parents and children. There were, however, major lags concerning inclusivity and equity in teacher support for children. In three districts, fewer than 1 in 10 teachers reported taking extra measures for preschool children with disabilities. Similarly, across all districts, only a small proportion of teachers reported using any strategies to engage with hard-to-reach children and their families. A similar insight emerged from FGDs with parents who highlighted the challenges they faced in staying in contact with the school during the lockdown. Thus, there is a significant number of students with whom teachers did not regularly engage during the lockdown.

Table 24: Support provided to teachers and teachers' support for children (Teacher Survey). Percentage of those enabled.

	Support Provided to Teachers & Teacher's Support for Children (n = 156)						
	Have you received training to support preschool children's well-being?	Have you received training to support preschool children's protection from abuse and neglect?	Did you use strategies to help you get in contact with hard-to-reach preschool children and their families?	Were there any preschool children or families you targeted more than others with your support?	Did you take measures to support preschool children's psychosocial well-being	Did you take measures to support preschool children's protection from abuse and neglect while they were not in school?	Did you take any extra measures to support preschool children with disabilities while they were not in school during the COVID-19 times?
Bahawalnagar	40%	47%	7%	33%	80%	60%	7%
Chakwal	29%	35%	29%	29%	71%	71%	24%
Chiniot	14%	18%	9%	18%	32%	14%	14%
Faisalabad	38%	46%	21%	17%	67%	63%	29%
Kasur	33%	50%	17%	39%	89%	56%	17%
Lodhran	23%	45%	23%	23%	68%	55%	9%
Multan	33%	44%	11%	28%	78%	67%	6%
Sargodha	25%	35%	10%	20%	75%	50%	15%
Total	**29%**	**40%**	**16%**	**25%**	**69%**	**53%**	**15%**

Financial Support for ECE Staff During lockdown (n = 156)		
	When schools were closed, did you receive a salary?	Did you receive any special support from the government or your school during this time?
Bahawalnagar	100%	0%
Chakwal	100%	0%
Chiniot	95%	0%
Faisalabad	100%	4%
Kasur	94%	6%
Lodhran	91%	5%
Multan	100%	0%
Sargodha	100%	0%
Total	97%	2%

Conclusion

In conclusion, the COVID-19 pandemic disrupted early years schooling in Pakistan. Its impact transcends quantifiable learning gaps. This study, leveraging MELQO tools and qualitative methods, unveils a deeper understanding of how home environments, teacher support, and systemic challenges intertwined to shape children's academic and socio-emotional well-being during this period.

Play-based learning emerged as a beacon of hope, highlighting its potential for low-cost, sustainable engagement even in resource-constrained settings. Parents, despite facing their own struggles, demonstrated a commendable willingness to support their children's learning. Teachers, too, displayed remarkable resilience, utilising low-tech solutions to maintain connections and nurture well-being.

However, these efforts were hampered by pre-existing inequities and traditional parenting mindsets. Limited access to technology, coupled with inadequate teacher training and positive parenting practices in early-years pedagogy, exacerbated the challenges in marginalised communities. Bridging these gaps requires a paradigm shift in how we approach early childhood education (ECE) in Pakistan, by going beyond filling learning gaps to more holistic pedagogical regimes. Policymakers and educators must rise to the occasion by prioritizing ECE as a cornerstone of national development and strong foundational learning. Context-specific strategies are crucial, focusing on:

- **Investing in Early Childhood Development (ECD) Professionals:** Equipping teachers with specialised training in ECD practices, particularly play-based pedagogy, empowers them to effectively support childrens holistic development.
- **Promoting Inclusive Play-Based Learning:** This low-cost, engaging approach fosters essential skills across diverse contexts, narrowing the equity gap and ensuring that all children benefit from its advantages.
- **Strengthening Home-School Partnerships:** Collaborative efforts between teachers, parents, and communities can create a supportive network that empowers families to nurture their children›s learning journey through positive parenting.
- **Leveraging Technology Responsibly:** Technology can bridge geographical divides and provide access to learning resources. However, its integration must be mindful of equity concerns, gendered access challenges in low resource settings and potential challenges of digital safety and literacy.

The pandemic may have exposed ECE's vulnerabilities, but it also ignited a spirit of resilience, care and innovation. By harnessing this momentum, Pakistan can move beyond simply recovering from learning losses and build a more robust, inclusive ECE system. This investment in the youngest generation will pay dividends not only in academic improvement and social emotional learning, but also in shaping a more equitable and prosperous future.

SECTION TWO

Systems, Learning and Technology

> I. Purpose-Driven Education Systems
> II. Desired Code Vs Desirable Codes: Language Learning in a Multi-Cultural Context
> III. PAL Network's ELTU Project: Foundational Learning supported by Indigenous Resources Experiences
> IV. A Scalable, Digital Learning Experiment: Analysing Children's Group Dynamics in Pratham's PraDigi Programme

THIS section looks at various education systems, learning environments and technological interventions.

This section starts with an essay on *Purpose-Driven Education Systems*. It gives an overview of the different systems that have been able to become 'more coherent for learning', which in turn have resulted in considerable learning gains. Using case studies from Brazil, Mexico, Tanzania, Kenya and India, the essay describes how system shifts were undertaken for more learning coherence. The study finds that multiple factors must come together to make this transition possible, including political will, explicitly stated learning goals, the commitment to adhere to them, and clear communication of the goals to the entire system. Describing the successful shifts made by these systems from less coherent to more coherent, the essay argues that the 'route to change is through the heart of an education system – its purpose'.

The second chapter *Desired Code Vs Desirable Codes: Language Learning in a Multi-Cultural Context* argues that much 'unlearning' may be necessary for children belonging to smaller, indigenous and minority communities to find a cultural 'fit' as able functionaries in their societies. The reason is that most textbooks followed in schools are biased towards the majority speech groups, their legends, grammar and morality. It further shows that what the children learn in the school system is control over an elite code that may suit them well in their future professional lives. However, they do not learn about the cultural context in which they are expected to use this Desired Code. The authors believe that this monistic approach to language leaves them in a difficult situation, because they have to function in a familiar and natural multilingual setting in the local contexts that demand code-mixing in the Desirable Codes. In contrast, all they learn in an apparently 'seamless' school setting encourages them to shun the mixing of speech codes. The chapter then proposes how through a mediating multilingual approach, a new kind of school curriculum could be built for such plural cultural contexts.

The theme of plural culture and multilingualism continues in the third chapter *PAL Network's ELTU Project: Foundational Learning supported by Indigenous Resources Experiences*. This study shares the experience and learning from the Every Language Teaches Us project, a multi-country, multilingual project to source teaching-learning resources from native and less-privileged languages. The chapter describes the efforts to promote community and indigenous knowledge to support foundational literacy and numeracy in children. The project is based on the argument that without teachers to help children navigate the educational content during the school closures learning gains were limited for young learners, as many learn through a second language or languages other than their mother tongue. This situation would have exacerbated the learning gap. The ELTU project that went on in eight countries helped in building a repository of indigenous language resources. These resources adapted for learning were used to strengthen the children's literacy and numeracy while also contributing to revitalising native languages.

This section ends with a technological intervention in India that studies how group dynamics play in such interventions. *A Scalable, Digital Learning Experiment: Analysing Children's Group Dynamics in Pratham's PraDigi Programme* explores issues related to children's group dynamics, identity and learning observed in Pratham's 'PraDigi Open Learning Programme' implemented in rural regions of Uttar Pradesh, Maharashtra and Rajasthan, India. Analysis of children's intra-group and inter-group interactions is used to understand their adoption of self-learning in a developing context. Social constructs, group cohesion and group formation are also analysed to gain insights into the children's self-regulated group learning. PraDigi serves as a scalable model to overcome access barriers and iteratively design a digitally-supported learning programme that supports children's social, emotional and foundational learning. This study also focused on children's group-level identities and learning.

Purpose-Driven Education Systems
Michelle Kaffenberger

Introduction

The evidence base for understanding education systems, children's learning outcomes, and approaches that do and do not improve children's learning has expanded remarkably in recent years. The RISE Programme, a long-term, multi-country research endeavour which is investigating how education systems can become more coherent for learning, has sought to contribute to this growing body of work.[1] While it has generated theoretical and empirical work on the characteristics of a coherent system, what has been missing, but is slowly emerging, is an articulation of how systems shift from being incoherent to being coherent for learning.

The nominal purpose of an education system is to equip the children of a country (or region or district) with quality education. However, in practice, education systems serve many purposes and interests, some explicit (such as goals of social

---

[1] The programme includes research teams in seven countries in Africa and Asia, two political economy teams, and a team of thematic researchers at the directorate; all focused on research to overcome the learning crisis.

cohesion) and some implicit (such as providing economic rents to political or bureaucratic actors). When these purposes stray too far from the purpose of providing high-quality education, low learning outcomes result.

This essay highlights a short but growing list of examples of education systems that have successfully shifted to being (more) coherent for learning, resulting in large learning gains. A common theme across these examples is the restoration of learning as the core purpose of the education system. This has taken the form of strong political will, the commitment and dedication of leaders to explicit learning goals, and clear communication of these goals to the rest of the system. The commitment to learning goals then allowed other elements in the system, which in the RISE systems framework we define as finance, support, information, and motivation, to also align around these goals (Figure 16). Such political will and commitment have been spurred by new and widely-available information on low learning levels and by grassroot movements demanding higher-quality education.

Delegation	What one actor in the system asks another actor to do.
Finance	Resources provided to carry out the tasks.
Support	Assistance and training provided to carry out the tasks.
Information	Information used to evaluate performance on the tasks.
Motivation	Ways in which the welfare of the actors being delegated to is contingent on their performances. Can be extrinsic or intrinsic.

Figure 16: RISE Systems Framework design elements
Note: For more on the RISE systems framework, see Pritchett (2015), Spivack (2021) and Kaffenberger and Spivack (2022).

1. How systems have shifted to align for learning

There is a growing, though still limited, number of examples of education systems that have shifted from incoherence for learning to greater coherence for learning.

1.1 Sobral, Brazil

In just 12 years, Sobral, Brazil, went from being the 1,366th municipality for learning to become the top performer in the national basic education ranking (Crouch, 2020). Despite high levels of poverty, its national assessment scores are 80 per cent higher than would be expected for its level of education expenditure.

In 2000-2001, a learning assessment conducted by the municipality revealed that 40 per cent of primary school students could not read (Loureiro & Cruz, 2020). In response to these and other findings, Sobral's Mayor established seven education goals, out of which the top two focused on literacy for primary school children. These goals prioritised and emphasised literacy as a core purpose of Sobral's education system and one which everyone in the system would be working towards. Under the banner of 'alphabetisation at the right age', the goals were sharp and easy to communicate: 1) ensure all 6- and 7-year-olds learn to read and 2) ensure all students in Grades 2 through 6 who could not read, should receive remedial support and learn to read.

These goals drove a set of policies and actions which pulled on multiple system levers. Drawing on the elements in the RISE systems framework, the policies brought information (including learning-based monitoring systems with feedback loops so that teachers and schools could adapt instructions to align with children's learning levels and assessments of all children twice per year), support (structured lessons for teachers, well-aligned teaching materials, and professional development based on materials), and motivation (good communication across different levels and actors in the system, bonuses, awards, and public recognition events for teachers and school leaders) in line with learning goals. By ensuring that these system design elements were kept consistent with the learning goals that had been established, these sets of policies achieved a level of system coherence that enabled improvements.

The result was considerable improvements in early literacy. The clear establishment of learning goals and alignment of other elements of the system with the goals was possible primarily because of commitment to the purpose of learning throughout the system.

1.2 Nationwide Tusome Programme in Kenya

In 2009-2012 multiple learning assessments, including the Uwezo and the baseline for the Primary Math and Reading (PRIMR) pilot programme, showed very low student learning levels. This served as a 'wake-up call' for education leaders. The subsequent success of PRIMR led to a desire among government authorities for a nationwide scale-up to improve learning, which resulted in the Tusome programme (Crouch, 2020; Piper et al., 2018).

Tusome established national benchmarks for learning outcomes, and the clearly-established 'purpose' of improving foundational learning was communicated down the system to schools (Piper et al., 2018). This clarity of expectations and purpose enabled other elements in the system to be aligned with the benchmarks, which included support (drawing again on the elements in the RISE systems framework) delivered through well-structured year-long curricula, teachers' guides, structured lessons, formative assessments for classroom use, ongoing coaching for teachers, textbooks for students; and information whereby early grade reading and math assessments (EGRA and EGMA) were used to track learning, accountability mechanisms for coaches and supervisors. These efforts resulted in large learning improvements.

1.3 Puebla, Mexico

Puebla, Mexico, has the fifth highest poverty level out of Mexico's 32 States, yet it ranks among the highest in national education assessments. In 2011, a new administration took office, and the new State Secretary of Public Education established three education objectives: universal school attendance, universal persistence and completion through upper secondary school, and universal learning achievement above the minimum level on national assessment (Crouch, 2020). These goals constituted a shared commitment with all children's school attainments and learning achievements.

From these precisely-established goals, a programme was implemented initially in select lower-performing schools and later more widely. The programme brought support, keeping in line with the targets, with well-designed and structured materials that were distributed to schools, teacher training focused on quality, not quantity, and locally recruited training facilitators from among the best teachers/principals/supervisors; information, by using a new mid-year Grade 2 assessment allowing time to course correct, assessments in Grade 5, identification of at-risk children for targeted attention, and school visits by decision-makers; and motivation, by giving facilitators/supervisors new honorary positions with status and prestige (Crouch, 2020). This package of system improvements, affecting multiple system design elements and aligned with the established purpose of improving schooling and learning, resulted in significant gains. In recent years, Puebla has had one of the fastest rates of improvement in the PISA (Programme for International Students Assessments) and is a prominent outlier for achievements relative to poverty levels.

1.4 Tanzania's 3Rs reform

Between 2006 and 2012, pass rates in Tanzania's primary school leaving exams more than halved, and in 2012 only 31 per cent of students who took the exam passed. These results were compounded by poor results in foundational skills on Uwezo assessments and subsequently in EGRA and EGMA. The poor learning performance spurred the government to take action to improve learning outcomes (Komba & Shukia, 2021). It took action by instituting the 3Rs curriculum reform, with the specifically delegated purpose of improving the 3Rs, namely reading, writing, and arithmetic in the early grades, specifically Grades 1 and 2.

Implementing the reform involved aligning many parts of the system with the newly-established goals. This included providing support to teachers and schools by developing and supplying new curricula, textbooks, and teacher instructional materials; in-service teacher training; school-based continuous professional development modules; and training for head teachers to support school leadership. Further, new information aligned with the delegated goals was provided in the system through the introduction of an annual Grade 2 assessment. The government also received financial support from Global Partnership for Education (GPE), United Nations Children's Fund (UNICEF), and United States Agency for International Development (USAID).

At least nine organisational actors were involved in designing and implementing programmes related to the 3Rs reform, ranging from the Ministry of Education, Science and Technology (MoEST), the Tanzania Institute of Education (TIE), GPE, UNICEF, USAID, and others. While the number of actors involved presented coordination challenges (Komba & Shukia, 2021), the clear, common, delegated goal of improving foundational literacy and numeracy enabled an environment in which many actors were able to undertake separate tasks and still achieve coherence for a common goal, ultimately making progress in the learning outcomes (Hwa et al., 2020). An external evaluation of the reform found that it achieved significant, positive increases in children's learning in both Kiswahili and mathematics (Rodriguez-Segura & Mbiti, 2022).

1.5 Pratham and Government Partners in India

Pratham, arguably among the largest and most successful education NGOs, launched its ASER assessments in 2005 under a theory of change that information on (low) learning could empower individuals to hold governments to account and spur political commitment to learning and, ultimately, improvements to the learning outcomes. Indeed, 15 years later, ASER results have been heavily cited by education authorities in India and informed education policies at both national and State levels.

Partly because of low learning results revealed in ASER assessments, multiple State governments have committed to improve learning in schools. Fifteen states have partnered with Pratham to support and train teachers in instructional techniques to ensure that children master foundational literacy and numeracy. The partnerships have also resulted in using

ASER-like assessments in classrooms for teachers to have continuous information on learning levels and improvements. Further government interest and partnerships with positive results emerged as well, one of them being Uttarakhand State's work with Room to Read on foundational learning. Additionally, ASER assessment questions have been incorporated into some State-level assessments, to provide ongoing information on learning improvements at the State level.

Findings from ASER assessments over many years also contributed to the establishment of foundational learning goals by the Government of India in the new National Education Policy 2020, and the associated national mission on Foundational Literacy and Numeracy. It is too early to gauge the effects of these new learning goals, but the political attention to foundational skills is itself an achievement.

1.6 Fostering Commitment for the Purpose of Learning

Many education actors, including national education leaders, non-governmental actors, and international donors and funders, want to know how to improve education system coherence for learning to improve learning outcomes. Actions have been taken to foster a commitment for a clear purpose of improving learning outcomes and allow other elements in the system to align for the same. Many involve more extended time frames than typical development 'projects'. However, by facilitating the reorientation of a system (whether at the national, regional, or district level), they have the potential to produce substantial and sustained gains.

One way that a commitment to the purpose of learning has been fostered in a variety of contexts is by conducting or funding learning assessments. These have spurred political and citizen-led attention and action and empowered champions within the education system to bring about change.

Findings from learning assessments as catalysts for spurring commitment to learning improvements appear in multiple examples above. These learning assessments were not primarily intended or being used for management accountability but rather for driving policy and programmatic attention and action. In Tanzania, Uwezo, EGRA, and EGMA drew attention to low learning; in Kenya, Uwezo results and baseline assessment for an education pilot project similarly achieved attention and action for learning. In Nicaragua (not discussed above), an EGRA conducted in partnership with the government spurred immediate actions to improve learning (Gove & Wetterberg, 2011). In Senegal, on the other hand, an EGRA did not drive immediate government action but was used by the civil society to draw attention to low learning (Gove & Wetterberg, 2011).

Of course, new information on learning does not always drive attention or action. The use of such assessments may be more politically feasible or desirable when a new government is formed rather than in the middle of an administrative term. In some places, the effectiveness of such assessments to drive policy relies on the presence and prominence of civil society actors who can use the results to advocate for change, which leads to the second purpose.

A second purpose has been fostered in contexts that have achieved learning improvements through the work of domestic think- and do-tanks. Domestic think tanks and evidence-informed, action-oriented civil society actors can significantly influence what politicians prioritise and act on. These entities create domestically-relevant research and knowledge, develop and maintain ongoing relationships with government actors, and advocate for reform from within a country.

Pratham, and its ASER assessments, have successfully driven attention and action on foundational learning in India. Central Square Foundation (also in India) engages with education decision-makers in addition to implementing education programmes. It has also advocated focusing on foundational learning in India's new National Education Policy. The Centre for the Study of the Economies of Africa (CSEA) in Nigeria provides research and analysis and a forum for policy dialogue between government stakeholders, the private sector and civil society actors.

SMERU, in Indonesia, similarly produces policy-relevant research and engages with the education ministry to improve learning. The INOVASI programme works directly with Indonesia's Education Ministry to implement education programmes and has been partnering with and advocating for government officials to prioritise learning, especially foundational skills, as schools reopened, following the COVID-19 school closures. In Nicaragua, the success of EGRA results in bringing about political action to improve learning is in part attributed to a local NGO, Centro de Investigación y Acción Educativa Social (CIASES), that the project-lead Research Triangle Institute (RTI) partnered with to implement the assessment. CIASES' high-level connections with the ministry and ongoing presence and influence on the ground enabled the new information on learning to translate into government dedication to action.[2]

---

2   For more see: Gove and Wetterberg, 2011.

A third change has been fostered at high levels of government through supporting future leaders today. Many of the successful examples above were driven by the dedication of a small set of leaders or bureaucrats who chose to prioritise a commitment for the purpose of learning. There are many examples of investing in future leaders from both within and outside the education sector.

Vanderbilt's Graduate Programme in Economic Development was established in 1954 to provide training in economic development to students from developing countries. The programme has trained future finance ministers and heads of central banks. Developing or facilitating access to similar, high-quality programmes for education could support future education leaders. The World Bank runs an Africa Fellowship Programme for young African scholars, a model which could be tailored for those focused on education. The African Leadership Academy in South Africa trains young people with the goal of '[transforming] Africa by developing a powerful network of young leaders who will work together to address Africa's greatest challenges'.

In the education sector, the Teach for All network is made up of national organisations in 60 countries that 'recruit promising leaders and train and support them to teach in classrooms for at least two years. Through this classroom experience and through cultivating ongoing connections with alumni, communities, and partner organisations, they seek to encourage young people to dedicate themselves to leadership in education. In another example, a consortium of universities, including the Lahore University of Management Sciences (LUMS), University of Cape Coast, Ghana, and University College London, have partnered to offer an 'education systems' course, training current masters' students on changes in education systems.

The Association for the Development of Education in Africa (ADEA) invests in capacity development for education policymaking. This includes efforts like Education Research in Africa Award, which invests in African researchers and African research capacity to inform effective education decision-making. The Brookings Institution hosts the Echidna Global Scholars Programme, which selects leaders and scholars from developing countries, provides residency at the Institution for them to research on improving learning outcomes in their country of focus, and supports them to take action when they return to their countries. These types of efforts are undertaken with a long-term view, facilitating the dedication of current and future education leaders to children's learning.

All these efforts and more have contributed to commitments to learning in a variety of contexts. Change is possible, and the short list of successful cases is slowly growing. This essay argues that the route to change is often through the heart of an education system – its purpose. Building and driving commitment to learning for all children, and instilling that commitment at all levels of an education system, maybe a critical first step towards the large-scale learning improvements that are needed to ensure quality education for every child.

Desired Code Vs Desirable Codes Language Learning in a Multi-Cultural Context

Udaya Narayana Singh, Conchúr Ó Giollagáin and Gordon Wells

1. Global South and Learning Issues

A considerable learning gap in the Global South is a known phenomenon. Irrespective of economic progress in Global South nations such as India and Kenya, the gap is ever-increasing; research has shown that despite increasing educational resources and government expenditure, the improvement in children's learning outcomes has not grown proportionally. This mismatch can be attributed to the fact that much of the resources have been used to increase children's enrolment in schools with lesser attention to educational quality. The existing learning gap widened because of a global pandemic situation during 2019-2022, especially among the section that had no access to online alternatives. Therefore, teaching-learning in such countries requires a re-look, especially to consider how the dislocations caused by pandemic-like situations can be plugged. This paper examines the disconnect between 'unconnected people', children's foundational education, and the language diversity of their socio-cultural environments.

An emergency situation such as the COVID-19 pandemic heightened the acute challenges of education management in many resource-starved Global South societies. Some of them lag in education because of poor economic health of the country or society and cannot achieve the desired teacher-student ratio, while others lack the physical infrastructure that directly impacts learning (as in Sudan, where only 2 per cent area has electricity). The other issue that immediately attracts our attention is the extent of the linguistic diversity of these regions. There are, of course, exceptions, such as Burundi, which is mainly monolingual with Kirundi as the main language; Somalia, where the population predominantly speaks Somali and eight other minor languages; and Guinea-Bissau which has Portuguese as the legacy language and Guinea-Bissau Creole as another official language (plus five more). However, most countries lagging in learning outcomes also happen to be linguistically diverse such as India (with 3500 plus mother tongues and 400 plus more populous languages) and Papua New Guinea, with 820 languages. Equally diverse linguistically are Indonesia, which has 742 languages, and Nigeria, which has 516. They are not exceptions. Evidence suggests that less linguistically diverse regions are more accessible in terms of education planning.

The challenge for educators in the Global South is to not allow learning gaps and maintain continuity in all kinds of learning environments, including different kinds of linguistic environments. What the children learn in the school system in many of these countries is control over an elite Desired Code that may suit them in their professional lives, but they do not get to know about its cultural contexts. However, in some speech communities, this monistic approach to language teaching leaves them in a difficult situation because they have to function in a natural multilingual setting that may demand code-switching and mixing in the Desirable Codes. The gap between the two codes has widened in the Global South as time went by, compared with developed nations.

However, there have been pockets in the Global North with serious issues of language preservation in the middle of a live multi-cultural space, where there are less fortunate smaller speech groups that decides their strategies differently. For instance, in some situations, such as in Scotland, one may disfavour code-mixing in Gaelic and English, as that leads to lesser and lesser use of the marginalised speech forms. As against this, many speech groups in Sikkim in India happily integrate some Nepali in their everyday communication as the latter emerged as a lingua franca here. Thus, the linguistically homogeneous context seems to be like a utopia.

In the 1960s, Bernstein made an important suggestion concerning how two sociolinguistic codes work, marking social inequalities based on language use. Bernstein (1971) talked about two general types of codes: Elaborated and Restricted. Those belonging to the middle and upper middle classes handle elaborate codes with many options and alternatives to choose from as they communicate. In the case of a restricted code which is used mostly by the working class, the number of these alternatives is severely limited. Psychologically, their distinction depends on the extent to which each facilitates (Elaborated Code) or inhibits (Restricted code) our speech orientations. The purest restricted codes happen in predictable situations, as in protocols, religious services, weather and party talks, or in some story-telling situations. The predictability comes from the general condition where the members of a speech group have a common and extensive set of closely-shared identifications and expectations. The speech here is likely to be fast and fluent, with articulatory clues reduced – where a lot is predictable, condensed and local – with a low level of vocabulary choice and syntactic selection. Those privileged to handle elaborated codes show very little predictability at both levels.

The proposal of 'Desired code' vs 'Desirable Code' in this paper is neither an extension of Basil Bernstein's 1960s dichotomy of 'Elaborated Code' as against the 'Restricted Code,' nor is it strictly comparable with this dichotomy. Bernstein's purpose was to explain the poor results of the working-class students in their mastery of languages – for which he made their membership in a given societal class responsible. He was not dealing with multilingual contexts. Later, Bernstein (1971) suggested that the learners or speakers belonging to the working class should use mostly restricted code because they were raised in a particular kind of social condition. Their socialisation process did not make them proficient, unlike their middle-class counterparts, in the use of both elaborated and restricted codes. Whereas an elaborated code had many options and details to plan a detailed conversation, a restricted code would always require to be precise, condensed and short – to understand which one needed to be a member of this class. In this paper, the Desired Code is generally a colonial legacy or an elite majority language that must be mastered to climb the social ladder. In comparison, what is being described as the Desirable Code recognises the plurality or multiplicity of languages in the school system, which needs to be more tolerant and accommodating to allow multilingual upbringing and expressions.

2. More about the 'Learning Gap': Could Unlearning be a Strategy?

With the onslaught of COVID-19, one has learnt that life and business can all wait until one can get back on one's feet. But the trouble is that while all other things can wait, childhood cannot. Winthrop and McGivney (2015) from the Brookings Institution raise an essential question in this context. It took us 200 years to bring – so far, 90 per cent of children to school (Figure 17). But they also remind us that innovative solutions for the hapless 10 per cent need to be thought of. They say: 'Without a fundamental rethinking of current approaches to education, it's going to take another 100 years for children in developing countries to reach the education levels achieved'[1] in the Global North. But can one wait another hundred years to bring some parity between the North and the South? Some may argue that the mass education method may not be the only way to educate children properly. The learning problems get complicated as one looks at the bottom of the pyramid in developing nations (Singh, Singh & Banerjee, 2020). How knowledge passes on from one generation to another is decided differently in each cultural community. Nevertheless, the fact that most nation-states have accepted schooling as a sure-shot way to educate is undoubtedly true at this point of time in history, as this figure[2] from the Centre for Universal Education shows:

---

1 https://www.weforum.org/agenda/2020/08/internet-users-usage-countries-change-demographics/
2 Cf: http://www.brookings.edu/~/media/Research/Files/Reports/2015/06/100-year-gap-primary-education-winthrop-mcgivney/v1.png?la=en

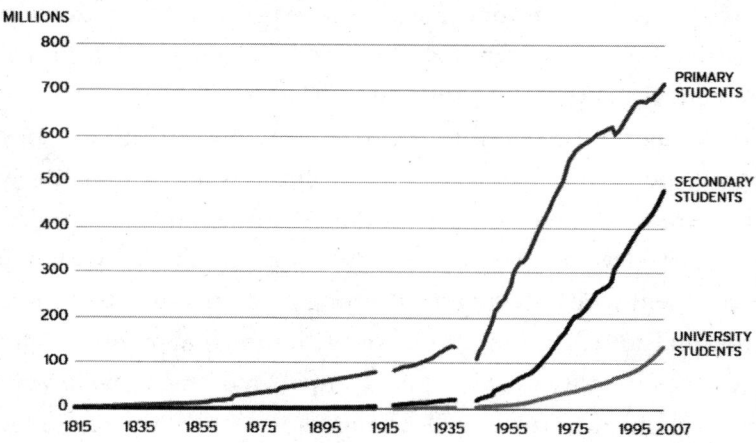

Figure 17: Progress in School Education: 1815-2007

Although there is a correlation between industrialisation and modernisation of the economy and production mechanisms and progress in establishing the modern-day school system, the lack of these factors is not necessarily the reason for the learning gap. They are not easy to find as there have been several other factors behind the spread of schooling on a large scale. One is the rise of nationalistic feelings or an urge to see one's own linguistic or cultural community on top. In addition, there is a desire to be on an equal footing with the world's other highly developed cultures or the rising consciousness of human rights. There is no point in determining whether less democratic countries or those with inferior economic strength contribute more to the learning gaps. Citizen-Led Assessments of learning abilities find fault with all kinds of systems and countries with varying GDPs.

While knowledge of agricultural activities and the acquisition of various skill sets associated with many arts and crafts were available in a community, with the expansion of production bases, even this traditional knowledge required institutional frameworks. These institutions became agencies for the development of a country's growth. The advent of technology and modernisation demanded that societies begin to think anew about how to increase their production, sales, and economies. As they devote energies to increasing productivity, many experiment with reducing the learning gaps, assuming that more efficient learning accomplishments will, somehow, contribute to greater productivity. Consequently, this achievement will reveals more about the nature of learning gaps – and how to bridge them. It is still necessary to look at the extent to which learning difficulties arise due to the huge gap between the school language and the home language. While this is true, one notices that there is considerable variation in the GDPs between countries with CLAs, and the per capita may not be that different. So this correlation needs to be further studied before making any generalisations. Notably, all the Global South countries with low learning outcomes of children's foundational learning were exploited or colonised in the past 200-500 years. That kind of subjugation must have also taken its toll on the education sector.

The colonial past of many nation-states has created a legacy of English education or Spanish medium or French ways of learning or a Portuguese system. The education managers in these states plan for foundational learning to demonstrate that children are enrolled and counted in the formal system – a statistical approach. However, dominant learning theorists of the Global North do not tell us that a lot of unlearning may be necessary for children belonging to indigenous communities to find a cultural fit, to function in their societies. In contrast, textbooks are generally biased towards the speech and grammar of the majority.

When history provides an opportunity for the political establishment to plan to bridge the learning gaps afresh, one must ask if it is necessary to push away the skills and knowledge that are no longer relevant today. In our minds, a change of perspective could be brought about only if we are willing to make these changes. Many institutions and organisations take a long time to realise that their long-standing perspectives, strategies, or tactics require a re-examination. Frozen syllabi do not encourage learning, as institutions are not 'future-fit', and pupils struggle with an 'unlearning' of redundant approaches. With new ideas, novel approaches and theories entering different fields, it may be necessary to take a few steps back and keep these new possibilities on par with the well-known and time-tested approaches.

Given the changing scenario, it may be necessary to re-evaluate which course of action would be the best. It would be essential to evaluate the novelty or newness of the solution offered to see if it provides a trigger to initiate 'unlearning'. If the World Economic Forum's Future of Work Report of 2016 adopted in Davos were to be believed, with the advancement of 'advanced robotics and autonomous transport, artificial intelligence and machine learning, advanced materials, biotechnology and genomics', over one-third of skills considered necessary in today's workforce would have changed. *Five years on and despite massive disruptions, we have not witnessed marked changes in how we survive and live our lives. If we seek constant and quick-fix growth in all walks of life, it further disrupts the transmission of established perspectives and practices. As the process becomes more disruptive, the intensity of the 'unlearning' to relearn lessons becomes more challenging.*

The picture gets more complicated in some other geo-spaces. For example, in some highly plurilingual countries, the fluid and multidimensional linguistic boundaries at the community level adds a post-colonial versus a counter-colonial dimension to the contexts. Different situations arise in the context of the West Indies and countries such as Guinea-Bissau or Liberia. Here, the basilect to acrolect 'creole continuum' throws another kind of challenge to planners on the questions of language definitions (or even in defining what 'mother-tongue' is), in code-mixing evaluated against the earlier standards of linguistic purity and on approaches and issues of translanguaging as a classroom strategy in mediating a multilingual situation. It may also pose challenges for the acquisition of more elaborated codes in both the subordinated and subordinating languages.

On the theoretical plane, one learns from JS Mill in Utilitarianism (Ch IV) that 'The sole evidence it is possible to produce that anything is desirable is that people actually desire it' (as quoted in Haezrahi 1949: 40, underlining: Authors'). The actual position, based on the principle of Utility from Mill, is based on certain parallels he draws:

> The only proof capable of being given that an object is visible, is that people actually see it. The only proof that a sound is audible, is that people hear it: and so of the other sources of our experience. In like manner, I apprehend, the sole evidence it is possible to produce that anything is desirable, is that people do actually desire it…. No reason can be given why the general happiness is desirable, except that each person, so far as he believes it to be attainable, desires his own happiness.

This obliteration of distinction was contested later, and many argue that we need to unlearn it. Three distinctions of meaning were proposed by Haezrahi in favour of the distinctive pair and against Mill's doctrine: (a) dispositional, (b) emotive or propagandist, and (c) imperative or absolute. The argument is that if the 'end' proposed by the utilitarian doctrine is not perceived by people as an end, 'nothing could ever convince any person that it was so'. The difficulty in the current context stems from the fact that what the state deems desirable may not be desired by the parents of children, and vice versa. In such cases, we need to ask who must get to make a choice or who gets to decide what we must desire.

The planners would like to quote Plato (The Republic), where he paraphrased Socrates, who seemed to be arguing that 'individual desires must be postponed in the name of the higher ideal'. The second problem comes from Aristotle's connection between 'reason' and 'desire'. Aristotle agrees that even though desire provides us with a reason for a set of actions, it still cannot explain all purposive movements towards a goal. He suggested that perhaps 'reason' and 'desire' together might be guided by our imagination, making it possible for us to apprehend an object of desire and see that it is indeed desirable. This way, reason and desire will work together to determine what is desirable. The problem with this position could be evaluating the reasons or reasonability of our decisions vis-à-vis how our new generations must begin learning or how they need to be handheld to reach the requisite knowledge.

3. Desired Codes: Who Decides?

Given the problems raised in the previous section, it is genuine to begin by questioning who decides what our Desired Code should be. Kieran McConville (2019) starts with an observation very common in post-colonial countries:

> Picture it: You show up for your first day at school, and the teacher starts talking to you in a language you don't understand. You're now expected to learn to read and write in this language. Imagine if there were two new languages for you to learn. One more thing: **You're only 4 years old.** For most kids in Kenya, that's exactly the scenario they face when starting school. Language barriers in the classroom are ubiquitous in a country that has 2 official languages and 66 local languages.[3]

That is, of course, McConville's observation. But one must see if the situation was still the same despite the introduction of the Competency-based Curriculum. However, in general, the dismal picture of schooling of children belonging to smaller and indigenous languages is similar in all developing countries. Although this data is two decades old, Indian Census 1981 told us that only 23.9 per cent of children aged 5-14 years belonging to tribal communities attended schools in India – with some States such as Madhya Pradesh (16.4 per cent) and Rajasthan (18.4 per cent) faring poorly. But what was more alarming was the dropout figures: between Classes I and V, the dropout figure among children from these communities was 64.5 per cent compared to 47.9 per cent of general category non-tribal students. More than economic marginalisation, lack of parental literacy and facilities around the tribal hamlets, the

---

3   https://www.concernusa.org/story/language-barriers-in-classroom/

magnitude of dropouts and delays or stagnations in the lower classes have more to do with the medium of school instruction in these schools, which are far removed from their home languages (cf. Nambissan 1994: 2747).

One conjectures that global economic growth and the country's entry into education planning were closely related. Placing so many children in a closed space to be handled by teachers as subject or knowledge area specialists worked well in the economics of education. Further, in each cultural space, there have been champions of mass education to make citizens future-ready. Sometimes, the support came from administrators or philanthropists devoted to 'schooling' as against those who believed in a 'de-schooling' approach.

The institutions in the ancient world, being organisations that were engaged in validating new knowledge, also promoted mass education. In all such countries, school dropouts are viewed as socially dysfunctional and a liability to the State. Then there was always this question of whether the new knowledge must be made available only in the languages that were ripe to house the debates. Further, the industrial revolutions also resulted in the demand for 'trained' or 'skilled' recruits who must have undergone comparable training or teaching in schools. That, too, resulted in some comparable learners who have had a 'modern' education.

For technology to keep progressing, industrial institutions also needed similarly skilled products. Even for manning the assembly line, some common understanding was expected. The certification of their skills became important as well. Additionally, it was also required that they be ready to move to newer places and platforms. As the choice of medium was a matter to be decided by the state, some problems stemmed from there. Further, schooling for women changed the picture of family and social structure altogether. Lastly, indoctrinating the young mind has always been an important agenda of those who rule, and it is easier to do that with fewer languages in the education scenario. For ageing polities as well as for the new nation-states, the states desired what the curricula would be and what the modes of delivery could be. The parents or the cultural leaders of the indigenous groups had no say or very little say in such matters.

4. Desirable Codes: What happens to them?

In a British Council-driven 'Voices Magazine', Kerryn Dixon of the University of the Witwatersrand in South Africa makes a strong case for integrating learners' home languages into the life of the school in the context of Africa. The author gives seven reasons for teachers to welcome home languages in education. One could elaborate on these simple reasons behind this choice of the LOLT or 'Language of Learning and Teaching' (Veriava, Thom and Fish2017, Chapter 11: 'Language in School'; pp 207). These are recollected and paraphrased as follows:

i) By welcoming children's home languages, one acknowledges that multilingualism is a global norm and not an aberration that must somehow be gotten rid of. As a result, each new language introduced as a school language is creative enough to develop new knowledge tools and products. As time progresses, viewing each other's linguistic products (even non-school items such as views, news, comics, or serials on OTT platforms, or serious films and documentaries) is becoming a common thing as there is a creative explosion;

ii) Learners learn more and can independently think, discuss, and debate when they can use their home languages. Many take this knowledge back to their community elders who might not have had schooling or formal education. Such students understand and perform better, as they do not have to move between two languages which could add to their desired cognitive load;

iii) It could be an excellent discovery for multilingual and pluricultural schools, enriching the teachers and equipping them to be better education managers. As humans are naturally endowed to be trouble-shooters or problem-solvers, such schools or systems that encourage instruction through many languages help student-student and student-teacher communication – using several languages and channels, including body language. Typically, teachers may lack in the traditional grammar of the majority tongue, different spellings/pronunciations, or newer ways of conveying the same sense, but multilingual schooling may alter the scene. Using one's home language could often be a creative attempt to solve a problem using language resources. There is also a lesson for teachers in this sort of experimentation.

iv) In an exchange where no interlocutors are involved, or if they do not assume ownership of the communication, progress in teaching-learning would halt. In other words, using the home language would ensure that learners would also occupy an important space in this dyadic relationship and that it would not be a top-down approach. Some may argue that making space for not one but several languages would create a chaotic situation. Still, since any act of mediating in a multilingual situation teaches us to make sense of the possible chaos or misunderstanding, this strategy indicates that 'there is space here for all of you!'

One has reasons to believe that when children feel their home language is not despised but rather respected, they are more than willing to continue the engagement in the classroom.

v) Kerryn Dixon (2018) argued, 'Using home languages can provide insight into other cultures. For example, tjoepstil in Afrikaans describes being absolutely silent, chon in Korean is the bond between friends, and hüzün in Turkish is a form of deep sadness. If your class reads a book together that is full of surprises....',[4] A multilingual space opens the possibilities of viewing the world through varied lenses provided by different languages.

vi) Seeing and hearing home languages can make school a safer place for children from indigenous or minority groups, displaced persons and refugees, and give them an impression that, like their home, their school is a safe place which is devoid of linguistic prejudices and phobia. In fact, Kerryn Dixon suggested that schools should encourage all learners to come up with their own multilingual signs for their school. This would be symbolic as it would instil a feeling that they are included in decision-making and active in the school life.

vii) Writing and speaking in home languages strengthens connections between school and home. Learners can write or audio-record messages from school to home, like lists of essential items for field trips, in their home language. Children often translate for their parents. Respecting these abilities acknowledges the skills children have

---

4 https://www.britishcouncil.org/voices-magazine/reasons-for-teachers-to-prioritise-home-languages-in-education

developed and recognises their valuable role in the family. In an alternative scenario where such small groups would enter online learning platforms in the future, this might also become a source of inspiration for many others who would not have been able to physically enrol in a remotely located institution. In fact, these children may become an instrument of change in many cultural communities. There have been many experiments, such as 'Hybrid Learning', where children's group play and creativity have been proven.

5. On Language Teaching Methods & An Eclectic Approach

It has been mentioned in various papers in this volume what assessment surveys such as ASER[5] or National Achievement Survey (NCERT) tell us about India's learning gap. Some pertinent facts are that about one-fourth of the children in the 14–18 age group cannot count currency correctly. Many more cannot add weights correctly in kilograms. Moreover, one in every seven children cannot 'read' or recognise a map of India, and above one-third of children cannot name the Indian capital cities.[6] About 79 per cent cannot name the State they live in, and 58 per cent cannot locate it on a map in response to this task. This is surely a matter of concern for teacher-educators.

Even if we agree that universal education (EAA[7] or SSA in India) was supposed to lift all linguistic groups in the country

---

5   See ASER 2014, or even ASER 2020 provisional report at http://img.asercentre.org/docs/ASER%202020/ASER%202020%20REPORT/aser2020fullreport.pdf
6   CF. Banerji & Duflo (2015) for more details and possible solutions.
7   See UNESCO 2015.

to the next level of development via the 'learning ladder' (Govinda, 2020), we have somewhere veered off course and landed ourselves in the quagmire of un-education, where schooling and education are no longer effective. It was wrongly believed that the language of the colonial masters could be adapted to fix all our divergences quickly. It has been argued by some that since the establishment of western education in India, and particularly after the School Book Society was set up in India in 1816, an over-emphasis on the uniform westernisation model led to the 'breakdown of modernisation' in this country.

A collapse of many erstwhile and existing political institutions and orders has also been seen in the last seven decades, resulting in mistrust, corruption, unrest, and violence. As this depressing situation requires to be changed, one needs to positively encourage the plural ethos in planning for languages, culture and education through a set of organised state interventions. Even as an agreement on the need to plan languages ensues, and NEP 2020 India, which champions the cause of mother-tongue education, is certainly a step in this direction, there is a realisation that parents of children belonging to smaller speech groups must also be engaged in this debate on mediation.

Economists tell us that the 'impressive aggregate growth' across developing nations has trickled down to the poor (Ahluwalia, Carter & Chenery, 2009). The disparity between growth and social development is directly linked to the lopsided distribution of wealth and opportunities. While growth is usually managed and viewed from a top-down perspective, social development is bottom-up, and we speculate that the disconnect between these two viewpoints is partly the reason for our not fulfilling our commitment to the poorer sections of society – the BoP or Bottom of the Pyramid (Wagner & Castillo, 2014). It is now becoming increasingly evident that for effective and successful implementation of social engineering policies in India, an inclusive dialogue is required which considers the voices of her diverse cultural and ethnic groups and an amalgamation of top-down and bottom-up perspectives, bringing us to the critical question of finding space for such confluence.

The dismal situation is that India's linguistic landscape has shown a significant degree of change over the last many decades. Talking about what our project in descriptive linguistics should be, Einar Haugen, way back in 1974, reminded us in 'The ecology of language' that literary and linguistic scholars would do well to pay attention to all smaller speech forms of an area, rather than devote energy on discovering the grammatical patterns of only well-known significant languages.

While biologists preserve or maintain a single species of organism in a container, isolated from all other species, languages cannot be tied down under such conditions because human beings are 'interacting species' (Morgan 1969: 34). Peter Mühlhäusler (1992: 164) rightly mentions that 'Preserving languages involves putting them into man-made artificial environments such as grammars and dictionaries, high literature, or giving language kits to surviving speakers. Such measures are unlikely to succeed unless the question of language ecology is seriously asked. These languages have to be allowed to interact and mingle to draw from or contribute to each other and create a multilingual ethos where even the smallest has a chance to survive.

This paper, thus, raises a question as to whether a mediating multilingual eclectic approach could help us design a new kind of school curriculum for such plural cultural contexts.

6. Conclusions: Mediating Multilingualism

This paper seeks to encourage further debate on whether a visual ethnographic method or what we call the Mediating Multilingual Approach could help design a new kind of audio-visual text. Developers could create school curricula based on such material to make them more appealing to minor speech group children in such plural cultural contexts. To elaborate further, under the project titled, 'Mediating Multilingualism'[8], Global South and Global North institutions and researchers from India, Ireland, Jamaica, and Scotland worked together to explore the potential synergies, informed mainly by the centring of the post-colonial experience of language education and language policy formation outlined above. From this point of view, a short 'case study' presentation of the Scottish island precursor elements in the overall project may be informative to identify the possible commonalities, as well as points of potentially significant difference (for example, concerning the dependability of access to online and digital tools and resources).

As the title suggests, this paper suggests an eclectic approach where the project foregrounds linguistic diversity (multilingualism) as a founding principle and seeks to explore the core processes through which such a principle can be given practical effect (or mediated). One of these may

---

[8] https://www.uhi.ac.uk/en/research-enterprise/res-themes/humanities-and-arts/language-sciences-ininstitute/projects/mediating-multilingualism/ and https://mediatingmultilingualism.com/

be technological, for example, in relation to adjusting the balance of emphasis placed on oral versus written skills in both education and wider society (Wells 2020[9]). But the term 'mediating' includes many shades of meaning, allowing a wider analytical lens to be cast over the field than one driven solely by new technical affordances whose global reach, as already noted, can be quite variable. Further, it should be pointed out that the Scottish Island Voices project,[10] on which Mediating Multilingualism draws, itself took significant inspiration from earlier Global South initiatives in practically-minded and educationally inclusive work, such as that of the Barefoot College of Tilonia, Rajasthan, India, its Children's Parliament[11] initiative and the facilitation of 'Barefoot Photographers'.[12] Cross-generational work and the de-mystification of media work through the production of User Generated Content are also, and indeed partly resultant of, hallmarks of the Island Voices approach. These are only some examples of how the bridge between Desired and Desirable Codes could be built.

In this context, it may be particularly appropriate to exemplify Island Voices' work by referring to its coverage of the Uist and Barra Children's Parliament, a short-term project that took place around 2008-2011. Mindful of the surrounding bilingual Gaelic-English community, even though local educational provision (particularly at the secondary level) was

---

9 https://guthan.wordpress.com/2020/05/18/studies-in-culture-and-education/ (This URL links to free or pre-publication versions if institutional access is not available.)
10 https://guthan.wordpress.com/about/
11 https://barefootcollegetilonia.org/education/
12 http://news.bbc.co.uk/1/shared/spl/hi/picture_gallery/05/south_asia_villagers0_barefoot_college/html/1.stm

largely English-only, care was taken to produce video material equally in both languages. The video material consisted of short home-made 'documentaries' in plain language, introducing a topic and sketching the context, complemented by talking head 'interviews' with participants, including project workers, parents, and, crucially, young people themselves speaking naturally in both English and Gaelic. This indexes parity of esteem between both languages and affirms, in particular, the often-neglected primacy of speech in an educational context where emphasis and prestige tend to be associated more with the written word.

These films formed just one part of the overall project's more comprehensive 'Generations' theme. Hopefully, in the end, a picture is created in the microcosm of a particular 'language eco-system' under existential threat, which may help to stabilise its meaning and value for its members. In the meantime, it is also hoped that international comparison of models from other contexts and cultures and wider global initiatives such as the Bangladesh-inspired International Mother Language Day,[13] fruitful cross-fertilisation of ideas may continue, with benefits all around for both South and North, wherever growing, or previously unrecognised cultural diversity demands closer attention.

It bears repeating that researchers and practitioners from the Global North are well-advised not to attempt to foist ready-made solutions from their own contexts on to colleagues in the South. Indeed, it could well be argued that despite the relatively munificent resource in time and money devoted to

---

13   https://www.sfc.ac.uk/news/blogs/Blog-78997.aspx

measures for supporting minority or minoritised languages, for example, Irish or Scottish Gaelic revitalisation, the results failed to deliver significant success or even relevance to the needs, educational and otherwise, of the vernacular communities. Despite localised successes, the overall track record is not good (see Ó Giollagáin et al. 2007; 2020). Given the level of threat to global ethnolinguistic diversity, there is onus on those involved in the language sciences to give relevant practical and moral support to speakers of subordinated languages. This support should have three interrelated objectives:

- Opening up a societally-relevant, credible focus on the educational and other institutional concerns and requirements of subordinated cultures and societies.
- Assisting them to capture, curate and enhance their collective socio-cultural assets as educational resources, as ethnographic validation and as risk-managed retrieval of potentially vulnerable or endangered socio-cultural wealth.
- Developing an empathetic ethnography in collaboration with threatened communities to explore societal, institutional and collectively organised options for improving their socio-political standing in relation to the cultural group(s) with which they compete for societal salience.

Without this shared perspective, the language sciences could be increasingly viewed as an extractive or even an exploitative and unconcerned institutional endeavour.

PAL Network's ELTU Project
Foundational Learning Supported by Indigenous Resources Experiences

Adrián D Cetina Catzin, Winny Cherotich Ngeno, Indrani Roy, Rajarshi Singh and Felipe Hevia de la Jara

1. Introduction

Indigenous individuals form roughly 5% of the globe's total population yet account for approximately 15% of the globe's poorest people (Hall & Gandolfo, 2016). Despite the apparent minority, when compared to 95% of the non-indigenous population, indigenous groups account for most of the cultures and languages of the world. It is estimated that nearly 5,000 indigenous groups speak 96% (approximately 6 to 7 thousand) of the existing languages in the world (García-Alix, 2003). Unfortunately, 40% of the indigenous languages are in danger of extinction, jeopardising the cultures and knowledge systems of the native speakers of these languages (Biddle Meehl, 2018). The United Nations continues to emphasise the critical nature of reviving and maintaining native languages and highlighting their meaningful impact on linguistic and cultural diversity (Gray, 2018).

Meanwhile, in the field of education, a rich body of literature has continuously pointed out that when it comes to indigenous peoples and multicultural contexts, education must be adequately resourced, culturally appropriate and courteous of cultural roots (May, 1999; Lee, 2007; Kana, 2017). However, this has rarely been the case as historically, most post-industrial education systems and programmes have been used to homogenise and integrate diversity and indigenous populations into the wider society.

Even in the context of modern education systems, there are just a few systems that have worked closely with indigenous peoples in the development of policies and curricula of their education (Taylor, 2018). The cost of such an approach has been the loss of many cultures, dialects, and knowledge. Languages are also subject to a life cycle – they are born, they live and they die (Mufwene, 2017). However, when languages are lost or become extinct, entire repositories of ideas, concepts, realities and culturally differentiated thoughts are wiped off. This study focuses on how the current education systems do not take into account the indigenous knowledge and ways of teaching-learning, how they favour non-indigenous knowledge and methods of teaching-learning, and the additional challenges that students who are not native to the dominant culture face while having to learn through a second or third language.

Social and cultural studies have described a common phenomenon in multicultural settings, where one group becomes more powerful than the rest (Sonn, Bishop, & Humphries, 2000; JanMohamed & Lloyd, 2014). As a result, this dominant group significantly influences many aspects of social life in certain territories (geographical boundaries, official languages, social organisation, norms and systems). Likewise, minority languages and cultures are not only swallowed up by the interests of the dominant culture but get trapped within geographical and political boundaries designed to favour the dominant culture (Hale, 2004; Postero, 2007). For minorities, such framework translates into challenges they have to face to overcome their disempowerment. Education is one of the critical areas in which such operationalisation becomes evident (Bozkurt, 2019). Minority groups face various challenges from pre-primary and primary to university-level education. These barriers are experienced throughout the educational pyramid.

Thus, even under normal circumstances before COVID-19, it was essential to develop culturally responsive teaching-learning strategies to address the learning gaps created by challenges such as learning via other languages and points of view. With the exacerbation of learning gaps experienced during the COVID-19 global health crisis, it became crucial beyond the scope of the traditional education system.

Despite government support for distance education and blended learning programmes during the school closures due to the pandemic, most education systems in Low-and Middle-Income Countries (LMICs) could not adequately support children's learning in hard-to-reach areas (Elsamadony, Fujii, Nerini, Kakinuma, & Kanae, 2022). Most distance learning content was not mapped to children's local contexts. Without teachers to guide them, out-of-school learning remained inaccessible.

This study also discusses the importance of developing culture-based teaching approaches and materials that the PAL Network's ELTU (Every Language Teaches Us) project aimed to create. The ELTU project conveyed the principles of foundational learning with the belief that indigenous languages and cultures had the resources to facilitate education during any pandemic and develop the skills indigenous children needed to succeed in non-indigenous education systems. By using indigenous languages and knowledge to create teaching and learning materials, ELTU also focused on revitalising these languages and enhancing the significance of their knowledge systems.

The sections that follow look at the challenges indigenous children face in traditional education systems, especially during times such as a pandemic. The significance of teaching-learning in the mother tongue is emphasised, as is the role of the foundational learning approach. The Every Language Teaches Us initiative, which addressed the need for teaching-learning materials in indigenous mother tongues, is explored along with its inception, development and implementation. The insights and learnings from the project are presented in this study, and further action has been suggested.

2. Background and Framework of Every Language Teaches Us

The general quality of education in places where indigenous children reside, which are often more distant and impoverished, is also typically worse (Renganathan, S., & Kral et al., 2018). Consequently, the rate of quitting school is higher for indigenous students than for non-indigenous children. For example, in Ecuador, indigenous students are 30% more prone to quitting school compared to non-indigenous children who also have a literacy level of 72%, compared to the general norm of 91%; in Bolivia, indigenous students complete elementary school at an approximate rate of 55%, in contrast to approximately 81% for non-indigenous students; and, throughout Vietnam, indigenous groups have a literacy level of 17%, compared to the 87% level of the public-school population (Biddle et al., 2018). In addition, the World Bank estimates that school closures during the COVID-19 pandemic worsened the learning crisis in Low-and Middle-Income Countries (LMICs), 'sharply increasing the learning poverty to an estimated 70%' (World Bank, 2022).

These predictions are perhaps grimmer for indigenous children. The outbreak of COVID-19 increased not only learning gaps between indigenous and non-indigenous students but also the barriers that indigenous children needed to overcome to continue their education. Most indigenous children did not have resources for distance education, so their education was deeply affected (Power et al., 2020). The previous remarks are significant, especially in LMICs where there is a lack of initiatives that focus on reducing learning gaps and enhancing the learning of indigenous children. For example, in Mexico, the work on the indigenous languages has primarily focused on documentation efforts to preserve indigenous languages. While the Federal government implemented bilingual and intercultural education initiatives, they were used as political tools for alphabetisation and integration of rural areas (see, for example, Naranjo 2011, Dietz & Cortés 2019). Just like in Mexico, existing indigenous education programmes in other LICs and MICs have been framed on the basis of political interests (see, for example, Jacob, Cheng, & Porter 2015).

The ELTU project was conceived to address the issues mentioned above and alleviate the needs of indigenous children, in the process revitalising indigenous languages. Furthermore, the project incorporated the literature on Early Childhood Education (ECE) and foundational learning to introduce indigenous teaching resources such as songs, stories, proverbs, rhymes, puzzles and more. These resources provide indigenous children with culturally relevant teaching-learning experiences that improve their foundational learning skills, such as reading, comprehension, mathematics and critical thinking.

2.1 Learning from the Mother Tongue and Culture

Globally, growing acceptance and appreciation of indigenous knowledge and educational approaches as workable and valid forms of education has initiated a re-examination of the importance of acknowledging and integrating cultural diversity into education. High-Income Countries (HICs) such as Canada, New Zealand, and the United States of America have provided examples of the positive results of teaching and learning approaches supported by indigenous perspectives and knowledge, which have helped achieve meaningful learning among indigenous students (Goulet & Goulet, 2014; Potter & Cooper, 2016; Pihama, Morgan & Smith, 2019; Nishanthi, 2020). For example, a senior school in Alberta, Canada, uses a separate indigenous children's room as part of a graduate training programme in which skilled indigenous consultants are on hand to help students with problems impeding their academic progress. And in regular classroom sessions, teachers offer customised tutoring to indigenous children based on their areas of need, like language acquisition, or areas that appeal to indigenous children, like cultural and athletic activities (Taylor & Bell, 2018).

Similarly, in other schools in the US, Canada and New Zealand, indigenous children's learning outcomes were improved by adapting teaching-learning approaches to support mother-tongue learning and creating a supportive network to guide children in and out of classrooms.

These results align with studies on mother tongue learning that show us that the better children's language skills are in their mother tongue, the faster and easier is to learn about other things in other languages. On the other hand, when learning happens through a second or third language –as in the case of many indigenous students – meaningful learning and progress becomes more difficult. This is especially true at young ages when children do not have mastery over such languages (see, for example, Atkinson 1987; Ndamba 2008; Yadav 2014; Nishanthi 2020). Similarly, studies in this area have underlined the importance of building strong relationships between ECE and mother tongue to improve the children's learning in multicultural environments (see, for example, Ball 2010; Abidogun & Adebule 2013; Awopetu 2016). In other words, mother tongue and culture-based teaching approaches can greatly improve the students' cognitive development, knowledge and ability to learn new things in other languages while developing solid skills and nurturing their knowledge in their native language. Despite these highlights, the positive results from indigenous-oriented education in High-Income Countries (HICs) and the advocacy of international organisations such as the World Bank and the United Nations, challenges remain for many LICs and MICs whose systems favour the non-indigenous teaching-learning frameworks. ELTU was conceived to help lessen these challenges and reduce the education gap that was created by the lack of culturally appropriate approaches to education for indigenous students (Pihama, Morgan & Smith, 2019).

2.2 Foundational Learning and Multicultural Environments

The Center for Regional Cooperation for Adult Education in Latin America and the Caribbean (CREFAL) describes foundational learning as a type of educational approach that is needed in multicultural contexts –the type of education that acknowledges the individuality of ethnic groups absorbed within the 'education for masses' policy and provides them not only the tools to overcome analphabetism but also for the challenges of a continuously changing world. Whereas CREFAL's view of foundational learning addresses its importance for the education of adults, it also underlines the crucial aspects that apply to the education of indigenous children: 1) foundational learning offers a viable option of education in multicultural contexts to provide minorities with better opportunities in the global world; 2) foundational learning provides students with indispensable skills that are needed to overcome the obstacles of an education that overlooks the heterogeneity of cultural views and processes of learning that may be present in the classroom. In this regard, Morrison, Woika & Breffni (2009), Arrow (2010) and Beeharry (2021) have outlined how foundational learning can benefit education in early childhood, underlining how building strong transferable skills and knowledge in young students facilitates future learning. Arrow (2010) uses the case of kindergarten students in New Zealand to show how working on developing emergent foundational skills in these young students favours future conventional literacy and makes a difference between good and poor achievers.

Most indigenous students grow up in a multicultural environment, so adding this eco-sociolinguistic perspective to the equation is essential. This approach directs attention to the importance of harmonising different multilingual ecologies in multicultural contexts to address the instrumental, emotional and psycho-social needs of students with diverse cultural backgrounds. It is expected that initiatives ignoring how intertwined indigenous peoples' lives are with the global world will likely fail as facing the global challenges of indigenous languages and cultures, including the education of indigenous children, requires an impartial framework. Such a framework needs to consider the cultural and social transformations of indigenous groups, i.e. most of them are no longer isolated, and there have been changes at the cultural and social levels.

Along with these remarks, the ELTU project conveys the principles of foundational learning, mother tongue learning-teaching, and early childhood education. The keystones supporting this initiative are not language revitalisation nor linguistic documentation; instead, the project focuses on foundational learning for indigenous children incorporating mother tongue teaching-learning and locally sourced materials to enhance their education. By bringing indigenous mother tongue resources into the domain of modern education, the project ultimately contributes to the revitalisation of these languages.

3. PAL Network and the ELTU Project

HICs have led the way in transforming the discursive dimension of education policies regarding minorities and indigenous groups into formal educational programmes and systems (Pihama, Morgan & Smith, 2019). The ELTU project was a major initiative in this direction in the Global South. The project was initiated and led by the People's Action of Learning (PAL) Network, a south-to-south group of 17 organisations across 15 countries in Asia, Africa, and the Americas. Having conducted large-scale citizen-led assessments and actions that were aimed at improving learning, PAL Network was in a unique position to carry out this enterprise. The project took place simultaneously in India, Kenya, Mexico, Mozambique, Nepal, Pakistan, Tanzania, and Uganda. Learning resources were collected from indigenous, endangered, minority and other low-resource languages in these countries to aid children's foundational learning by developing teaching-learning materials in children's mother tongues.

With the participation of NGOs and individuals from indigenous communities, the ELTU project directed attention to the vital role that non-governmental organisations and individuals can play in shifting different paradigms that affect minorities despite the size of the initiatives and budgets.

ELTU also looked at developing a documentation experience in which participation is a prerogative of the audience, inviting an indirect revitalisation method. Therefore, during the fieldwork and data collection stage of the ELTU project, working with the local population was fundamental for identifying and documenting teaching and learning resources.

3.1 Participating Countries and Organisations

The ELTU project emerges as an initiative that resonates with the United Nations' advocacy for indigenous languages and cultures and the PAL Network's interest in improving learning outcomes. Accordingly, as a sponsored project of PAL, the scope of the ELTU project covered indigenous and at-risk languages from America, Africa and Asia, where the PAL Network is present. Whereas indigenous and at-risk languages in these areas face similar challenges, one must be aware of the political and linguistic contexts that surround them. Table 26 shows the linguistic landscape of the participating countries.

Though spread across three continents, all selected countries share some common features. All of them were former colonies and therefore bear the legacy of having an official language that is not the mother tongue of most of the population. This legacy has also continued to impact their language and medium of instruction policies. For example, English has official language

Table 26: Linguistic landscape of participating countries

KENYA	MOZAMBIQUE	TANZANIA	UGANDA
• According to The Constitution of Kenya Review Committee - CKRC (2000), the number of languages in Kenya is 70. • English and Swahili are the official languages of Kenya. • English is used as the medium of instruction from Grade 4.	• Mozambique is a multilingual country where most of the languages belong to the Bantu language family. • The Indigenous language Makhuwa is spoken by 4 million people, according to the 2007 census. • In 1975 Mozambique adopted Portuguese as its official language and as the medium of instruction.	• There are 126 languages spoken in Tanzania. • Kiswahili is the national language of Tanzania. It is the mother tongue of 10% of the population. It is also the medium of instruction in primary schools. • English is Tanzania's official language and the medium of higher education.	• Uganda has 41 languages currently being spoken. • English has been the official language of Uganda since its independence in 1965. It is used in all formal contexts and is the language used in education and governance. • Luganda and Swahili are used as languages of wider communication.
INDIA	**NEPAL**	**PAKISTAN**	**MEXICO**
• The number of languages in India is estimated to be around 500. • Hindi and English are the official languages of the country. • The schools in different Indian States follow a three-language formula where the State language is taught alongside Hindi and English.	• There are 123 languages spoken in Nepal. • Nepali was made the national language by the constitutions of 1959 and 1962. • The 1990 constitution gave the people a fundamental right to get primary education in their first language.	• There are about 70 languages spoken in Pakistan. • Urdu and English are the official languages and also the languages of instruction. • 48% of the population speak Punjabi. Urdu is spoken by 8% of the population.	• There are 68 native languages. Spanish is the dominant language. • 21.50% of the population self-identify as indigenous (INEGI, 2015). • 60% of the indigenous languages are close to disappearance.

status in Kenya, Tanzania, India, and Pakistan; Portuguese is the official language of Mozambique, and Spanish is the official language of Mexico. In all these countries, including Nepal, these official languages play a dominant role in education. All the countries participating in the project are linguistically diverse, with languages from different families. To ensure that many languages were brought into the ELTU fold, PAL Network worked through member organisations actively working in Foundational Learning in these countries.

3.2 Resource Selection

The project aimed to collect a wide variety of learning resources in as many languages as possible. However, the focus was on six genres considered ideal for enhancing oral ability and fluency and suitable for use in PAL's learning camps. It was believed that using these could also positively impact language ideologies by catapulting the prestige of marginalised languages and balancing hegemonic linguistic hierarchies via early childhood education.

The genres and their use as learning resources are described below:

Riddles – These are essential in developing inferential comprehension and increasing vocabulary and verbal and cognitive skills in early infant language acquisition.

Proverbs – These help to understand moral values and norms that act as practical guides for appropriate cultural communicative behaviour, such as language etiquettes. They allow linking previous knowledge with new information.

Tongue-twisters – They also help to develop fluency, increase vocabulary and aid in identifying characteristic meaningful identical sounds. These are also helpful in elevating fluency proficiencies in early language acquisition.

Legends – These allow cultural and linguistic reproduction, increasing oral and writing skills.

Songs – They help to acquire lyrics and poetic genres using metaphors and rhythm, prosodic and kinetic patterns, and help in language fluency and memorising.

Measures of Weight and distance – They facilitate in aggregation and disaggregation processes for learning arithmetic operations.

3.3 Implementation of the project

The project was implemented in three phases, with each stage having multiple action items. The following visual representation gives an overview of the implementation:

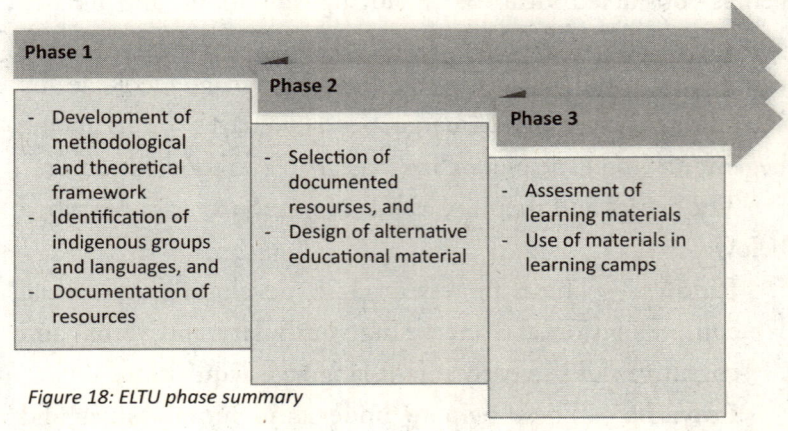

Figure 18: ELTU phase summary

3.3.1 Training Sessions

Training for the project was to be carried out within one month. However, given that the situation in each country was different, multiple sessions were organised beginning in May 2021. Mexico was the first country to hold a training session, followed by Kenya, Tanzania, Uganda and Mozambique.

The Asian countries joined in when many of the COVID-19 restrictions were lifted. Training sessions with India, Pakistan and Nepal were held in September 2021.

Each of the participating organisations underwent training in two phases. In the first phase, PAL partners were briefed about the project, its goals and expected outcomes in the form of data. Due to COVID-related restrictions, the training took place primarily online.

In the second phase, selected language champions (the term used by PAL Network to refer to its citizen volunteers) or the enumerators responsible for collecting data and interacting with the local communities to collect the indigenous resources were initiated into the project. It was felt that the champions needed to understand the relevance of the work they would do. Therefore, they were briefly introduced to the ideas of language endangerment, learning poverty and revitalisation. They were also informed that the data would be used as teaching-learning materials in learning camps, so indigenous language material which was appropriate for teaching was required.

Training workshops were conducted in multiple languages, as many participants did not speak English. Therefore, to ensure a better reach of the idea of the project, training workshops were held in Hindi (India), Spanish (Mexico), Urdu (Pakistan), Nepali (Nepal) and Swahili (Tanzania).

The training module was enhanced to include a walkthrough of the Kobo Collect App to collect data. During the training, the champions were encouraged to collect sample data to ensure that everyone was technically equipped to handle this mode of data collection. Later, an exclusive training session on using KoboCollect App helped all participants to become familiar with the platform interface and tools.

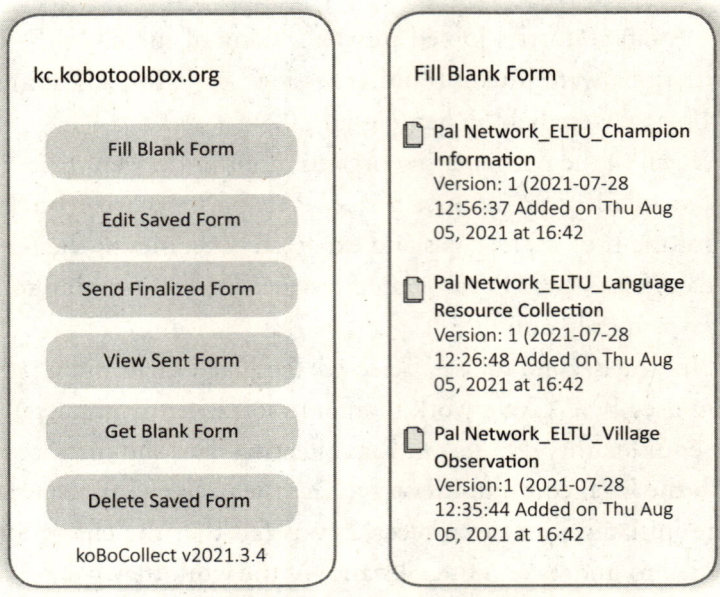

Figure 19: KoboCollect Tools and Forms for ELTU

3.3.2 Field Work

As the project entered the data collection stage, the pandemic raged across the world. This situation compelled the PAL team to rethink strategies and tools for effective training and data collection. Virtual meetings, remote training and digital tools became the support of the project. They allowed its operation by overcoming the limitations that were laid out by the pandemic and limitations of more rudimentary methods.

This situation made KoboCollect the preferred mode for collecting resources in many locations, as the tool allowed online and offline data collection and worked seamlessly across browsers and android smartphones. Data from the field could be directly uploaded to the project's servers in real-time (while participants collected the information on-site) or if that was not possible, it was done when a reliable internet connection was

Figure 20: Photo of data collection in Nepal

available. For example, Mozambique, Tanzania and Uganda conducted the data collection exercise using the Kobo Collect App online. India, Kenya and Mexico used offline and online data collection options, while Pakistan and Nepal only collected offline data.

A detailed questionnaire was developed to enable the language champions to easily collect language samples and send transcriptions and voice recordings. The data collection took two and a half months.

Table 27 shows the region and the languages covered at the beginning of the project.

3.3.3 Data Collation and Creating a Database

At the end of the data collection phase, it was found that songs, legends and riddles were the most common genres in all the languages. In addition to the primary genres, over 300 other resources were collected, showcasing greetings, days of the month, seasons and names of plants and animals.

Table 27: Project locations and languages

Country	District of implementation	Languages	Country	District of implementation	Languages
Pakistan	Gojal	Wakhi	**Tanzania**	Arusha Rural	Maa (Masai)
	Kalash	Khowar		Ilemela	Sukuma
	Thar region	Dhatki		Mwanga	Pare
	Southern Punjab	Saraiki		Kisarawe	Kiswahili
Kenya	Turkana County	Ng'aturkana	**Mozambique**	Nampula	Macua
	Tana River County	Pokomo, Orma			Ekoti
Mexico	Quintana Roo, Yucatan, Campeche	Yucatec Maya	**Uganda**	Bugiri	Lusoga Lusamia / Lugwere
	State of Puebla, Mexico, San Luis Potosi	Nahuatl		Kayunga	Luganda Ruluuli / Lunyala
	Oaxaca	Mixe Ayuujk		Kaseese	Lhukonzo Rwamba
	Chiapas	Tseltal Maya		Yumbe	Aringati Kakwa
Nepal	Makwanpur/ Kavrepalan-chowk	Tamang	**India**	Kabirdham	Baigai
	Kathmandu Valley region	Newari		Jhansi	Bundeli
	Okhaldhunga/ Bhojpur	Rai		Puruliya	Kurmali
	Far-west Hill region	Doteli		Bikaner	Marwadi
	Myagdi/Baglung	Chhantyal		Kishanganj	Surjarpuri
	Himalayas	Hyolmo			

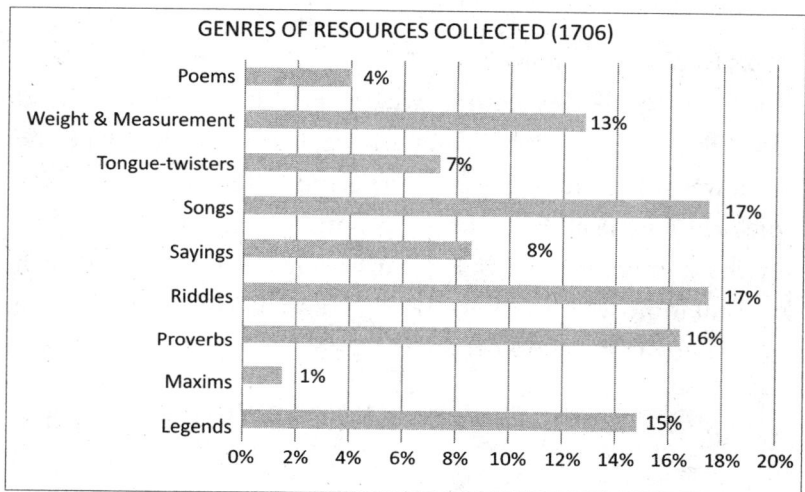

Figure 21: Distribution of genres

The resources were collected from 36 languages, as seen in the distribution below (Figure 22). Most of the champions reported that collecting data for units of weights and measurements was difficult as the indigenous language terms were not in use or had been forgotten. There was a useful insight in this which demonstrated two things: one about the nature of genres suitable for teaching and learning, and the second about the shrinking domain of the use of indigenous languages.

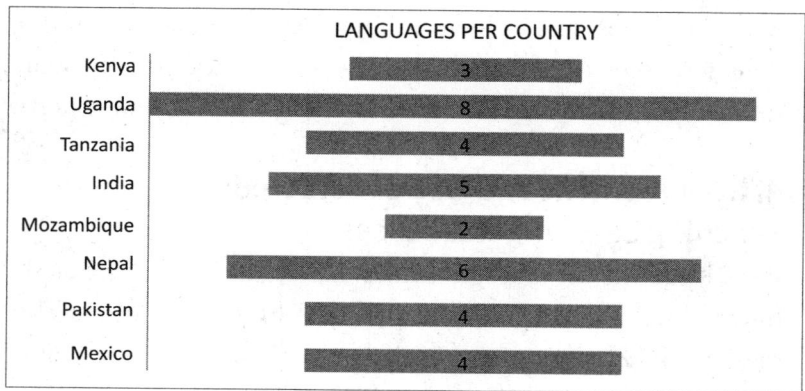

Figure 22: Language distribution

3.3.4 Data Verification Phase

In a project of this nature, where the data is to be used as teaching material, it becomes essential to verify it. Once the data was collected, they were sorted into different genres. Every piece of language data had to be transcribed in either English or the dominant language; a translation was then provided in consultation with the informant. The final output had to be verified by language experts.

Language: Yucaytec Maya | **Country:** Mexico | **Type of resource:** Riddle	
ORIGINAL LANGUAGE	ENGLISH
Jach mejen, bek'ech yéetel chowak u koj. Waa a k'áat a túuxt malo'ob óolal, Je' máaxake' a k'áat, u beytal a wa'alikti' ku bisej. Ba'ax lelo'. R= Ts'unu'un.	It is small, its beak is thin and long. If you want to send good thoughts It doesn't matter who it is you can tell them to take it. What is it? R = Hummingbird

Figure 23: Sample resource

It is important to note that some of these languages were endangered and had very few speakers; therefore, finding language experts who could verify data of the native speakers was a daunting task. However, the PAL members put in all their resources to ensure the data was authentic. In Pakistan, for instance, each item was vetted and signed off by an expert.

4. Development and Use of Selected Teaching Learning Resources

PAL Network set out guidelines based on which materials for teaching and learning were selected by the countries. The materials had to be age-appropriate, contribute to the social and emotional development of the child, enhance comprehension and vocabulary, aid in developing reasoning abilities, promote storytelling and narration or teach a basic mathematical concept.

Another round of orientation was held for the project leaders of each country between February and March 2022, where the guidelines on selecting language data for teaching materials were discussed.

RESOURCE SELECTION CRITERIA

Instructional materials:
- Should support the educational philosophy, goals and objectives of the ELTU project (to improve literacy & numeracy).
- Should be appropriate for the age, emotional and social development, and ability level of the learners for whom the materials are selected.
- It is important to remember to keep the child at the center of the selection and ask-what is the child going to learn with this resource? Is this material suitable for his/her age, will their learning experience be better?
- Should be diverse with respect to levels of difficulty, reader appeal, and should present a variety of points of view.
- Should have aesthetic, cultural, literary, of social value.

SELECTION CRITERIA CONTINUED

- Should foster respect for cultural diversity. Should foster respect for men, women, the disabled, and minority groups and should portray a variety of roles and lifestyles that are open to people in today's world.
- When selecting materials ask:
  - Does this have potential to enhance comprehension and vocabulary?
  - Does this enhance memory?
  - Does this aid in developing reasoning?
  - Does this help build storytelling and narration skills?
  - Does this help in understanding a basic mathematical concept?
- Should be designed to motivate learners to examine their own attitudes and behaviors.
- Should be selected taking into account the relevance, originality and copyright for new and previously published instructional materials.

Figure 24: Sample slide- Resource selection

Each country devised different ways of using the language data based on their ongoing programmes. In Kenya, Mexico and Pakistan, the teams developed detailed techniques for using different genres that could be used in Learning Camps to enhance children's learning. The team from Nepal worked on making print materials from the resources collected in various languages.

The first learning camp sessions ran between March and June 2022. Training was first given to session facilitators, demonstrating how to incorporate the collected resources in the sessions with children.

The following is an example of an activity developed using indigenous songs in learning camps in Pakistan where Saraiki, Wakhi, Khowar and Dhatki language resources were used.

	Teaching Techniques/Activities
1.	The facilitator gives the participants the lyrics of a regional song and asks them to listen carefully following the lyrics. They can use any of those included in Annex 5.
2.	After having listened to it, the facilitator invites everyone to sing it, no matter if they are out of tune. The facilitator should sing along with the group to motivate them.
3.	At the end of the song the facilitator will ask if they have already heard the song (or danced to it if it is rhythmic), if they like it or not and why they like it. The interventions are voluntary and the facilitator comments that songs are texts written in verse to which music can be added, such as the one that has just been sung. There are different types of songs, for example: folk songs, popular songs, art songs, children's songs... Songs can also be used to improve reading skills.
4.	Form teams of four people and each team member is given a copy of the same song. There will be one song per team.
5.	The facilitator will explain that they are going to do a collective reading of the song, each team member will read aloud one verse and then the whole team will read it chorally.
6.	Afterwards, each team will discuss the song they read: what does the song talk about, who did they write the song to, what part of the song did they like the most, what did they not like? The facilitator will go around the teams to get the reflections and opinions of the participants.
7.	Each team should compose a verse of a song. You can suggest that they set it to music from a song they all know.
8.	In plenary the teams sing the verse of their song they composed.
9.	In a following session they can continue with the complete writing of their song.

Figure 25: Techniques & Activities

The survey done at the conclusion of the camps showed an overwhelmingly positive response to the ELTU resources, as seen in Figure 26. The assessment of the result showed that the materials not only engaged the students but also helped their learning. A popular suggestion was to use multimedia to make the materials more engaging. Considering that the audios and videos were also part of the resource collected, this suggestion was not out of reach for future learning camps.

5. Key Takeaways from the Project

The project garnered enthusiastic responses from participants across countries. In most cases, the enumerators who were speakers of indigenous languages understood the value of preserving their language and were aligned with PAL's vision throughout the project. At the project's culmination, a survey was done among the participants. They were asked whether 'ELTU addresses the social problem of lack of use of indigenous learning materials to support children's foundational learning'. Most of the participants Strongly Agreed with the statement, while the rest Agreed.

For the statement, 'The scale of the project was adequate for your country', there were mixed responses from the participants. In Uganda, Tanzania, Mozambique and Pakistan, the participants Agreed; the response from Kenya was neutral while Nepal had participants disagreeing, and Indian participants either Disagreed or Strongly Disagreed.

Participants also largely Agreed with the statement, 'Villages and participants would be interested in participating in projects such as ELTU'.

A few reactions from the participants (translated into English from their native languages) are given below:

Insights from the Learning Camps

An overview of the feedback received from the learning camps in Pakistan

Insight 1

32 out of total 46 students surveyed in Pakistan strongly agreed that the indigenous language resources made it easier to learn the language.

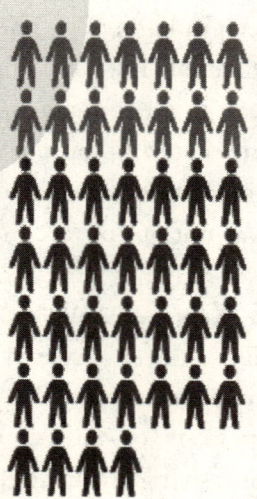

Insight 2

80%

Most of the Facilitators in Pakistan strongly agreed that ELTU resources were useful for them in the learning camps.

Most popular resources

Songs and stories were the most popular resources used in the learning camps in Pakistan.

Improved learning outcomes

Learning camp observers unanimously felt that including local language materials improved the learning outcomes.

Figure 26: Learning camp insights

Was engaging and encouraged the participation of elderly people irrespective of their academic qualification.

While collecting the resources from villagers, I saw a very clear image such as – everyone was interested and agreed to participate; also, they agreed to get reading materials in their Indigenous language. Someone says that we have forgotten a lot of word lists, and many words have been mixed with Bengali; we have been trying but haven't been able to find our actual words. If we are not having a good opportunity, we will forget our language...please save us and our language.

...during resources collection, we found that younger children were enjoying legends, songs etc., while their parents or old people were telling in front of us. It seems that when we will use it with children, it will help them to understand language strongly.

First of all, we ourselves at least got the awareness that endangered language could be revived and preserved from our own level rather than depending on some authorities. We still need to work more on languages and materials.

The survey also asked the participants for suggestions on how they saw the resources being used. Some of the responses were:
- Curating appropriate lesson plans/videos/guides so anyone who wished to learn any local language could do so easily.
- Scaling up the project to cover larger areas.
- Including more languages.

The project made evident the 'double-edged sword' of technology. While it is essential to keep in mind the role that globalised communication technology platforms have played in endangering minority and marginalised languages worldwide

(David et al., 2007), it is also crucial to understand its potential as a means to strengthen the endangered languages. In fact, the ELTU project found in technology the necessary tools to overcome the limitations that arose from the COVID-19 pandemic. Therefore, technology cannot be done away with, as it is essential in democratising research and learning.

6. Conclusion

The seed of the ELTU project was how to address the learning gap that was getting worse due to school closures. The goal was to aid children's foundational learning by developing teaching-learning materials in children's mother tongues. The project spanned eight countries across three continents and covered 36 languages. One thousand seven hundred six language resources were collected in all.

The dearth of teaching-learning materials in these languages is not just a problem for the children. In countries such as India, Mexico and Nepal, where there has been a push to teach in children's mother tongue, teachers often are at a loss as to how to translate this intention into action. Galla (2010) notes that the paucity of teaching-learning materials that is culturally appropriate and accurate is a challenge for teachers of endangered languages. By focussing on the genres that would be most suitable as teaching-learning materials, ELTU aimed to address this inadequacy of materials.

For indigenous teachers and students, incorporating these strategies into schools frequently improves educational efficiency by enhancing an education system that is consistent with an indigenous individual's inherent perceptions, experiences, dialect, and norms, hence attempting to make the transition into adult life easier for children (Goldman & Racine 2021).

For non-indigenous learners and instructors, this kind of education usually significantly increases knowledge of personal and collective customs that are related to indigenous societies and people, thus fostering better respect for their beliefs and understanding of diverse cultural situations.

Most of the languages that ELTU focused on fall under the category of Shifting (scale 7) or Threatened (6b) on Fishman's Graded Intergenerational Disruption Scale (1991). By tapping these repositories of indigenous culture and knowledge, the project tried to give these languages a new lease of life by using them as learning resources in learning camps, creating print educational materials and creating a free digital database. Thus, fulfilling another aspect of the project, that of language revitalisation.

Though not originally intended as a remote or online project, due to the circumstances arising from the COVID-19 pandemic, ELTU also turned out to be an example of successful remote collaboration. All the participants, whether it was the research team, executive team, country coordinators or field enumerators, worked from different locations harnessing technology to bridge the physical distance.

Among the tertiary gains that might come out of projects like this is parental and especially maternal involvement in the education of their children. Studies in this book, such as Rebuilding with Mothers as Partners: How and Why Mothers Engage with their Children in Rural India? show that mothers hesitate to play an active role in their children's education if they are less educated themselves. It is not hard to see that if teaching and learning materials are available in the children's mother tongues, mothers could become 'partners in their children's education'.

The chapter Mitigating Learning and Development Losses for Children in Early Years: Evidence from Pakistan in this book discusses that during school closures, Early Childhood Education gets less attention. If there are disruptions similar to the pandemic in future, learning resources in mother tongues would hopefully help the young learners at home among indigenous language speakers.

Though the above outcomes met the goals set out at the start of the project, they are but a drop in the ocean when seen in terms of the work that remains to be done. As the participants pointed out, it is necessary to increase the scale of the project and include more languages to make a better impact. It is hoped that the ELTU project can be seen as a beginning of such initiatives in the Global South and that similar large-scale interventions are conceived and executed for strengthening foundational learning using the mother tongue.

A Scalable, Digital Learning Experiment Analysing Children's Group Dynamics in Pratham's PraDigi Programme

Rajarshi Singh and Nishant Baghel

1. Introduction

The Annual Status of Education Report (ASER), a nationwide assessment of children's foundational learning by Pratham, first showcased the disconnect between schooling and children's learning in 2005. It showed that 52% of children in Grade 5 across rural India could not read a Grade 2-level story in the language of instruction. Unfortunately, this has not improved in the past two decades. Similar citizen-led assessments (CLAs) by PAL Network members showed the prevalence of this learning crisis in South Asia, Africa and the Americas. Estimates in 2019 showed that the learning poverty in low-and-middle-income countries was 53% (World Bank, 2019). Disruptions related to COVID-19 deepened this global learning crisis. The distancing of formal education has disproportionately affected children who were already disadvantaged. Children at the bottom of the pyramid faced more significant risks of learning loss, lower access to learning opportunities and higher chances of dropping out of school not just in India but across all systems in developed, developing or under-developed regions (Rose, 2020).

Research shows that without a minimum proficiency in foundational skills, children are unlikely to gain many 'years of learning' despite going to school (Wadhwa, 2020). Similarly, Kaffenberger (2021) also demonstrated that short-term learning losses continue to accumulate unless they are addressed directly. Supporting foundational learning as early as possible improves children's educational resilience and ability to cope with educational shocks (IIEP, 2015; Duckworth, Akerman, MacGregor, Salter, & Vorhaus, 2009).

It is in this context that Pratham's PraDigi Open Learning Programme is explored. Pradigi is a community-based, digitally enabled open-learning intervention that spans multiple cognitive and non-cognitive skills (Singh, Sharma, & Verma, 2017). Its implementation model encourages parental participation and contextualisation of learning activities.

Children from various groups learn within these group settings—an organic space for self-directed learning. Furthermore, children's shared 'social experiences' develop contexts for growth, social interaction, and learning (Kam, Mathur, Kumar, & Canny, 2009). Children's groups serve as 'tiny publics' (Fine, 2012, pp. 19-33), where members share affiliations and grow.

This chapter focuses on how children work together and their modes of learning together in a group setting. The results of learning improvement to quantify the academic gains of participating in the PraDigi programme and the understanding gained by children's participation, performance, group work, and identity development in the programme are also discussed in this essay.

PraDigi utilises data and feedback. Data from different phases of its evolution are used to draw insights into how to structure technology-supported education interventions to aid children's learning in low-resource contexts throughout rural India.

2. PraDigi – an overview

The PraDigi Open Learning Programme is an out-of-school intervention designed to expose children to learning opportunities within their community by giving them access to contextualised content and nurturing a learning environment. It showcases Pratham's take on scaling digitally-supported group-based learning in rural India. PraDigi's iterative design has created an open learning space for children and youth. After its launch in 2015, the programme expanded to reach more than 40,000 children across Uttar Pradesh, Maharashtra, and Rajasthan by 2017. At the time of writing, in the Covid years 2021-22, it had directly helped more than 100,000 children in India.

In the initial phase between 2015 to 2017, tablets were loaded with content on science, mathematics, general knowledge, English and Hindi or Marathi and distributed in the villages targeting children aged 5-8 years. The content was regularly updated. Children were encouraged to form 'learning groups'. Each tablet was shared by two groups and each group had approximately five members. Children were responsible for the maintenance and care of their tablets.

The content was delivered through a dedicated application that worked offline and an internet connection was not provided as part of the programme. The application also tracked the content usage of children. Participants were informed about the content and group tracking was done by programme facilitators. These facilitators also regularly interacted with children, recording their feedback about their learning experience and programme participation. This feedback was then used to update the lessons. For example, in the second year of the programme, the content was made interactive based on the feedback. At the same time, more than 70 role-play-based English learning content was added, along with science videos on simple experiments and games to improve language and mathematics.

Locally-recruited programme facilitators were trained to engage with children, encourage them to form their groups and manage their learning – including scheduling learning timetables for themselves, choosing what to learn, setting learning goals, and participating in group activities. Youth from local communities coached the groups.

In 2018, the programme launched learning centres equipped with a Raspberry Pi, a low-cost single-board computer, a monitor, a keyboard, a hard drive, a webcam, and a microphone, at the cost of USD 200. This computer setup enabled restricted access to 350 select educational websites and housed digital content that was created by children. This new feature was rolled out in 1,000 villages. Pratham partnered with local youth and community champions to coach the children. The principle of 'education for education' helped create a youth network of 6,000 coaches in 1000 villages. Mothers' groups for children in Grades 1-2 were also provided tablets for activities.

These villages continue to serve as 'demonstration sites' for the programme model and products. The content gets updated periodically by using local Wi-Fi hotspots. A schematic map of the programme's evolution is shown in Table 28.

In addition to PraDigi's direct outreach, the teaching-learning digital content has been distributed to an additional 200,000 children. Learning content was tracked for 19,800 groups. Learners engaged with the PraDigi app for 12-14 days a month for an average of 55-60 minutes per day. Children viewed 70+ million minutes of content over 18 months. A controlled

Table 28: Evolution of the PraDigi model

2015	2016	2017	2018
Project Initiation	**Content Trials**	**Trigger Methodology Trials**	**Consolidation**
3,000 tablets preloaded with content and distributed in 400 villages in UP, MH, RJ. 2 groups of 5 children each share the tablet and mothers given charge of tablets.	Contextualised content creation for English conversation and science. 70+ role-play-based English learning videos and Science videos on simple experiments. Games aimed at math & language learning.	Project Based Learning (PBL) approach was tried to explore 'out of digital' experience. Children started creating learner-generated content. Programme expanded to 1,000 villages and a RCT evaluation was set up in 300 villages.	Mini course approach was tried by fusing group learning with MOOCs (massive open online courses). Village committees were setup to increase community engagement. Youth from community signed to be coaches.

trial with 139 treatments and 99 control communities found that children in the programme outlearned their counterparts in science, English and Hindi; they also showed 12 percentage points higher performance in school curricular subjects (World Economic Forum, 2020).

PraDigi's digital infrastructure is maintained and supported by parents, youth, and community members. The programme challenges the notion of a learning pyramid and its hierarchical structure by helping children manage their learning with assistance from trained facilitators and youth champions. Sub-village level communities and *mohalla* based activities support children's foundational learning and guide them in 'learning to learn'.

PraDigi asks a simple question – if children in cities can learn about melodies and maestros, why cannot children in rural villages? Furthermore, the programme also taps children's

creativity and latent talents by engaging them as content creators. PraDigi has three core pillars:
- **Social Structure** – This comprises of community stakeholders who actively participate in children's learning
- **Digital Infrastructure** – Mobile devices and robust technology placed in the hands of children, which is used for self-organised learning and project-based activities
- **Learning Content** – A wide array of contextualised content is created in the form of videos, games, and applications

The programme's hybrid model blends social, digital and content support to create a responsive learning environment. Its content is goal-driven and not grade-driven. It goes beyond identifying foundational learning gaps and plugging them. An overview of the content map for different grade groups is shown in Figure 27.

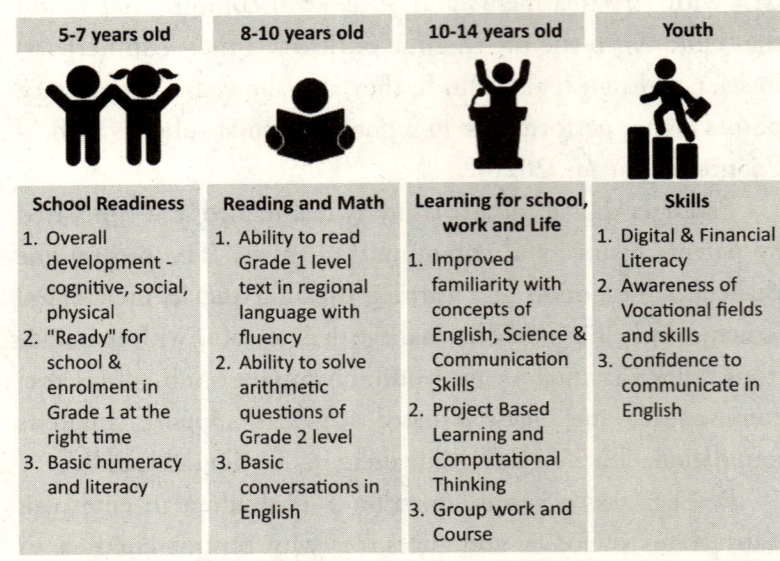

5-7 years old	8-10 years old	10-14 years old	Youth
School Readiness	**Reading and Math**	**Learning for school, work and Life**	**Skills**
1. Overall development - cognitive, social, physical
2. "Ready" for school & enrolment in Grade 1 at the right time
3. Basic numeracy and literacy	1. Ability to read Grade 1 level text in regional language with fluency
2. Ability to solve arithmetic questions of Grade 2 level
3. Basic conversations in English	1. Improved familiarity with concepts of English, Science & Communication Skills
2. Project Based Learning and Computational Thinking
3. Group work and Course	1. Digital & Financial Literacy
2. Awareness of Vocational fields and skills
3. Confidence to communicate in English

Figure 27: Learning content and progression

Going beyond academic achievement, PraDigi helps children to appreciate the value of teamwork, presentation, communication and group management skills. Its architect, Dr Madhav Chavan (2013, p. 224) summed up this outlook of child-friendly learning and education by stating that education needed to 'move away from the age-grade system. Instead, we need an age-stage system that allows children to meet learning goals in both the social and academic sphere when they are ready, transitioning to each stage at their own pace'. The following section shows that this philosophy is well supported by evidence from research into children's foundational learning, play-based pedagogy and resilience.

3. What is PraDigi's teaching-learning philosophy?

PraDigi believes in improving children's learning through 'controlled exposure to challenge' (Neill & Dias, 2001). Unlike traditional curriculum-based instructions (Sparapani, Perez, Gould, Hillman, & Clark, 2014) it harnesses children's natural inquisitiveness by encouraging opportunities to experiment with technology and activity-based learning. This approach has shown to improve children's cognition, linguistic awareness, social competence, foundational learning, motivation and attitude towards learning, and scholastic achievement (Ahlqvist, Larsson, Rosen, Allodi, & Rydelius, 2019).

PraDigi adapts and adopts five strategies to support learning in a child-friendly environment, namely, (1) Contextualised play-based learning, (2) Mother/local tongue content, (3) Level-appropriate learning material, (4) Using technology for education, and (5) Learning by doing. Experiments to maximise participation and engagement from the learner groups have shaped the programme's 4Ex Experiential Learning Framework. It involves four stages (1) Expose learners to new concepts, (2) Explore opportunities to know more about a topic of choice, (3) Experiment with construct to develop understanding and, (4) Exchange their learning with other learners.

Research shows that learners' resilience has a long-lasting impact on their learning journeys (Jackson & Martin, 1998) and is a crucial driver of children's success, especially during adverse conditions (Waxman, Gray, & Padron, 2003). During the COVID-19 school closures, many digital technologies and measures were simply 'ported' from developed countries to the Global South. These disregarded local innovations and inclusive approaches and simply followed top-down policy (Glewwe, Hanushek, Humpage, & Ravina, 2011; Loreman, Forlin, & Sharma, 2014). PraDigi, on the other hand, is an example of a home-grown digital learning solution that supports children's learning by promoting social accountability (Fox, 2015) and local participation.

PraDigi combines a community-based approach with discovery and game-based learning. It is aligned with how children learn through exploration, trial and error, and social collaboration. Considering the critical role of a teacher or guide in children's interaction with game-based pedagogy (Hang, 2017), the programme engages youth volunteers and facilitators. El-Shami observes that games are activities where 'players meet a challenge to achieve an objective and win' (2001, p. 15). Much of PraDigi's content and activities are aligned with his criteria for effective games, as outlined in Table 29.

Unlike many commercially available Ed-Tech products in India that are mapped to age/grade-level curricula, PraDigi is tailored to children's capability levels. It takes high-quality and affordable learning in vernacular languages to rural households

Table 29: Features and criteria that make games useful learning tools

Value as a game	Learning issues	Trainer-friendly
Fits with content, design, objective	Repeats and reinforces key learning	Requires minimal advance preparation
Is challenging and engaging	Gives immediate feedback	Fits time, space and cost constraints
Adds variety and energy	Provides safe practice of new skills	Fits trainer competencies
Has objective, measurable results	Develops understanding of concepts	Is flexible and adaptable
Yields worthwhile amounts of learning	Provides meaningful challenges	Is non-disruptive to surroundings
Has a suitable strategy for winning	Stimulates many senses	Is easy to support
Works with various numbers of players	Promotes intense dialogue, discussion	You like it
Has a high fun-factor	Provides social contact, group work	
	Has realistic, complex experiences	
	Has analysis, interpretation, reflection	

across India (Sampson et al., 2019). Since learners demonstrate higher gains when teaching-learning instruction is aligned with their learning levels (Banerjee et al., 2016), PraDigi's open curriculum is aligned with learners' needs. It also encourages learning by doing, an ideal pathway for learning through play (Krithika, 2019). Lenaiyasa (2004) extolls the significance of play in children's development as it 'occupies a significant amount of time' in a child's life. Pradigi's play-based pedagogies promote teamwork and cultural values which ultimately enhance children's resilience.

Children associated with PraDigi are active stakeholders and content creators as well. In the past, the programme has used content created by children (Ex. Mummy's interview', a video interview of a participant's mother by the participant) to help other children learn. The programme's content is dynamic, simple to understand, culturally aligned and urges hands-on engagement with science and learning experiments. It also promotes teaching-learning in children's language by using native languages for instruction (Mandillah, 2019).

4. How did children learn and participate in the programme?

Children tend to empathise with each other – older children take care of younger ones, and those with better learning outcomes support others. Their openness to accommodate alternate views is also observed in Pratham's PraDigi programme and is a key driver of group work and social architecture of the programme.

The tablet provided as part of the programme is shared by two groups, each with an average of five children. Having come together of their own volition, the groups devise and follow a mutually-agreed tablet-sharing mechanism. Children within a group nominate a member in charge of the tablet. Those responsible for the tablets fell into one of the following categories: (1) Children who managed the tablet by ensuring each group got equal time and access to the tablet, (2) Children who had access to charging facilities and could ensure that the tablets were charged daily, and (3) Some children whose parents commanded 'respect' in the village. Sometimes the child responsible for charging the tablets also served as the defacto group 'leader', overseeing the management of activities.

Although the programme did not directly build structures, children found means of exercising management structures that worked for them. For instance, in the context of tablet management, a child who was initially made responsible for the tablet lost the privilege because of ineffective management of the shared resource.

Despite the heterogeneity of the groups and children's relationships with their groups, the commonly observed feature of children's eagerness to share experiences, knowledge and curiosity inspired mature group dynamics. During group work children learnt non-academic skills such as teamwork, articulation, listening and negotiation.

An overview of group formation and selection of group leaders is given here:

- Most groups had mixed gender composition. Only a small fraction were either all-girls or all-boys groups. Girls led a significant proportion of mixed-gender groups. Group leaders consciously took the responsibility of guiding others in their learning.
- Group leadership was based on merit. Children with better learning outcomes tended to take up the role of leaders. It should be noted that merit-based selections occurred within rural communities that otherwise have social barriers and communal and gender inequity issues.
- It was observed that some groups had a rotational system for selecting leaders depending on the children's competence in specific tasks. For example, a child skilled in video-making led the video-making projects, while another who was better at maths helped others during maths lessons. This task-oriented view of leadership shows children's focus on successfully completing activities that were interesting to them – improved learning outcomes seem like a by-product of their focused engagement.
- Instances of leaders leading by example by participating actively and helping others were also observed. These groups were generally harmonious and functioned efficiently.
- There were a handful of groups where some children took

authority without taking much responsibility for helping the group.
- It was also observed that in a few but significant instances, advanced learners from upper grades (ninth, tenth or higher) helped manage younger children's learning. This seeded the programme's later engagement of youth volunteers as children's learning coaches.

The programme's discovery-based learning removed the fear of failure, encouraging experimentation. Even though the relationship between children and their groups was heterogeneous, the unifying feature was the children's willingness to help others learn and share their learning. Children's natural curiosity and tendency to question enhanced the group dynamics. Within the group, they also learnt non-academic skills such as teamwork, articulation, listening and negotiation. At times, the more advanced learners took it upon themselves to manage the learning sessions of other group members, ensuring that every child understood the core content of the lessons. Such group learning activities that cut across learning levels, grades, gender and social strata are novel and not visible in school-based learning environments in these communities.

5. What were the learning gains of the participants?

Children in PraDigi were assessed at multiple checkpoints to keep track of their learning progress. A combination of ASER (for language, English and maths) and subject-specific assessments are used for the baseline and subsequent rounds of assessments. Facilitators conduct household surveys based on one-on-one assessments in the spirit of Citizen-led Assessments.

Each child's assessment data is tracked over time.

In 2017, Pratham initiated a quasi-experimental trial in 294 villages in Rajasthan, India to understand the impact of different treatment variations, comparing the learning gains across a digital intervention, a print intervention and control locations. Children were assessed using the standard ASER tools and subject tools over two years. Assessments of four subjects, English, Math, Science and Hindi, were designed based on the school curriculum and conducted across treatment and control villages. Since the content in year two was different and more advanced than in year one, new assessment tools were made for children's subject assessment in year two. These subject assessments had common anchor items.

Five children were randomly sampled from each grade between Grades 5-8 from each village, making a total of 20 children from every village. The final sample size for this exercise was 5,540 children. The villages with variations of the treatment were selected from three blocks of Dausa, Bassi and Sikrai, while control locations were from Rajgarh. The villages had similar ASER results and socio-economic conditions. The survey rollout across the villages is outlined in Table 30, and the location and year-wise rollout of treatment interventions are summarised in Table 31.

Table 30: Coverage and timeline of the impact evaluation study

Census	March – May 2017
Baseline (year 1)	August – September 2017 (Four subjects assessed)
Endline (year 1)	March – April 2018 (ASER + four subjects assessed)
Baseline (year 2)	August – September 2018 (ASER + four subjects assessed)
Endline (year 2)	March – April 2019 (ASER + four subjects assessed)

Table 31: Location and year-wise rollout of treatment and control

Block	Year 1	Year 2
Rajgarh	Control	Control
Sikrai	Intervention in the community using print materials	Print materials + Digital intervention in the community
Bassi	Print materials + Digital intervention in the community	Print materials + Digital intervention in the community
Dausa	Print materials + Digital intervention in the community and schools	Print materials + Digital intervention in the community and schools

To understand the impact of the novelty of the digital device in a self-learning context, the variation of interventions across Sikrai and Bassi studied. In Sikrai, the digital intervention was introduced only in year two, while in Bassi, it was included from year one.

Throughout the programme, the children's engagement with English content was consistently high across all communities. The surveyors conducted an oral assessment of English. Student response was recorded and analysed. The average performance of children in English oral assessments across different blocks is shown in Table 32.

Table 32: Performance in English Oral Assessment

	Average % Score in English Oral Assessment			
	Baseline Y1	Endline Y1	Baseline Y2	Endline Y2
Rajgarh	59.4	62.7	64.8	67
Sikrai	60.4	63.8	67.6	71.1
Bassi	61.7	67.7	70.5	72.6
Dausa	60.2	66.3	68.6	71.3

Table 33: Change in performance across years (between treatment and control groups)

	Change in score Year 1 and Year 2			
Blocks	Year 1		Year 2	
	Δ in % score	S.D	Δ in % score	S.D
Rajgarh	3.4		2.2	
Sikrai vs. Rajgarh	0.3	0.01	1.2*	0.03*
Bassi vs. Sikrai	2.2***	0.2***	-1.3*	0.1*
Dausa vs. Bassi	0.2	0.01	0.7	0.02

(Refer to Bassi vs Sikrai under the column for Year 1 and Sikrai vs Rajgarh under the column for Year 2)

In both years, the blocks with the first year of digital intervention in the community have shown the largest and most significant progress. Digital and print intervention in the community were both introduced in Bassi from Year 1 and continued in Year 2. In contrast, Sikrai, which had print material intervention in the community in Year 1, got digital and print intervention in the community in Year 2. On comparing Bassi to Dausa, to understand if simultaneous interventions in school and community has an additional impact, no additional advantage is seen by adding a layer of school intervention.

Table 34: Change in performance on Anchor Items across Years 1 and 2

Blocks	Change in the score of Anchor Items in Year 1 and Year 2			
	Year 1		Year 2	
	Δ in % score	S.D	Δ in % score	S.D
Rajgarh	4.8		-3.5	
Sikrai vs. Rajgarh	1.2	0.0	3.4***	0.1***
Bassi vs. Sikrai	3.2***	0.1***	-2.1**	0.0**
Dausa vs. Bassi	0.6	0.0	0.7	0.0

(Refer to Bassi vs Sikrai under the column for Year 1 and Sikrai vs Rajgarh under the column for Year 2)

A similar trend is seen when Anchor Items are compared over the two years of intervention. The progress in Bassi in Year 1 is equal in magnitude to the progress in Sikrai in Year 2.

The data suggests that the digital intervention in the community has a positive and significant impact on the English scores, with significant progress in the first year of the intervention. In rural environments where English is not freely available, there are significant improvements in children's oral language skills through self-learning with digital devices. Most interestingly, the year-on-year gains are sustained, indicating that engagement levels were high enough to promote learning gains. A more detailed view of children's use of the tablet content is presented in the next section where data is presented not just from the quasi-experimental trials but from all the locations.

6. What were the children's engagement with the content like?

Usage data were collected and analysed to understand how the groups of children used the device. Two indicators used frequently across digital interventions are the Average Days per Month the learning content is accessed and the Average Duration of content access per Day. For this programme, data from October 2017 to May 2020 were analysed to determine the device usage patterns by groups of learners.

In 2017, the programme was introduced into 600 new communities. Figure 28 shows that the usage trend dips from an initial high level to stabilise over a period of time. This confirms the decreasing novelty of the device over time. However, the usage trend also closely follows the programme activities in the community. From April to July 2018, devices were taken away from the community for maintenance and repair. In July 2018, the devices were deployed again in the communities but with new content. The usage jumped up in this period due to renewed interest in exploring the content on the devices. In February and March 2019, structured courses in science were introduced, and groups were encouraged to enrol in the courses. An uptick in usage was seen during this period. In April 2019, a new set of 'off tech' activities were introduced. In these activities, the groups engaged in projects around science and life skills outside the device. The content on the device acted as a 'trigger' for these activities. There is a drop in the usage of the device after the introduction of these activities. The groups were using the device not to learn from the apps but to record videos of the projects they were creating.

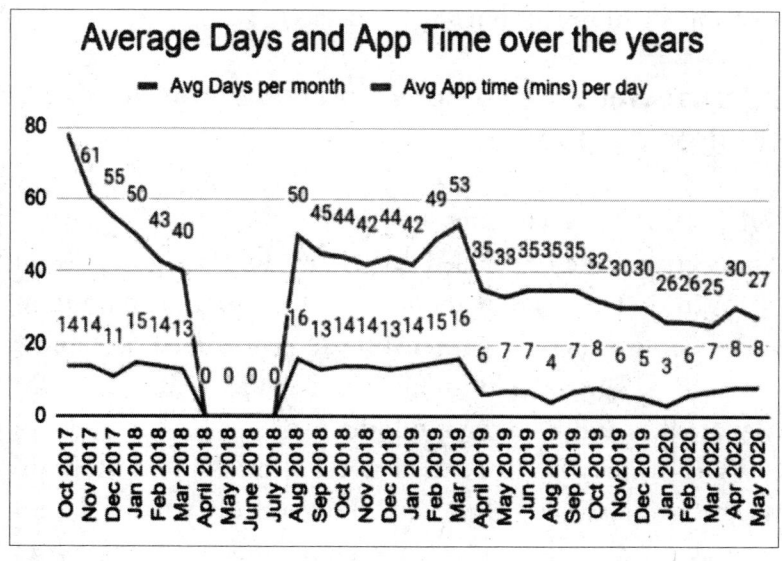

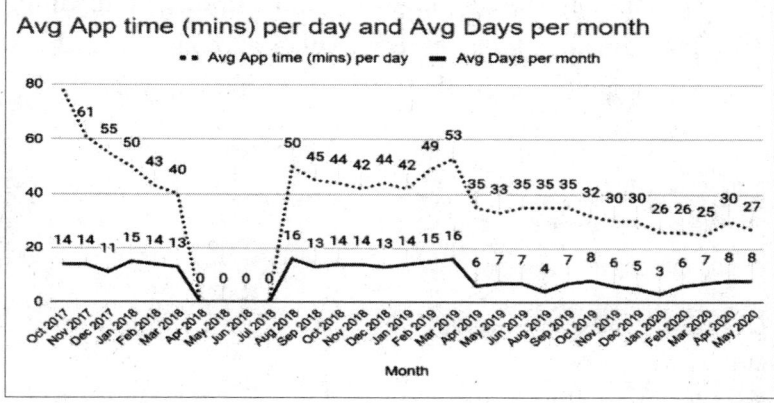

Figure 28: Device usage patterns (Oct 2017- May 2020)

Evidently, the interaction with the devices closely follows the programme activities and the stimulus given to the groups. In a controlled scenario where the only factor influencing the usage of the devices would have been their availability, the usage would have followed a steadier trend. Engaging groups in learning activities on the devices requires the creation of a learning environment outside the devices.

7. What were the composition and dynamics of children's groups?

7.1 Group Characteristics

This section presents detailed data about children's groups from 2015-2017. Information about group formation, composition and group names were gathered by all programme facilitators across the programme locations in the States of Uttar Pradesh, Maharashtra and Rajasthan in India.

The primary language used across Uttar Pradesh is Hindi, while in Rajasthan, there are different dialects of Hindi used as per Census 2011. There are considerable differences between children's home languages and Hindi, the medium of instruction in schools, especially in Rajasthan. Marathi is the primary language in Maharashtra. As shown in Table 35,

Table 35: Profiles of States with PraDigi

State	Medium of instruction	Population % (as % of the overall population of India- 2011 Census)	Groups (as % of groups in the programme)	BPL population and ranking as per capita income
Uttar Pradesh	Hindi	16.50%	47%	19.43% (28th)
Maharashtra	Marathi	9.29%	36%	17.35% (1st)
Rajasthan	Hindi	5.6%	17%	14.71% (22nd)

Maharashtra is the most prosperous of the three. The villages in Aurangabad which were part of this intervention had better access to electricity, schools and roads.

Data from 6,018 groups from across 400 communities was analysed. All the children were aware that data on their groups and group activities was being monitored for research and programme improvement purposes. A total of 2,825 groups were distributed between Sitapur (26%) and Unnao districts (21%) of Uttar Pradesh. Aurangabad district in Maharashtra had the highest number of groups, i.e. 2,173 unique groups (36%). Ajmer district in Rajasthan had 1,020 groups (17%). Figure 29 shows the district-wise distribution of groups across the States.

The distribution of 400 communities across districts and blocks is given in Table 36. Pisangan block in Ajmer district of Rajasthan had the largest average number of groups per village. In comparison, the Hilauli block of Unnao (Uttar Pradesh) had the least number of groups per village.

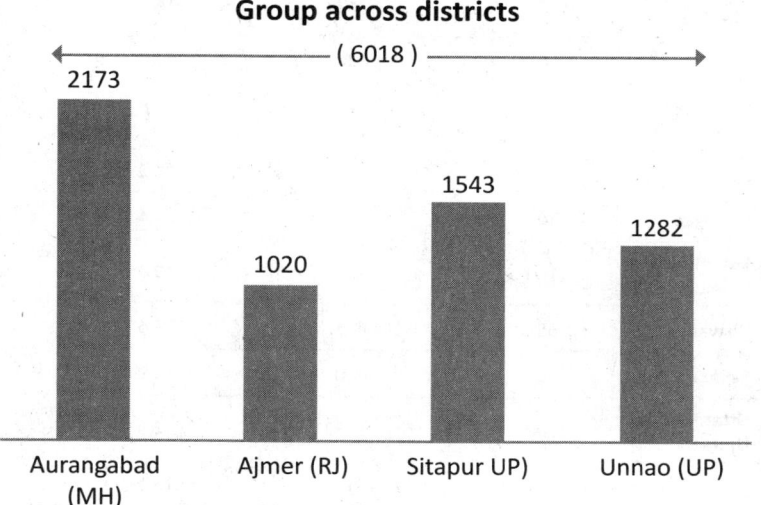

Figure 29: Distribution of groups across districts

The children's groups were characterised based on their members (a) Gender, to account for differences related to educational access, (b) Foundational literacy competence, to understand behaviour linked to learning outcomes and (c) School enrolment status (government versus private). While the programme included out-of-school children, the analysis showed that most were enrolled in schools. The groups were classified using the following parameters: the fraction of girls in a group, the fraction of readers (children who can proficiently read a Grade 2-level text in the language of instruction), and the fraction of government school students in a group. Children's reading competency was measured using the ASER tool.

Surprisingly, the percentage of all-boys groups across the

Table 36: Villages and Groups per District and Block

States/District	Count of Villages	Count of Groups	Groups per Village
Villages per District and Block			
Maharashtra Aurangabad	150	2173	14.5
Khultabad	100	1382	13.8
Phulambri	50	791	15.8
Rajasthan Ajmer	50	1020	20.4
Pisangan	50	1020	20.4
Uttar Pradesh Sitapur	100	1543	15.4
Biswan	65	883	13.6
Sakaran	35	660	18.9
Uttar Pradesh Unnao	100	1282	12.8
Asoha	54	817	15.1
Hilauli	46	465	10.1

programme was as low as 3% compared to 8% for the all-girls groups. As much as 16% of groups had less than one-fourth girls, 21% had more than one-fourth girl members and 41% had an equal or higher representation of girls in their mixed groups. There was considerable variation across the locations: Ajmer, Rajasthan, had 20% groups without girls compared to 12% in Aurangabad, Maharashtra. Incidentally, Maharashtra also had the least proportion of all-girls groups. Ajmer had the highest proportion of all-girls groups, which reflected the State's prevalent gender norms. Maharashtra had a higher proportion of groups with either less than 25% or between 25-50% of girl members. Uttar Pradesh had the highest proportion of groups, with more than 50% girl members. Table 37 gives the details.

Table 37: Fraction of Girls in Groups across Districts and Blocks

States	Fraction of Girls in Groups					
	None%	Less than 25%	Between 25-60%	More than 50%	All%	Total%
Maharashtra Aurangabad	12%	21%	26%	38%	3%	1%
Khultabad	11%	21%	28%	38%	2%	64%
Phulambri	14%	21%	22%	38%	6%	36%
Rajasthan Ajmer	20%	15%	18%	34%	13%	1%
Pisangan	20%	15%	18%	34%	13%	1%
Uttar Pradesh Sitapur	12%	14%	20%	44%	11%	55%
Biswan	13%	13%	18%	45%	11%	57%
Sakaran	11%	16%	21%	42%	10%	43%
Uttar Pradesh Unnao	11%	13%	19%	46%	11%	45%
Asoha	12%	12%	19%	47%	10%	64%
Hilauli	11%	14%	19%	45%	12%	36%

Although the programme supported children's learning in various subjects, the group's learning level was benchmarked against ASER which assesses children's foundational literacy and numeracy. 'Readers' are defined as those children who can fluently read at least a Grade 2-level text in the medium of instruction (Hindi texts in Uttar Pradesh and Rajasthan, and Marathi in Maharashtra). Groups in Rajasthan were most polarised, with 40% having members who were all readers. In comparison, Maharashtra had only 21% of all-reader groups. On average, in 78% of the groups, at least 50% of children were readers. This points towards children's strategy of focusing on educational competence while forming groups. A smaller proportion of groups with no readers or fewer than 25% of readers was observed. This skewed distribution indicates children's empathy and willingness to help each other. Table 38 summarises the distribution of readers across groups in the programme.

Table 38: Fraction of Readers in Groups across Blocks and Districts

States	Fraction of Readers in Groups					
	None%	Less than 25%	Between 25-60%	More than 50%	All%	Total%
Maharashtra Aurangabad	9%	8%	12%	50%	21%	1%
Khultabad	11%	9%	15%	52%	14%	64%
Phulambri	6%	6%	8%	47%	32%	36%
Rajasthan Ajmer	10%	3%	7%	39%	40%	1%
Pisangan	10%	3%	7%	39%	40%	1%
Uttar Pradesh Sitapur	7%	7%	11%	45%	31%	55%
Biswan	5%	6%	9%	47%	32%	57%
Sakaran	9%	9%	13%	41%	29%	43%
Uttar Pradesh Unnao	3%	3%	7%	51%	35%	45%
Asoha	3%	2%	6%	54%	34%	64%
Hilauli	3%	5%	10%	46%	36%	36%

French and Kingdon (2010) note that educational production is influenced by the child, household and school-level inputs. Despite the public policy being focused on schooling, children in rural communities 'show a rapid migration' to private low-cost schools (Kingdon, 2017). Even though one expects segregation of children attending public and private schools, the distribution pattern of children's enrollment status across the groups provides a contrary view. A healthy average of 33% of groups have 'more than 50%' children enrolled in public schools, suggesting that children in the PraDigi programme seem to have overcome the socio-economic and educational divisions based on school type, as detailed in Table 39.

Table 39: Fraction of Group members in Govt. Schools across Blocks and Districts

States	Fraction of Govt School students in Groups					
	None %	Less than 25%	Between 25-60%	More than 50%	All %	Total %
Maharashtra Aurangabad	27%	7%	10%	37%	18%	1%
Khultabad	26%	8%	12%	39%	15%	64%
Phulambri	30%	6%	7%	33%	24%	36%
Rajasthan Ajmer	18%	5%	8%	35%	34%	1%
Pisangan	18%	5%	8%	35%	34%	1%
Uttar Pradesh Sitapur	13%	8%	9%	37%	34%	55%
Biswan	16%	9%	10%	33%	32%	57%
Sakaran	8%	7%	8%	41%	37%	43%
Uttar Pradesh Unnao	37%	9%	8%	24%	22%	45%
Asoha	47%	5%	6%	22%	19%	64%
Hilauli	20%	15%	11%	28%	26%	36%

The children's groups were heterogeneous. The variations were not an outcome of random assignment but rather of children's self-selection and self-formation of groups. This shows that children valued strong group work and strong academic teams, irrespective of gender composition and enrolment in public/private schools.

In the following section, the names adopted by children's groups and the process of naming are analysed which is also indicative of decision-making and group dynamics. This analysis of group names uses a socio-linguistic lens.

7.2 Group Names

Names and naming are key constructs of socio-cultural spaces and are closely related to the identity and identification of individuals and groups (Aldrin, 2016). In matters of 'formalised' naming, children have very little say (Lareau, 1987). However, in the PraDigi programme, children exercised the responsibility of naming their groups – an act that has socio-cultural undertones in the context of children's communities. The transference of naming rights also suggests a transfer of power to children themselves. The semantic analysis also offers insights into the cultural landscapes that affect the overall environment. Observations of the naming processes of groups are also provided, using accounts from field notes. Two important processes related to group formation and naming are: (1) Children formed groups of their own volition and were free to select group members, (2) Children were provided with no restrictions on the names they could select. Analysis of sample responses of some groups informs that the decision tree for naming (how children name their groups) – provides glimpses of how children exercise their democratic voice to adopt social

identities that they can identify with across rural communities in Uttar Pradesh, Maharashtra and Rajasthan. A total of 6,018 children's group names (from Phase 2) were analysed. Children used a total of 1,497 unique roots to name their groups. The key steps in analysing group names included:
- Developing an exhaustive table of group characteristics and group names created,
- Standardising the spellings of group names (using Latin script),
- Associating names to root words (Ex. Shiv Ji and Shiv Dev mapped to the root name 'Shiva'),
- Classification of root words (Ex. Gulab categorised as a flower)
- Creating a frequency table of unique root words across geographies (see Table 40).
-

Some patterns in the naming schema that stand out very clearly are detailed below:
- In Maharashtra, a high proportion of groups were named after historical figures compared to Rajasthan and Uttar Pradesh
- In Uttar Pradesh, 16-40% of the groups named themselves after flowers or vegetables (Hilauli had the highest propensity for this behaviour)
- Religious names were most popular (38%) in Rajasthan
- Naming groups after celebrities or pop culture were not popular
- While flower names were popular in Maharashtra, fruit names were not
- An average 8% of the group names had English root words
- Objects of reverence (*agni, aasman* etc.) were most popular in Uttar Pradesh

Table 40: Root word distribution across categories

Root Words	467	412	482	282	293	312	121	1497
Other	5%	5%	3%	0%	2%	1%	0%	
Caste Related	1%	1%	2%	0%	0%	0%	0%	
National/Democratic	8%	9%	2%	9%	8%	12%	9%	
Location	9%	6%	1%	5%	4%	10%	12%	
Festival	0%	0%	0%	0%	1%	1%	0%	
Local Location	0%	0%	0%	0%	1%	0%	0%	
Geographic	3%	3%	0%	1%	2%	2%	0%	
Religious	11%	10%	38%	6%	2%	3%	3%	
Kids-Relgion/Culture	1%	0%	1%	0%	0%	1%	0%	
Mythology/Historic	2%	2%	1%	1%	1%	1%	0%	
Historic King/Queen	12%	10%	4%	0%	0%	0%	0%	
Common Identifier	1%	0%	1%	0%	0%	1%	0%	
Noun/Adjective	15%	16%	10%	11%	12%	16%	4%	
Object	2%	6%	4%	12%	15%	11%	3%	
Study Related	1%	1%	1%	2%	5%	2%	2%	
Animal/Bird	1%	1%	1%	5%	5%	6%	9%	
English	5%	7%	9%	7%	9%	7%	13%	
Fruit/Vegetable	0%	0%	0%	16%	15%	8%	20%	
Flower/Flora	12%	9%	3%	11%	8%	8%	20%	
Popculture	1%	0%	2%	1%	0%	2%	0%	
Brand	2%	2%	1%	0%	0%	1%	1%	
Famous Person	0%	2%	2%	0%	0%	0%	0%	
Politician/Statesman	5%	5%	6%	7%	5%	4%	%1	
Food	0%	0%	0%	1%	1%	2%	0%	
Person	5%	5%	7%	1%	2%	1%	2%	
Total	1382	791	1020	883	660	817	465	
Block	Khultabad	Phulambri	Pisangan	Biswan	Sakaran	Asoha	Hilauli	
District	Aurangabad		Ajmer	Sitapur		Unnao		
State	MH		RJ	UP				

- Nouns and adjectives (*aadarsh, abhilasha,* dharya etc.) were uniformly popular (13%) across all blocks except in Hilauli
- Names of pre-Independence and post-Independence leaders were popular across all locations in Uttar Pradesh and Maharashtra but not Rajasthan
- No specific trend was noticed showcasing caste-related names (Ex. the last names of group leaders). They were uniformly unpopular.

The decision chain for children naming their groups is outlined in Figure 30. The list is not exhaustive. It is based on interactions with a few groups and their members during field visits. The decision chain has four components, (1) Source, (2) Process, (3) Purpose, and (4) Use of group names. The arrows indicate the pathway followed by the children's groups. Each component is further analysed to understand its value concerning children's group dynamics and identity.

There are five primary sources of group names. Given the semi-formal structure of the programme, innovative and imaginary names (such as nonsense words) were not used. Interestingly, a significant majority of the names were associated with tangible entities. There are different sources from where children adopted the group names. Programme staff were trained specifically not to dictate names, but in some instances, they had to provide examples of group names and some groups adopted these names. These names were not only homogenous and but there is also evidence of a high degree of emulation across programme staff.

The other sources of names included the immediate village environment, cultural surroundings, media and school environs, and finally, names borrowed from other groups. Each source is mapped to four processes of adopting the name for groups, namely, acceptance of a proposed name, adoption after intra-group discussions, following suggestions of a group leader or other authority figures, and non-democratic decisions by specific children (usually the leader). The third component which is purpose is understood as what the adopted name adds to the group. The gains are broadly described below:

- **Marking identity:** The group can buy into a self-developed identity associated with their chosen name.
- **Emulating role models:** The group consciously adopts the name of a role model. It gives them confidence and perceived vigour to achieve their learning goals.
- **Internalising socio-cultural identity:** Adopting the prescribed norm and pre-existing social identity that children have come across.
- **Following norms:** Accepting naming and cultural norms to reduce any friction in getting access to the tablet.

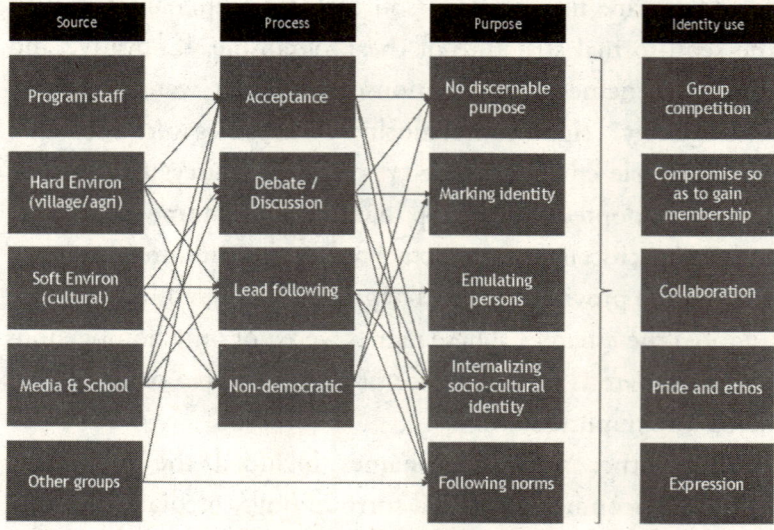

Figure 30: Group name process decision chain

The association of group names with identity encouraged positive social learning behaviours, such as a sense of belonging during child-friendly learning competitions and games. Some groups with names such as 'Australia', 'New Zealand', and 'India' emulated a friendly rivalry as seen on cricket pitches. Such groups collaborate and compete with each other to effectively and efficiently go through the learning content. Self-naming groups also encouraged collaboration. There were instances where groups using common names, for example, 'Kela' (banana) and 'Santra' (orange), worked together to go through their digital content. Sometimes these groups shared the same tablet and depended on each-other for charging or other infrastructure-related issues. When groups adopted names of role models or historical figures, a sense of pride and common historic ethos was also observed. This was especially true when groups adopted names of heroes from history, such as Shivaji in Maharashtra or religious figures, such as Saraswati in Rajasthan. Some groups borrowed the names of other groups to gain access to the programme and its activities. For example, two all-girl groups named themselves 'Gulab' (rose) to allow their parents to permit them to participate in the programme. Each group told their parents that the other one was participating in the programme to convince them.

Some clear patterns emerged on investigating the semantic content of the names chosen by the children. Religious symbolism was ingrained in the children's minds, which was revealed by names such as Bhole Shankar, Bholenath, Bismala (sic), Edgah, Ganga (Ma), Ganeshay Namah, Ganpati (also, Ganesh), Gautam (Buddha), Garib Nawaz etc. Tara saptak in rural areas seems to be a common label, as many stories are woven around the existence of different pairs or combinations of stars in the sky. Additionally, consumables, FMCG brands and products such as '5-Star' (famous and affordable chocolate) are popular. Adopting names with a prefix and star (ex: 3-Star to 9-Star) was commonly observed, indicating an affinity to point systems or an understanding of grading scales.

Many idealistic words and concepts were observed, such as 'Aadarsh' or 'Aakansha' etc. It is possible that parents played a role in suggesting such 'high culture' names. Heroes, real-life as well as imaginary, have always been inspirations, and therefore we got Kabirdas, Laxmi Bai, Ahilya Bai and Ambedkar amongst others.

Modern-day personalities like 'Baba Ram Dev' and Mary Kom also inspired children's group names. Patriotism and national pride were also reflected in several names. Computer games, cartoons and food names (Ex. Jalebi, Santra, Samosa, Rasgulla) are other sources of naming. Place names occured very frequently as well. Lastly, film-inspired group names such as 'Bahubali', and 'Bajrangi Bhaijaan' were also.

In summary, group names personalised a scale-friendly large-scale learning experiment. Social innovation of self-administered and managed group learning enables democratic learning practices across groups in the villages.

Aligned with the SDG framework, the PraDigi programme successfully balanced the need to scale using digital technology with individualism to enhance children's learning experience. In the last section, we discuss the ramifications of performance and naming on children's participation.

8. Conclusion

PraDigi provides a unique opportunity for children to take up curated learning content outside the school environment. Children's groups are free to explore and set the pace of their learning journeys according to their needs. In the absence of performance-related penalties and being outside their school rooms, children are known to participate without fear. They ask questions, clear their doubts, share queries and explanations, and work together as a unit, fully engaged with their learning tasks. In this manner, children's groups empowered individuals as much as individuals empowered the groups.

In many cases, the groups negotiated the content together and moved ahead, once everyone had understood the lesson. They also worked together to create models, act out videos, take notes and fill in worksheets mapped to the content, all on their own. Children used other features on the tablets, especially the camera application and some personalised their tablets with photographs and put in popular music.

Pratham's facilitators were trained not to teach but rather to guide children through the content. They worked with the groups to enhance their active participation. They prodded groups with questions, cleared doubts or directed children to places where they could discover the answers. Notably, almost half the facilitators had prior experience in Pratham's traditional teaching-learning interventions. They were also trained to increase community participation. Villagers, especially mothers and youth, were encouraged to support children's learning.

The excitement over digital and tablet-based learning was very visible. Guardians personally ensured the safety of the devices in many cases. The concept of self-learning out of school, sans a teacher to instruct children, was novel to the communities. With time they appreciated how children were organising their learning. It was observed that children gravitated more towards material that was relatable to their immediate surroundings, characters they could identify with and videos that went beyond being mere audio-visual adaptations of their textbooks. These insights specifically shaped creation of new content.

As the programme progressed, children choose their topics through the iterative process of trial and error. Content is regularly updated every six to eight weeks. Constant feedback from children is collected to improve programme processes and content. Detailed analysis of children's usage, especially the popularity of different lessons and length of sessions during specific content use, are also used to re-analyse content features and update lessons. For example, during a visit to Neemtikar village in Uttar Pradesh, it became clear why a video named 'Golden Girls' about an Indian sprinter winning a medal at the Asian Games was not doing well with some groups, especially those with girls. On questioning a group of mostly girls who had named themselves Gulab Gang, it was found that they objected to the athlete's attire. The girls discussed why they would not watch this particular video. This demonstrated a discussion-led and collegiate-style participatory mechanism and provided an example of an otherwise marginalised group asserting their opinion.

The nature of decision-making itself was different across groups. Some activities were driven by their leaders convincing the others about what was best for them, while in others, each child was given a chance to pick a lesson turn by turn. Some groups followed a lesson plan set by an older youth and coach responsible for guiding the group.

PraDigi has evolved and experimented with different mechanisms to improve children's participation and learning. It aims to develop child-driven and child-friendly learning spaces where they can explore and grow, collaborate and not just compete. The programme delivers a learning solution that bypasses two critical barriers to quality education across rural India: poor access to quality learning and the absence of a learner-centric environment. This programme has successfully empowered children by helping them realise the value of asking questions, working in groups, getting their communities involved in their learning, developing and evolving their own/ group identities, and taking leadership roles. Analysis of group dynamics and group names demonstrates the possibility of children learning various executive functions to manage and govern their learning experiences. Albeit anecdotal, children who are part of the programme are visibly more confident and better communicators of original ideas while also showing improved learning outcomes.

The positive impact of quality education on children's growth and social development is well established (Payton et al., 2008; Hanushek & Woessmann, 2007). Plato, in his polemic on education (Plato & Cornford, 1945), says, 'Enforced exercise does no harm to the body, but enforced learning will not stay in mind. So, avoid compulsion, and let your children's lessons take the form of play'. This quote is the inspiration for the PraDigi programme to create democratic learning environments where children are comfortable and learn well through group work and collaboration.

SECTION THREE

Scaling and Role of Partnerships

I. An Education-Knowledge Bridge: Building Better by Advancing Evidence Use in Education
II. Education Advocacy in Uganda: Capacity of Civil Society Organisations At Sub-national Level
III. The ALiVE Project in East Africa: Can Collaborative Action Drive Learning Outcomes? A Critical Examination

HOW can learning outcomes be improved by scaling up practices in education, what makes collaboration and partnerships work are the themes of the third section of this book.

The first chapter *An Education-Knowledge Bridge: Building Better by Advancing Evidence Use in Education,* argues that despite immense progress and many important initiatives, the communities of research, policy, and practice are often independent islands of activity, making worthy but uncoordinated attempts to bridge the education and knowledge gaps. This is even more so when considering evidence that emerges from civil society organisations, that are focused on applying and refining interventions. Their experiences are rarely reflected in policy or implementation choices. The study draws upon a critical comparison of the education and health sectors' use of evidence for decision-making and discusses how this evidence can be used to build better education practices. The findings of this study are used to propose concrete approaches that will allow routine application of evidencefrom civil society to strengthen education practices at scale for improved learning outcomes.

The second chapter, *Education Advocacy in Uganda: Capacity of Civil Society Organisations At Sub-national Level,* describes the partnership efforts of Uwezo with multiple civil society organisations (CSOs) at the district level in Uganda. These partnerships carried out independent national assessments of children's literacy and numeracy and raised public awareness about educational issues. This study examines the situations of Uwezo's partner CSOs, with a focus on education advocacy. In August-September 2020, data was obtained using a mixed-method approach through semi-structured interviews conducted by telephone or Zoom and a survey questionnaire that was distributed and collected by email. The study presents the findings of this survey. It shows that nearly all Uwezo's CSO partners consider advocacy a part of their mission. The study also highlights the issues faced by the CSOs, such as severe financial constraints and the directions in which the partnerships can be improved, such as staff training in resource mobilisation and research methods.

The final chapter, *The ALiVE Project in East Africa: Can Collaborative Action Drive Learning Outcomes? A Critical Examination* examines the effectiveness of the collaboration process and its contextual dynamism for the Regional Education Learning Initiative programme called ALiVE (Assessment of Life Skills and Values in East Africa). The study employed a qualitative approach and a phenomenological research design to inquire, learn and reflect on the collaboration process of East African partner organisations for developing contextualised assessment tools. It was found that partners have personal motives for joining the collaboration alliances and stay in the collaboration only if their motives are fulfilled. Further, partners would collaborate if their vision and goals reflect their needs and when there is an opportunity to learn from diverse perspectives, make decisions collectively and agree on solutions collectively.

An Education–Knowledge Bridge Building Better by Advancing Evidence Use in Education[*]

Suzanne Grant Lewis, Evangeline Nderu, Aleesha Taylor and Randa Grob-Zakhary

1. Introduction

The gap between what we know and what we do in education lies at the heart of a global learning crisis, which demands dramatic and urgent system improvement. Despite immense progress and many important initiatives, the communities of research, policy, and practice are often independent islands of activity, making worthy but uncoordinated attempts to bridge the gaps. This is even more so when considering evidence that emerges from civil society organisations that are focused on applying and refining interventions. Their experiences are rarely reflected in policy or implementation choices.

Building on Education.org's global COVID School Reopening Tracker[1] (Education.org, 2021a), an analysis was conducted to interrogate the causes of such barriers and find

---

[*] This document is an abbreviated adaptation of a White Paper and was specifically prepared for the PAL Network Conference 2021. The full White Paper, with a complete list of contributors and organisations analysed, can be found at https://education.org/white-paper.

[1] The COVID-19 Tracking and Analysis site is no longer being updated but the dashboards and analytic reports are accessible at https://education.org/covid-19.

feasible opportunities for improvement. The findings highlight that lack of new research is not the greatest obstacle to progress but it is the failure to access and use what we already know. Furthermore, there is strong consensus and political will around the urgent need to better access and use country and community evidence in education dialogues and decision-making at local, national, regional, and global levels.

While there are outstanding examples in education that address this challenge, but they are efforts to build upon but are sufficient alone. Therefore, this paper draws upon a critical comparison of the education and health sectors' use of evidence for decision-making. It identifies what can be done to accelerate improvements in education by making more effective use of the evidence that should be driving education policy and practice and puts forth an appeal and roadmap for collective action to span the knowing-doing gap by building an 'Education Knowledge Bridge'. The proposed Education Knowledge Bridge aims to lift experiences and voices into a sustainable evidence architecture. Finally, findings are used to propose concrete approaches that will allow us to routinely apply evidence from civil society to strengthen education practices at scale for improved learning outcomes.

2. The Challenge

In the education sector, we often look towards the health sector for inspiration. We explored the important differences between ways that the health and education sectors work with evidence. Our goal was not to uncritically 'copy and paste' from health to education, nor to underplay many challenges in the health sector, but to stimulate critical thinking about how to accelerate progress in education, particularly for the most marginalised young people.

The differences between the health and education sectors are most stark during a crisis. As COVID-19 swept across the globe, the health sector responded quickly on multiple fronts, testing, collecting data, utilising existing R&D protocols to develop vaccines, refining treatment guidance and rapidly increasing system capacity. While there were numerous failures and policy mistakes, rapid improvements in treatment protocols and survival rates were achieved globally in only a few months as the health sector used its well-established knowledge bridge to learn and adapt while simultaneously treating patients.

In contrast, education systems worldwide experienced the largest closure of schools in history. There was an absence of data on the educational impact for children in the context of growing inequity, ad-hoc distance learning provided to a minority with little evaluation of quality, and policy confusion over good practice for reopening, which had serious implications for the most marginalised.

There are substantial differences, of course. Education does not have diseases, pills or cures. A quick blood test can reveal COVID-19 antibodies, but it cannot tell us if a child understands calculus. Yet, there are also many similarities. Firstly, patients and students are people. Secondly, patients/students respond very differently to the same intervention, and doctors/teachers often need the skills of a social worker to understand what is most likely to work.

Health is far from a perfect parallel, and many health experts are quick to point out significant deficiencies, particularly in its focus on treating disease rather than prevention and well-being. Nevertheless, health offers inspiration to inform our thinking (Chalmers, 2022). So, how does the health sector work to bridge the knowing-doing gap?

In the past forty years, the health sector has turbocharged the quantity and quality of research available,[2] but its success is a result of much more than volume alone. Sector-wide capacity has been built to create comprehensive and systematic syntheses of evidence that has been through trust-building processes that strive for independence and transparency. These syntheses are the foundation for actionable guidance that is user-centric, reflecting the actual challenges faced by policymakers and practitioners. Results are communicated by dedicated translation specialists so that evidence is shared beyond the narrow group of experts. Over time, the process has become more inclusive, with greater awareness of gender and ethnic diversity. Underpinning this approach is effective coordination and alignment of incentives and culture across the health sector communities of research, policy and practice.

In the education sector, despite massive progress and many important initiatives, critical parts of knowledge infrastructure are still either missing or nascent. The communities of research, policy and practice are often independent islands of activity, making worthy but uncoordinated attempts to bridge the gaps. According to our analysis, for every synthesis developed

---

2   The evidence-based medicine (EBM) movement was profoundly motivated by the 1972 book by Archie Cochrane, "Effectiveness and Efficiency: Random Reflections on Health Services". After his death, in the early 1980s, clinical epidemiologists and doctors in Canada, the UK and the US began to publish on how to better appraise medical literature to improve clinical treatments which were overly reliant on the habits of individual senior physicians or the marketing efforts of pharmaceutical companies. In 1989, UK obstetrician Iain Chalmers published 'Effective care in pregnancy and childbirth', based on systematic reviews and clinical trial registries, the first evidence-based textbook on treatment. The UK Cochrane Centre was founded by Chalmers in 1992, funded by the National Institute for Health Research, and a year later he, Sackett and other EBM pioneers founded The Cochrane Collaboration (now Cochrane), to build the global evidence base of synthesized reviews of healthcare interventions and published them in the Cochrane since 1996.

in education, health produces 26 syntheses.[3] In addition to this volume gap, education syntheses, compared to the ones in the health sector, are sporadic, incomplete and less likely to be connected to policy and practice challenges. This means that existing education research is rarely translated into actionable guidance and is hardly used by policymakers and practitioners to inform their decisions. Teachers and education policymakers, unlike doctors, are often left to guess what the evidence says. Education.org seeks to catalyse the formation of an Education Knowledge Bridge that tackles the global learning crisis by making more and better use of the evidence we already have.

3. Method

The methodology for this paper consists of four complementary elements: (1) An analysis of 88 global and regional education knowledge organisations, identifying of key informants and analysis of 26 interviews, including with PAL Network members that were carried out between May 2020 and January 2021, (2) Case studies of organisations currently working on issues relating to this paper were conducted to understand their role and contribution, (3) A review of 80 major reports and eight collaborative knowledge initiatives in education was conducted, and (4) These analyses were then complemented by a rigorous comparative analysis of the infrastructure and culture of the health system with evidence generation and used it with that of the education sector. This analysis considered the strengths and weaknesses with an eye towards accelerating progress in education.

---

3   See Appendix E: The synthesis volume gap – Health vs. Education in Education.org (2021) A White Paper to Advance Evidence Use in Education. https://education.org/white-paper .

4. What Will It Take to Build an Education-Knowledge Bridge?

An Education Knowledge Bridge will build on existing good examples and enable the capacity for developing and using comprehensive and up-to-date syntheses, accelerating progress towards SDG4. The analysis reveals five capabilities that are present in the health sector knowledge bridge, which were judged to be absent or nascent in education.

4.1 Capability One: Research Generation, Promoting Use and User Orientation from the Outset

It is essential to make better use of existing evidence. However, research generation also remains a challenge, especially in education, where quantity, quality and relevance must improve. It is inevitable that the volume and focus of research will have a significant impact on its future utilisation. Comprehensive syntheses could focus new research on evidence gaps, while stronger involvement of policymakers and practitioners in early research stages would help to ensure that scarce resources can tackle important challenges.

Encouragingly, building blocks for a future Education Knowledge Bridge are evident, though on a much smaller scale than in the health sector. One such bridge is the Knowledge and Innovation Exchange (KIX), established with a budget of US$75 million, to meet the global public good gaps in education. KIX brings together 68 low- and middle-income countries that are partners of the Global Partnership for Education to identify common policy challenges and facilitate knowledge sharing and evidence building (GPE KIX, 2020).

New research on health will start with an understanding of a specific challenge or obstacle in the treatment of a condition;

it is likely to be focused on filling gaps in the current knowledge and envisioning application in an existing treatment pathway. In contrast, education research is less likely to be focused on current problems of practice and policy and is more likely to be decided by researchers who identify questions of interest to them (Donovan, Snow & Daro, 2013; White, 2018) or that which they deem relevant. Again, there are encouraging initiatives in place. For example, Evidence and Gap Maps (EGMs), as championed by the International Initiative for Impact Evaluation (3ie), are a 'systematic evidence synthesis product which displays the available evidence relevant to a specific research question' (White et al., 2020).

By identifying gaps where little or no evidence from impact evaluations and systematic reviews is available, it is possible to support a more strategic approach for building the evidence base for a sector. EGMs have been combined to create megamaps such as the recent Mega-map of systematic reviews and evidence and gap maps on interventions to improve child well-being in low and middle-income countries, published by the Campbell Collaboration. This mega-map covered 333 systematic reviews and 23 EGMs (Saran, Albright. Adona & White, 2020). Such initiatives offer funders and academics greater insight into research needs and gaps, while potentially also reducing the risk of wasting scarce resources through duplication and repetition of what has already been researched.

Health research is also increasingly reflecting the needs of minority groups. Over time, the health research community has recognised its inherent biases towards patients of a particular gender, age or condition – realising that equity can only be achieved when data is collected from and reflects the differing needs of all relevant groups and contexts (Cochrane, 2019).

The question of 'what works?' has steadily been replaced with 'what works for whom, when, where and why?' with greater effort to increase diversity and meaningful participation in clinical trials (Cochrane, 2019; Challenger & Ferraro, 2020).

Currently, the vast majority of education research is conducted in contexts that are not representative of most of the global population, limiting the likelihood of its findings supporting a meaningful equity agenda (Siliezar & Joseph, 2020; Quam, 2016; Mulimani, 2019). However, there are encouraging innovations in the education sector. For example, The People's Action for Learning (PAL) Network's effort to forge South-South partnerships of organisations that are working across three continents to conduct citizen-led assessments which are aimed at improving learning outcomes by, among other activities, generating data through oral one-on-one assessments conducted in households. Another example is the Regional Education Learning Initiative (RELI) which is composed of 70 members in East Africa, promoting cross-organisational learning and exchange to improve education access and quality.

4.2 Capability Two: Synthesis - Building a Big Picture with Jigsaw Pieces

'Evidence synthesis refers to the process of bringing together information from a range of sources and disciplines to inform debates and decisions on specific issues. Decision-making and public debate are best served if policymakers have access to the best current evidence on an issue (The Royal Society, Academy of Medical Sciences, 2018).'

Extending the focus of policymakers and practitioners from individual studies to comprehensive syntheses is essential, as is shifting the frequency of syntheses from one-offs to routine updates. In education, it is necessary to broaden the types of evidence that are synthesised and to better reflect country-level data and contexts, which are poorly represented in most traditional research.

In health, a sector-wide synthesis process means doctors and policymakers rarely need to read, rate, and evaluate individual studies. Instead, they can draw on robust and comprehensive syntheses of evidence around specific, practice-focused themes or have confidence that the established treatment pathways will reflect the best-in-class evidence. These syntheses come from specialist organisations which conduct synthesis at scale. For example, Cochrane provides 8,500 systematic reviews in its publicly available and searchable library (Cochrane, 2019). Also, in health, a systematic review is a living document. Health sector syntheses are timely and updated regularly as new evidence becomes available.

The education sector has no systematic sector-wide process for synthesis at scale or a central library of the results. Most educational research remains isolated in individual journal articles, often one-off intervention studies, hidden behind paywalls. While there is no systematic sector-wide process, a smaller scale and high-quality synthesis work is underway. For example, the Education Endowment Foundation's (EEF) online Teaching and Learning Toolkit has synthesised and continues to update evidence about 35 school-based interventions (Education Endowment Foundation, 2017). While this and other critical building blocks exist, they are not sufficient to bridge the knowing-doing gap. Even when the results of existing efforts are combined, they confirm the small scale of synthesis work in the education sector which are relative to the need. Furthermore, there is no single place where work from these different organisations comes together in a form that is easy for policymakers and practitioners to find and engage with.

The health sector has also developed sophisticated synthesis methodologies and is increasingly incorporating broader types of evidence. Synthesis is understood as a complex undertaking that is fraught with methodological issues and potential bias. A systematic review should follow standardised processes to ensure that all practically available relevant evidence is identified, considered, rigorously assessed, and thoughtfully synthesised (Savitz, Wellenius & Trikalinos, 2019). The health sector has, therefore, championed more rigorous approaches to the process of synthesis. For example, GRADE (Grading of Recommendations, Assessment, Development and Evaluations) is a transparent framework for developing and presenting summaries of evidence and provides a systematic approach for making clinical practice recommendations (BMJ Best Practice, n.d.).

Used by more than 100 organisations worldwide, GRADE allows the quality of evidence and the confidence in recommendations to be assessed on a consistent scale. In a similar vein, the padlock symbol used in the EEF's Teaching and Learning Toolkit is an example of a confidence scale that is being used by one organisation working in education (Education Endowment Foundation, 2017).

Due to the larger volume of health sector research, it is inevitable that systematic reviews find a greater volume of eligible research. However, in other fields, such as education, where research can be sparse, alternative methodologies such as 'subject-wide evidence synthesis' are gaining interest

(Sutherland & Wordley, 2018, Barnett-Page & Thomas, 2009). Approaches that embrace a wider range of methodologies and sources are likely to have growing relevance. For example, GRADE- CERQual (Confidence in the Evidence from Reviews of Qualitative Research) addresses the need to assess confidence in qualitative research (Lewin et al., 2018).

4.3 Capability Three: Guidance - Answering the 'So What?' of Every Synthesis.

Synthesis is essential but not sufficient. The third part of the bridge is the capacity to develop evidence-informed guidance and recommendations from the synthesis. The process for developing guidance needs to be as robust as that of developing synthesis. Recommendations must be relevant, realistic and clear for the target audiences and contexts, as well as sensitive to the fact that cost is a limiting factor for policy.

The health sector has the infrastructure and well-established processes to create and disseminate guidance. Health syntheses routinely include 'implications for practice' in their conclusions. The health sector also systematically embeds the conclusions of syntheses into treatment recommendations (known as critical pathways), prescribing guidance, purchasing decisions and regulations (Kwan & Sandercock, 2003).

With less research to draw upon and without a systematic synthesis process to shape conclusions from the research that exist, educational policy development is a far less predictable and rigorous process. Education systems (that is, everything that goes into educating school students, including laws, policies, funding and regulations) are more likely to oscillate between stagnation and dramatic change in direction as they fall victim to political interventions, rather than having continuous improvement. According to the Organisation for Economic Co-operation and Development (OECD), looking at some of the best-resourced countries in the world, 'many OECD countries lack effective mechanisms to strategically integrate data and educational research into the process of evidence-based resource planning' and demonstrate 'systematic weaknesses in the ability to use data and research evidence can appear at every level of governance' (OECD, 2017).

Yet, building blocks are emerging. For example, the Global Education Evidence Advisory Panel (GEEAP), co-hosted by the UK Foreign, Commonwealth & Development Office and the World Bank, is composed of economists, educationalists, psychologists and policymakers and has released its first recommendations on 'smart buys' in education for low- and middle- income countries (The World Bank, n.d., The World Bank, 2020).

In health, new evidence is consistently being translated into guidance to improve the existing systems and practices. The sector is evolving over time through tweaks to strengthen the current practices rather than by adding entirely new or parallel systems. If a doctor wants to test a new idea or potential treatment, there are clearly defined mechanisms to ensure transparency, patient safety, ethical approval, trial delivery and publication of results, all within the mainstream system.

In education, teachers usually lack any similar support for innovation. While they sometimes enjoy greater autonomy in the classroom, the likelihood of innovation by any single teacher leading to improvements in the overall system is very low. Education organisations such as the Institute for the Study of Knowledge Management in Education (ISKME) – a non-profit organisation whose mission is to improve the practice of continuous learning, collaboration, and change in the education sector – are doing vital work to help schools in collecting and sharing information, particularly through Open Educational Resources (OERs) (Institute for the Study of Knowledge Management in Education, n.d.).

Meanwhile, the search for silver bullets in education sometimes causes pilots to be established, running alongside or parallel to the formal education system. An increasing body of scaling experience argues that these 'parallel pilots' that do not engage with the reality of the mainstream system are likely to drain resources and create unsustainable results (Saving Brains Learning Platform, 2019).

4.4 Capability Four: Implementation - Engaging for and Supporting Change at Scale

Turning guidance into policy and practice requires an improved capacity to implement change. It needs coordinated support from global players and local actors, bottom-up as much as top-down. Implementation plans must engage stakeholders with effective communication. They must be designed with rapid learning and adjustment in mind, aware that every new context has enormous implications for even the most established model. It is essential to resist implementing interventions without a critical assessment of their relevance for specific contexts.

With evidence-informed guidance in place, it becomes possible to focus on the challenges of implementing changes within a system. In comparing the capacity of the health and education sectors to do this, two important differences stand out.

First, the health sector invests funds in technical assistance and capacity building to implement research findings at the country level. Research in the health sector has established that 'passive approaches for disseminating [evidence] are largely ineffective because dissemination does not happen spontaneously' and 'too often, capacity-building efforts have been built around pushing out research-based evidence without accounting for the pull of practitioners, policymakers or community members or accounting for key contextual variables (e.g., resources, needs, culture, capacity)' (Brownson, Fielding & Green, 2018).

In the education sector, the building blocks are once again evident. For example, the UNESCO International Institute for Education Planning (IIEP) holds the UN mandate to support educational policy, planning and management. IIEP is 'committed to creating and sharing knowledge to support context-relevant analyses to improve educational policy formulation and planning. Training, technical cooperation, applied research and knowledge sharing are the four main activities through which IIEP accomplishes its mission' (IIEP-UNESCO, n.d.).

The UNICEF Data Must Speak initiative (DMS) helps countries 'unlock existing data to expand access to education and improve learning for all. DMS provides direct technical assistance in Chad, Madagascar, Namibia, Nepal, Niger, the Philippines, Togo and Zambia' (UNICEF, n.d.). In a strong example of private philanthropy and government stakeholders collaborating to improve policy delivery, the UBS Optimus Foundation provided funding to the Ministry of Basic and Senior Secondary Education (MBSSE) in Sierra Leone to undertake a systems-level analysis of education service delivery, with emphasis on identifying the disconnects between policy design and implementation (Education Partnership Group, 2020). The report supported the development of Sierra Leone's Education Sector Analysis preceding the new Education Sector Plan (2020-2025), a proposed restructuring of the MBSSE, and the establishment of a delivery unit.

Second, the health sector invests in learning networks so that implementers can systematically learn about how to implement evidence in practice. For example, the Joint Learning Network for Universal Health Coverage (JLN) is 'an innovative, country-driven network of practitioners and policymakers from around the globe who co-develop global knowledge products that help bridge the gap between theory and practice to extend health coverage to more than 3 billion people' in 34 countries (Joint Learning Network, n.d.).

Such networks are not unique to health, although it is (currently) difficult to point to activities at the scale of the JLN. Strong building blocks in education include the Millions Learning Real-time Scaling Labs, initiated by Brookings, which aim to 'strengthen scaling efforts through a forum for peer-to-peer learning in which lab participants discuss lessons learned and develop strategies to address challenges faced during their education interventions' scaling journey (Robinson & Winthrop, 2016)'.

Another promising example is the four Early Childhood Development (ECD) regional networks (Africa Early Childhood Network (AfECN), Asia-Pacific Regional Network for Early Childhood (ARNEC), The Arab Network for Early Childhood (ANECD) and International Step by Step Association (ISSA), which are member associations that act as regional learning communities, bridging the policy and practice domains to 'challenge existing knowledge and practice, and co-construct new approaches and models' (International Step by Step Association, n.d.). Also focused on early learning is the Saving Brains Learning Platform, which is a learning community of more than 100 NGOs who are using evidence-based approaches to scale early childhood development, and which are supported by a number of private foundations that understand the value of peer-based learning and networks to support change and scaling (Radner et al., 2018).

In both the health and education sectors, implementation research is a growing area of study which is fundamental to understanding evidence use. Implementation research seeks to better understand the real-life challenges of 'implementation –the act of carrying an intention into effect'. Embracing real-world challenges and complex contextual issues, this approach focuses on the users of research rather than the producers. Methodologically, it utilises a wide variety of qualitative, quantitative and mixed methods techniques that seek to better understand issues, including acceptability, adoption, appropriateness, feasibility, fidelity, implementation cost, coverage and sustainability (Peters et al., 2013; Moir, 2018).

4.5 Capability Five: Enabling Environment - Building a Culture of Evidence Use

Evidence use is a culture as much as a process. Interviews and analysis suggest that adopting new tools and processes is not enough. How we do it matters too, especially in education, where the culture and approach are distinctive. In reflecting on the health knowledge bridge, it becomes clear that its strengths are explained by something greater than just institutions and processes. The health sector has created an enabling environment – a culture of evidence use – that pervades its work. In comparing the health and education environments, three important differences stand out.

First, the health sector strives for independence and transparency in research and synthesis. Central to the health synthesis process is the engagement of large numbers of health professionals from numerous organisations, who act in volunteer or supporter roles. This helps with transparency, creates higher levels of buy-in and distributes costs across and around the sector so that central financing is not an overly influential factor in determining what gets synthesised and when. In education, it is possible to see certain stakeholders exhibiting a significant influence on what gets researched and when.

For example, research is sometimes commissioned by donors around specific agendas, which are linked to individual interventions who act funded by the same donors. Synthesis, when it happens, is often commissioned as a one-off study from a university department, think tank, or private research institution, with little transparency. The education sector has not yet matured to the same level of expectations regarding independence and transparency that are evident in health. However, both sectors, no doubt, have further to go.

Second, the health sector works to align incentives and culture between evidence creators (researchers) and evidence consumers (health practitioners). Doctors are immersed in a culture of research from the very early stages of their medical training. Many hospitals have specialist facilities for conducting research and trials, and contributing to clinical trials is a shared responsibility and opportunity for all who work in the sector. Ethics committees and other research infrastructure exist to support this.

The difference between hospitals and universities is much less stark than between schools and universities. Teaching hospitals and the work of academic practitioners mean that professionals routinely cross between these worlds, sometimes several times a day. Various incentives also encourage engagement in research. For example, hospitals can earn additional income by hosting and facilitating clinical trials for pharmaceutical companies; therefore, many have specialist research and development departments thereby making this an everyday and mutually beneficial part of their work (Northern Care Alliance, n.d.).

Schools and teachers, on the other hand, have fewer opportunities to learn about evidence in their training, conduct less frequent research, and usually lack the facilities and/or resources to do so. This means that mountains of data held by schools and teachers (e.g., related to student assessment) remain siloed in schools and are rarely analysed to help improve performance in the wider system.

Third, the health sector has dedicated translation specialists. Allied to the health sector are professions that focus on translating science into practice. For example, medical writers specialise in writing regulatory and research-related documents, disease or drug-related educational and promotional literature, publish articles such as journal manuscripts and abstracts, and content for healthcare websites, health-related magazines and news articles. To do so, they need an understanding of the key medical concepts and the ability to communicate scientific information to suit the different levels of understanding of specialists and lay audiences (Sharma, 2010).

In the education sector, it is common to find education journalists who write about it, but the education sector's equivalent role of a medical writer is difficult to find. Without it, too much valuable evidence remains hidden.

Individually, these differences between the health and education sectors are important but not necessarily dramatic. Yet, by ensuring capacity and good practice at every stage of the process (from knowledge generation to implementation support, facilitated by an enabling culture), the health sector ensures that the knowing-doing gap is bridged. The health sector knowledge bridge has taken decades to develop, and it continues to evolve. An equivalent Education Knowledge Bridge will inevitably look and function differently, but our analysis shows that many building blocks already exist.

5. Creating an Environment for an Education-Knowledge Bridge

Urgent action and greater persistence are required to strengthen and connect these building blocks into a functioning Education Knowledge Bridge. To create the enabling environment necessary for the Education Knowledge Bridge to emerge and evolve, we must:

5.1 Be User-centric rather than Focusing on Theory. This can be achieved by involving those who will utilise evidence in their decision-making from the start of the research process, prioritising the most relevant issues for their practice and policy challenges, making sure that recommendations are context-specific and communicate in a simple and actionable way. It is necessary to engage a wider range of users than those traditionally involved in policy dialogue.

5.2 Reinforce the Core Education System instead of Establishing Parallel Tracks. We must use evidence to build permanent infrastructures to continuously improve the mainstream education system rather than one-off efforts.

5.3 Safeguard Independence instead of being driven by Funding Biases. Credibility derives from a process that is independent, transparent and non-partisan at every stage. If synthesis processes are tied to verifying specific interventions, projects or themes, especially through the enthusiasm of a donor who is utilising restricted grants, credibility and trust in the entire process are placed at risk.

5.4 Leverage Networks instead of Reinforcing Silos. Much of the synthesis process in health is led by a network called Cochrane, made feasible by 82,000 volunteer members who are typically medical professionals. Their engagement in the process is mutually beneficial and gives further amplification and credibility to the results. The same principle is true when delivering change programmes. Success is supported and reinforced when networks of collaborators span academia, policy, practice, business, philanthropy, social entrepreneurs, unions and civil society.

5.5 Prioritise Equity, Avoid Averages. The greatest challenge in the learning crisis relates to marginalised children such as girls, children from minority communities, those living in poverty and children with learning differences and special needs. It is an even greater responsibility to ensure that evidence reflects and is used for the benefit of children at a great risk.

6. An Open Invitation to Engage in Bridge-Building

An effective Education Knowledge Bridge enables better utilisation of the evidence and resources that have already been paid for but sit largely unused. It contributes towards the goal of creating stronger, more equitable education systems, and better support learning outcomes at scale, especially for marginalised groups (i.e., girls, minorities, those in poverty, children with learning differences or special needs). It allows us to move faster and respond better, especially in times of crisis. Finally, an effective Education Knowledge Bridge encourages the democratisation of the culture around evidence and frontline voices, which are often missing in decision-making today.

Through the good work of many organisations, more fully documented in the full Education.org White Paper (2021b) from which this paper has evolved, critical building blocks for this knowledge bridge already exist. Education.org extends an open invitation to work together to transform these building blocks into a fully functioning Education Knowledge Bridge that tackles the global learning crisis through greater use of the existing evidence, so that all children have the opportunity to realise their potential.

If we are to accelerate progress towards SDG4, especially given the learning loss and ongoing disruptions of the current global pandemic, then we should seize the opportunity to connect and build on existing examples and current initiatives to create the kind of knowledge bridge that has transformed the health sector over the past forty years. Several actors need to come together at this point to contribute to the building of a knowledge bridge as robust as that of the health sector.

National and local education leaders need to invest resources in the capacity, culture and cultivation of political will to use the growing volumes of evidence in decision-making. Effective national research centres that are tightly linked to education planning cycles and long-term national policy agendas are essential.

Donors and research commissioners, including private foundations, multilaterals, bilaterals, and businesses, must address the gap between what research is funded and what research is used by advancing incentives that focus more on evidence use.

Existing education institutional knowledge actors must take action to increase the accessibility and use of knowledge products for policy and implementation to lift everyone's work.

Individual academics and researchers must start every research project by investigating the challenges that are being faced by policymakers and practitioners, and routinely engage them as partners.

Teachers and school leaders play a vital role by making frontline experience visible and contribute insights from every classroom to help set the research agenda and break down the academic-practitioner divide. Teacher organisations and teacher training colleges can help teachers to strengthen their evidence literacy.

Community voices and NGOs should actively surface their experiences and advocate for high-quality, evidence-informed decision-making that reflects local needs, especially those of the most marginalised groups.

The media can contribute by using its skills in translating the complex ideas to help ensure that the most essential information reaches those who need it in easily understood forms.

Everyone, including parents, families, learners and citizens, can and should support and participate in the revolution to make education a science-based sector, so that all children have access to quality education.

Education Advocacy in Uganda
Capacity of Civil Society Organisations
At Sub-national Level

Mary Goretti Nakabugo and James Urwick

1. Introduction

For ten years now, Uwezo has been actively engaging with many civil society organisations (CSOs) at the district level in Uganda. The purpose of this engagement has been to carry out independent, national assessments of children's literacy and numeracy and to raise public awareness about issues in education. The CSO selected for assessment in each district recruits volunteers who receive training. Following this training, they visit selected households to conduct assessments of the children and obtain survey data from households and primary schools. After each assessment exercise, Uwezo makes these findings available to the CSOs and other stakeholders at the district as well as national levels. In one of the recent national assessments (in 2018, reported in Uwezo, 2019), 32 CSOs (one for each district in the sample) participated. These CSOs had a variety of developmental purposes, including children's issues, literacy issues and faith-based agendas.

Since January 2020, Uwezo Uganda has been an independent, not-for-profit, national CSO, whereas previously, it was an education programme of the regional organisation

Twaweza East Africa. One of its major goals continues to be to engage with policymakers and raise public awareness (Uwezo Uganda 2020, 16-17). This goal requires efforts to strengthen civil society within the education sector, at local as well as national levels, promoting 'mutual accountability' between the providers of basic education and the families and communities that are intended to benefit from it. As major problems persist in the delivery of education – complicated further by the school closures due to the pandemic in 2020-21 – and as anecdotal evidence about the success of local advocacy is very mixed, it becomes imperative to achieve a better understanding of the challenges that collaborating CSOs face, at the district level and more locally. The intention is to strengthen Uwezo's advocacy and communications and its role in coordinating advocacy on educational issues. To some degree, the challenges in Uganda are likely to be relevant to other organisations in the PAL Network as well.

2. Literature review and conceptual framework

'Capacity building' has become a buzzword among organisations that are concerned with the delivery of services. As Cairns, Harris and Young (2005) point out, the contexts in which the concept of capacity building is used range from narrow organisational changes to attempts at wider social change (p. 875). The possible activities include analysis, planning, training, resource acquisition and alliance formation. Uwezo is aware of the difficulties that can occur in an asymmetrical relationship, in which one organisation seeks to build or promote capacity building in other organisations that have fewer resources or operate at a more local level.

The problems of asymmetry are well presented by Deborah

Eade (2007) regarding relations between international NGOs based in the Global North and their partners in the South whom they are trying to support. In Nakabugo et al. (2010) the discussion is about North-South Research Relationships in Higher Education that have been criticised for focusing too much on the one-directional 'transfer' of capacity from North to South, at the expense of genuine partnerships working, mutual learning and responsiveness to need.

Many of the same problems could occur between an apex national NGO, such as Uwezo, and local CSOs in the same country. For example, Eade mentions that energetic advocacy by a large NGO on behalf of smaller partners could unwittingly obscure their voices. There are also issues related to the policy agendas that lie behind funding from outside the country, on which a national NGO (as well as international ones) may depend. Donors with a focus on human rights may see the capacity building of CSOs as useful for monitoring of public services, but others with a more neo-liberal outlook may see them as potential substitutes for public agencies (Eade, 2007, p. 634). One of the implications of Eade's discussion is that capacity-building efforts need to be a process of mutual learning in which the apex organisation is self-critical and seeks to improve its own skills as well as those of the local partners.

Along with an awareness of these issues, an apex organisation also needs a systematic approach to assess the capacity of the CSOs that it wishes to support. It seems practical and sensible to follow the example of Austin (1994) in treating both intangible features, such as missions and strategies, and tangible resources, such as staff and equipment, as aspects of capacity. The ways in which these various aspects combine to produce outcomes are varied and difficult to predict. Evidence of outcomes is also important, but it needs to be understood in its social and political context.

In a well-known essay, Allan Kaplan (2000) argues that the intangible qualities of an organisation, which are the most difficult to observe and measure, are the most critical for its capacity. In his view, a clear orientation with the environment, a sense of purpose, a vision and a strategy are prerequisites for appropriate organisational structure, training and material resources (pp. 518-9). The argument implies that it may be difficult or impossible for a survey (as opposed to qualitative research) to capture some of the most critical aspects of capacity. Kaplan also underlines the importance of understanding the specific context in which an intervention is attempted. These considerations have influenced the choice of a mixed-method approach for this study.

Despite their varied characteristics, CSOs in Uganda face some common external problems in the national and international context. Over the past two decades, many developing countries have experienced conflicting socio-economic and political currents that affect civil society. On the one hand, civil society organisations (CSOs) have increased in number and become more formalised. On the other hand, political authoritarianism has increased in many countries, including Uganda, with restrictions on political choice, state violence against critics and both formal and informal constraints on the freedom of expression and association (Lynch & Crawford, 2011).

The global financial crisis of 2008-9 may have contributed indirectly to this second trend indirectly by reducing foreign aid and investment. But there are also risks that both international donors and national NGOs, in seeking to support development objectives, may, in the process, seem to endorse authoritarian practices (Cheesman & Fisher, 2020, pp. 78-9). Authoritarian and hybrid regimes favour the service delivery role of CSOs while discouraging their advocacy role and seek to redefine 'civility' in ways that deter criticism (Hammett & Jackson, 2017).

In the case of Uganda, NGOs are registered and monitored by the Ministry of Internal Affairs rather than a development ministry (Nkwatsibwe, 2019). As the Uganda National NGO Forum (UNNGOF) points out, they have faced intimidation by district administrators and security officials (UNNGOF, 2018, pp. 24-25). Most NGOs are not opposed in principle to regulation, which helps to prevent fraud. Yet, there are questions about whether the current NGO Act and Regulations (Government of Uganda, 2016, 2017) have made registration too difficult in practice for small organisations (UNNGOF, 2018, pp. 12-13).

Tensions between civil society and government bodies are common, partly because of constraints on parliamentary and electoral opposition to the ruling party (Kalinaki, 2014, pp. 155-312). These constraints leave NGOs on the 'front line' as monitors and critics of governance and of public service provision, thus increasing the risks that they encounter. On the other hand, the NGO Monitoring Committees at the district levels are helpful in diffusing tensions. The risks, too, maybe fewer for NGOs or CSOs that are concerned with education and social welfare than for those concerned directly with governance and civil rights. Thus, the CSOs contacted for this study did not complain about any intimidation.

3. Methodology

3.1 Research Questions

The major concerns of this research are the ability of the CSOs to act on educational issues and the usefulness of collaboration for the CSOs, especially with Uwezo Uganda. The questions guiding the research, therefore, fall into two following clusters.
Questions about effectiveness:
1. How far do the CSOs have coherent missions, a broad base of support and stable funding?
2. How successful are they in raising concerns about education with the district education authorities and with the schools?
3. What kind of concerns have they raised about education?
4. How far are they able to influence the policies and practices of the district education authorities and the schools?
5. What factors influence their ability to raise concerns and influence policies and practices (as specified in Questions 2 and 4)?

Questions about collaboration:
1. How far do these CSOs collaborate with other organisations?
2. Do they find the Uwezo national assessments useful for advocacy at the district level? How helpful were (a) the 2018 findings and (b) the volunteers they provided in 2018?
3. How can Uwezo improve its collaboration with these CSOs?

3.2 Research Approach and Methods of Data Collection

The study used a mixed-method approach of research, with both qualitative and quantitative elements. It moved from an exploratory phase to a more deductive one. In the first data collection phase, semi-structured interviews were held with senior representatives of eight district-level CSOs by telephone or via Zoom. The second phase was a survey of all 32 CSOs, for which a questionnaire was distributed and returned by email. The interview findings were used to construct the questionnaire in such a way as to obtain quantitative measures of key CSO characteristics and respondent opinions, as well as a few open-ended responses. The interview schedule and the questions are given in Annexes I and II.

The eight CSOs for the interview stage were selected purposively from the 32 that had taken part in the 2018 national assessment. Two cases were drawn from each of Uganda's statistical regions (Central, Eastern, Northern and Western). They vary in their mission, services provided, membership structure and size. Five of them included coordination of other CSOs in their mission, but others are relatively small entities that manage a school or an early childhood development (ECD) centre. Seven of these focus on children's issues or include them in their mission, but most of them focus on other issues as well.

A pilot interview was conducted with one CSO in a different district which had taken part in the 2015 assessment, but not of 2018. This resulted in minor amendments to the interview schedule. In all the cases, the interviewers took notes and obtained the informant's agreement for sound recording. It was explained that the identities of the informants and their organisations would not be used in the reporting. The interviews were completed by two research team members (Uwezo Uganda staff) during the week of 20th-26th August 2020.

The questionnaire was created by the lead researcher, reviewed by the research team and then distributed by email in the week of 21-25 September 2020. Before they were distributed, the CSO representatives (normally the senior executives) were contacted by telephone and asked to assist. The return of the questionnaire took about two weeks, and the Uwezo Uganda staff followed up by telephone where necessary. These procedures resulted in the return of 30 questionnaires from the 32 CSOs contacted (a 94% response rate). Because the sample was relatively small, the eight CSOs that provided interviews were asked to take part in the survey as well.

The researchers used the interview data, where appropriate, to construct binary or multiple-choice questionnaire items that presentd common alternatives. For example, a checklist for possible areas of focus of the CSOs distinguished between advocacy and provision of services. Another checklist identified educational issues which the CSOs acted upon. Perceived success in advocacy at the district level is rated for six items on a Likert scale. The questionnaire also gives opportunities for additional comments.

The use of distance methods for data collection enabled Uwezo Uganda to carry out this study even when there were restrictions on travel and face-to-face meetings because of the Covid-19 pandemic. The distance methods also resulted in very modest expenses and provided flexibility in the timing of the research.

3.3 Analytical objectives

The analysis draws on survey data and makes selective use of data from the in-depth interviews to interpret and elaborate the main findings. The main survey outputs are:
a) An overview of the missions of the CSOs, distinguishing especially between service provision, advocacy and coordination.

b) The variations among the CSOs in size, range of funding sources and membership structures.
c) A ranking of the educational issues on which the CSOs tend to focus.
d) A measure of advocacy satisfaction of CSOs with the impact of their own advocacy on educational issues within the district and factors that account for differences in this measure.
e) A summary of perceptions about collaboration with other CSOs.
f) A summary of perceptions about the contributions of the Uwezo 2018 Assessment to advocacy in the district.
g) Types of activity in which further collaboration with Uwezo Uganda is desired.
h) CSO priorities for the training of staff.

4. Findings

The sample consists of representatives of CSOs that have been collaborating with Uwezo in recent years, and is not necessarily representative of district-level CSOs in general. To some extent, Uwezo has chosen to work with these CSOs because of their apparent success and potential. This should be kept in mind as the findings are interpreted. The data also has limitations as there was an element of self-evaluation by the leaders of the CSOs, without the benefit of external evaluation. Informants were varied in the optimism or sober realism with which they described the achievements of the CSOs and the problems they faced. An important merit of the research, however, is that it obtained insiders' perceptions and priorities in varied local situations.

4.1 Missions, Size, Funding and Structure of the CSOs

CSOs vary in their emphasis on advocacy vis-à-vis the provision of services. Furthermore, there has been a historical shift towards advocacy. All but one of the 30 survey informants considered advocacy as one of the main functions of their CSO. In 28 cases, this advocacy was on a range of social issues, including educational ones. The questionnaire distinguishes between advocacy of social issues and advocacy of educational issues only, but these categories are discussed in an integrated manner in the analysis.

Most of the CSOs (24) provided welfare services to families and communities. Of the ten which managed a school or early childhood development (ECD) centre, all but one provided welfare services as well. An impression gained from the interviews, however, is that small CSOs managing a school or centre have less opportunity for advocacy, even if it is stated as part of their mission.

Another vital function of the CSOs is the coordination with other CSOs, as reported in 13 cases. Some of these were relatively large CSOs that were in many districts with explicit focus on a sub-region within Uganda (such as Lango or Teso). They included faith-based organisations with support from national sources.

Table 41 provides a classification of the CSOs according to their combinations of the four functions of advocacy, welfare service, school management and coordination of CSOs. They fall into an 'advocacy only' group and have seven combinations.

Two measures of the size of CSOs were obtained: the number of districts in which they worked and the number of full-time employees. In both cases, the distributions are positively skewed, with a few relatively large organisations.

Table 42 shows the numbers according to arbitrary categories of size, as well as basic statistics.

Financially, the CSOs depended mainly on grants and donations. International grants were almost as frequent as grants from within Uganda. Some were able to supplement their income by engaging in income-generating activities such as consulting, sales of goods and produce or renting out property. The Pareto chart in Figure 31 shows types of funding sources according to the frequency of occurrence in a total of 105 responses. On average, therefore, 3.5 types of funding sources were recorded.

Table 41: Numbers of CSOs by Major Functions

Functions	Number (percentage)
Advocacy only	4 (13%)
Advocacy and welfare service	8 (27%)
Advocacy and school management	1 (3%)
Welfare service and school management	1 (3%)
Advocacy and coordination of CSOs	1 (3%)
Advocacy, welfare service and school management	3 (10%)
Advocacy, welfare service and coordination of CSOs	6 (20%)
Advocacy, welfare service, school management & coordination of CSOs	5 (17%)
Total	30 (100%)

Table 42: Numbers of CSOs by size categories

Number of districts covered:		Number of full-time employees:	
Category	No. of CSOs	Category	No. of CSOs
1 only	11	0-10	15
2-10	17	11-20	11
11 or more	2	21 or more	4
Total	30	Total	30
Basic statistics:		Basic statistics:	
Mean	4.17	Mean	12.33
Standard dev.	3.82	Standard dev.	9.40

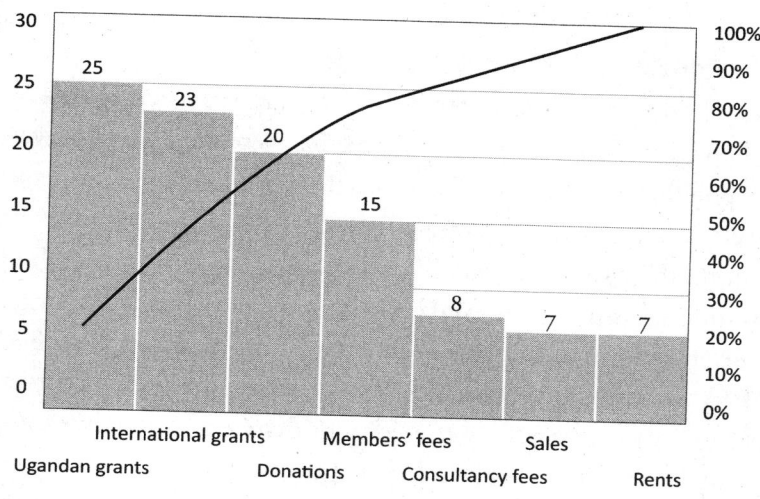

Figure 31: Types of funding in order of frequency

The governance structures of the CSOs were varied, but they tended to have a managing board or committee, as well as a secretariat with some full-time staff members. Some also had regular volunteer workers. Most of the CSOs had either an individual or an organisational membership system. A few had both types of membership or no membership. Figure 32 shows the distribution of the 30 responses:

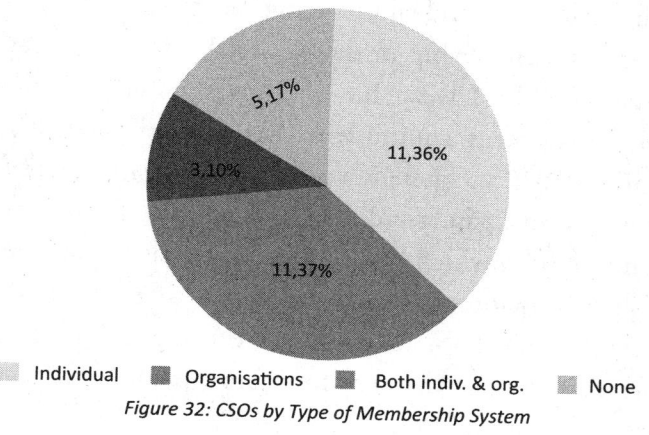

Figure 32: CSOs by Type of Membership System

4.2 Educational Issues Raised by the CSOs

The in-depth interviews enabled the researchers to assemble a list of 18 educational issues or concerns that were mentioned or were of potential interest to the CSOs. In the questionnaire, informants were asked to tick the ones their CSOs had taken action on within the past three years. They were also asked to mention any additional issues. This exercise helped to show how far Uwezo's current priorities were shared by partner organisations. Figure 33 shows 12 issues that attracted 19 or more responses in the survey. These issues were mainly related to primary education, but some of them cut across different levels of education.

In the issues listed, there is a natural break in the data after the issue of 'provision of learning materials'. Other issues attracted 13 or fewer responses. These 'lower priority' issues include provision for disabilities and other special needs, 'other teacher misconduct' and molestation of female pupils.

Of the 12 'priority' issues, Uwezo Uganda took poor learning outcomes as its main focus, but attention has also been given in the reports and planning to pupil and teacher absenteeism, physical facilities of the school, provision of learning materials and monitoring of schools in general. Through its membership in the Regional Education Learning Initiative (RELI), Uwezo has also given some attention to school management committees (SMCs) and parent-teacher associations (PTAs). There is a substantial consistency of focus between Uwezo Uganda and the CSOs studied. There are other areas, however, in which Uwezo Uganda needs to take the lead in raising consciousness, such as access to early childhood education, support for home-based learning, school hygiene and health issues and the need for more remedial teaching and less grade repetition in primary schools.

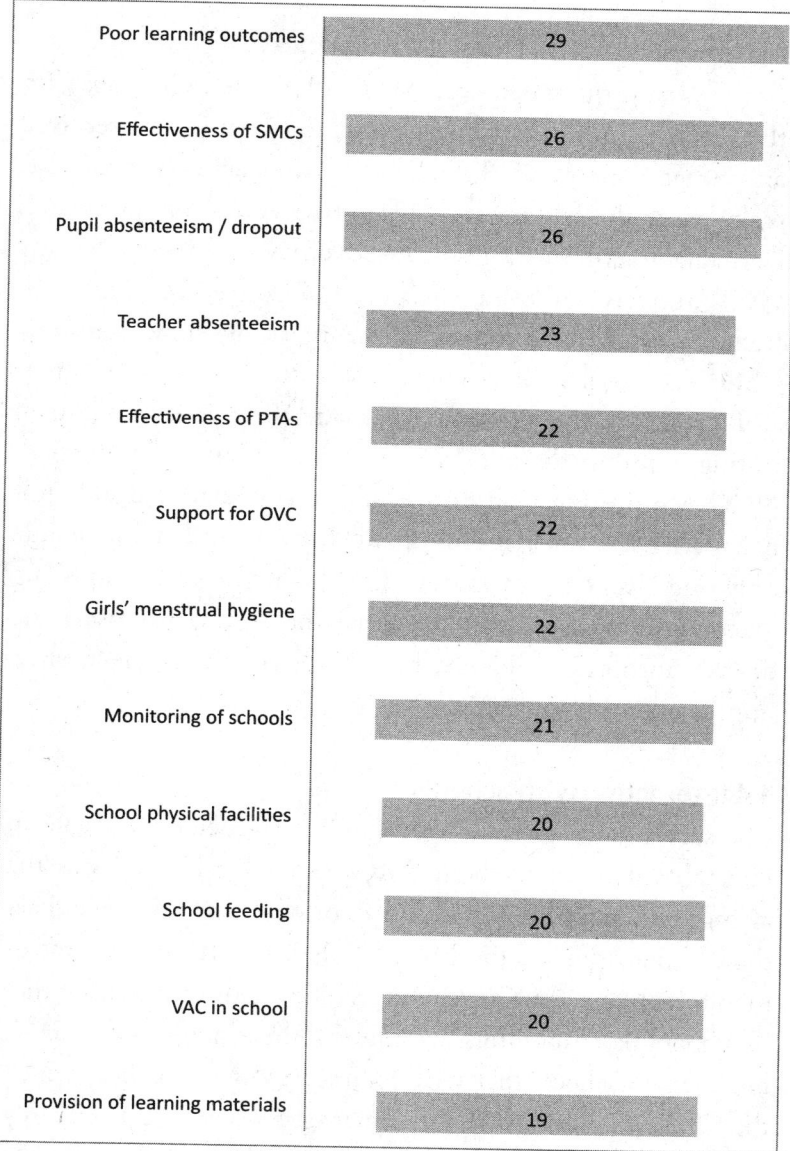

Figure 33: Education issues most frequently raised by CSOs

Abbreviations used: OVC = Orphans and vulnerable children;
PTA = Parent-teacher association;
SMC = School management committee; VAC = Violence against children.

4.3 Interaction with District Authorities

In the survey, the statement, 'My CSO is able to interact with the District Education Officer on educational issues', received an average response of 'Strongly agree' on the five-point Likert scale, while the statement, 'The district education authorities have taken action as a result of advocacy and reports by my CSO', received an average response of 'Agree' (see Annex II, Items 7a and 7b). Comments in the interviews show that some CSOs had regular direct contact with the district authorities, while some of the smaller ones made their concerns known through intermediaries. In these interactions, the district's NGO Monitoring Committee, if it was operational, was not necessarily the most useful channel, as it tended to include only one NGO representative. On the matter of action being taken, informants tended to agree that (in some cases) the district authorities did not have funds to make the desired improvements (Item 7c).

4.4 Interaction with Schools

The survey findings show that CSOs, in general, were able to interact with head teachers, SMCs and PTAs: 'Agree' was the average response to Items 7d and 7e on this issue. The interviews showed that some of the larger CSOs had extensive systems of monitoring: one had 'Citizen Accessibility Platforms', and another had school-based monitors. We infer that these monitors were SMC members in schools that were founded by the church to which the CSO was linked. CSOs that managed schools were primarily concerned with making these exemplary in their practices. On the question of whether their monitoring of schools had resulted in improvements (Item 7f), the survey informants were divided: 9 agreed, 12 disagreed, and 9 gave a 'neutral' response.

4.5 The Summary Measure of Impact Satisfaction

From the Likert-scale data on interaction with the district authorities and schools, a summary score was constructed showing the satisfaction of the informants with their own CSO's impact on educational issues. Item 7c, on funding available to district authorities, had to be excluded, but the responses to the other five items in Question 7 of the questionnaire were sufficiently consistent. For Items 7a, 7b, 7d and 7e, scores of 5 to 1 are allocated (where 5 = Strongly agree) and for Item 7f, which had a negative meaning, reverse scoring is used (1 = Strongly agree). On this basis, the sum of each CSO's scores on the five items is used as a summary measure of impact satisfaction. The value of Cronbach's Alpha for the item scores is 0.73, a sufficient level of internal consistency. Figure 34 shows the distribution of the measure.

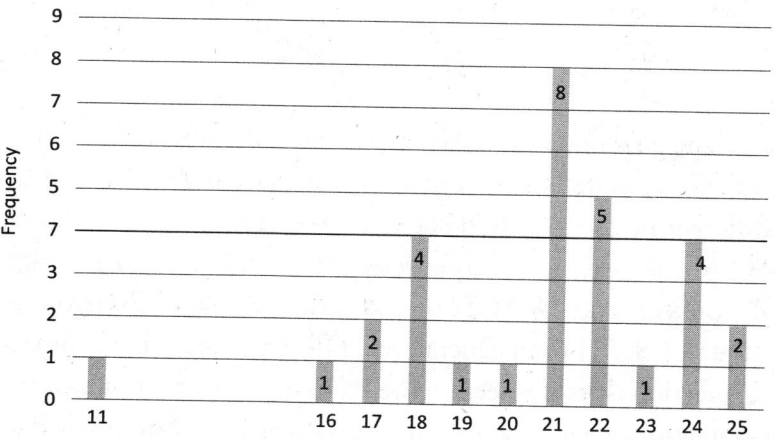

Figure 34: CSO satisfaction with their own impact in the district on educational issues

The level of impact satisfaction was quite high, with a mean of 20.63 and a standard deviation of 3.06. We hypothesised that the variation might be related in part to the size of CSOs, on the assumption that smaller ones have fewer resources for advocacy. Therefore, a comparison was done of the mean scores on the measure for CSOs that worked in one district only with those that worked in multiple districts (see Figure 35). The difference was in the expected direction, but for a small sample like this one, it was not statistically significant (t = 1.67). It may thus be inferred that size is a minor factor.

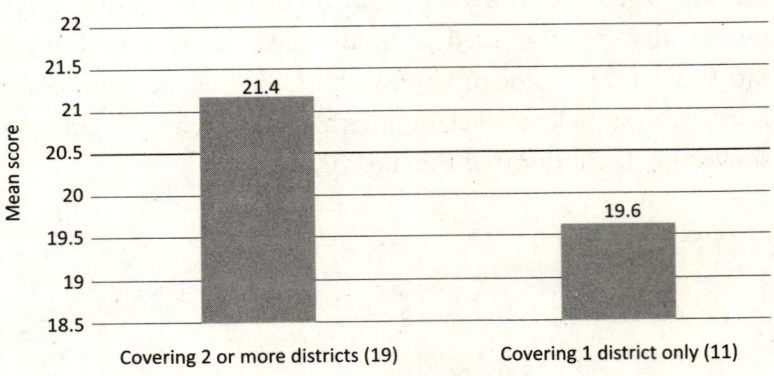

Figure 35: Mean scores of CSO impact satisfaction, by size category

The possibility of regional differences in impact satisfaction was also considered. But the mean scores were not significantly different in Uganda's four statistical regions, as Table 43 shows. When sub-regions are considered, the mean is relatively high for Bukedi at 23.0 (2 CSOs) and relatively low for Bunyoro at 18.0 (1 CSO), but in general, the differences are minor. Impact satisfaction does not seem to be related to poverty levels in the population, which increase on a gradient from South-West to North-East in Uganda.

Table 43: Basic statistics of CSO impact satisfaction scores, by region of Uganda

Region	Mean	Standard deviation	N
Central	20.5	2.95	6
Eastern	21.2	2.54	9
Northern	20.0	2.30	9
Western	20.6	5.06	6
Total	20.6	3.06	30

4.6 Patterns of Collaboration

Attitudes to collaboration with other organisations were generally very positive. Twenty-eight of the 30 survey informants confirmed that their CSO collaborated with other CSOs in the district for advocacy, and 29 agreed that collaboration made their advocacy more effective. As mentioned above, 13 CSOs played a coordinating role in regional advocacy networks. A further 11 informants confirmed that their CSO was a member of such a network. (The reference here is to regions within Uganda.)

From the perspective of Uwezo Uganda, these regional networks are potentially useful as vehicles both for communication of ideas and findings and for obtaining local knowledge in different parts of Uganda. In these processes, collaboration of the coordinating CSOs could be an important asset.

4.7 Perceived Effects of the 2018 Uwezo Assessment

Uwezo's national basic assessments are of particular importance for education advocacy. Therefore, the opinion of the CSO about the usefulness of the most recent (2018) assessment was also probed.

This assessment was within recent memory for informants. The responses had to be interpreted with care, as they reflected both Uwezo's efforts at dissemination and the capacity of the CSOs to absorb and use the findings and the volunteers.

In responding to Question 9 of the questionnaire, most informants (19) disagreed with the idea that the finding of the 2018 Assessment had taught them nothing new. All but one (29) agreed that the findings had been useful for advocacy within the district, and most of these (16) strongly agreed. Most informants (25) indicated that they had made more use of district findings than of the national ones. This result suggested that, in general, district findings were effectively disseminated.

The survey findings about the use of volunteers (from Items 9c and 9d) are rather inconsistent. A total of 23 informants confirmed that the volunteers they provided to Uwezo in 2018 had been useful since then for their own work. Yet many of the same informants indicated that they did not have the funds to make further use of the volunteers (a total of 25). This implies that many CSOs had not been able to use the volunteers systematically because of their inability to pay expenses but some volunteers continued to be useful as individual advocates. The interviews showed that, in some cases, the findings and the volunteers helped to increase the visibility of the CSOs. These findings are, reassuring for Uwezo Uganda. But the question of how to keep volunteers active in supporting education after the assessment and maximise their value deserves more attention.

4.8 Views about Future Collaboration with Uwezo Uganda

In the survey, informants were invited to express interest in collaborating with Uwezo in future national assessments and research and advocacy in the district. For research and advocacy, a distinction was made between education alone and social issues that are 'cross-cutting'. The examples of social issues (child welfare, family poverty and so on) were mentioned in the survey. As Figure 36 shows, most informants showed an interest in all the five areas suggested in the questionnaire (Question 10). They are shown in order of popularity.

Further national assesments	30
Educational advocacy	30
Educational research	29
Advocacy on cross-cutting_	28
Research on cross-cutting issuses	26

Figure 36: Areas for collaboration with Uwezo Uganda by the number of interested informants

The survey was also used as an opportunity to ask for indications of the training needs of the CSO staff. Question 11 of the questionnaire mentioned six possible areas for training and asked informants to designate each as 'high priority', 'low priority' or 'not needed'. Figure 37 lists the six areas in the order of frequency of 'high priority' responses.

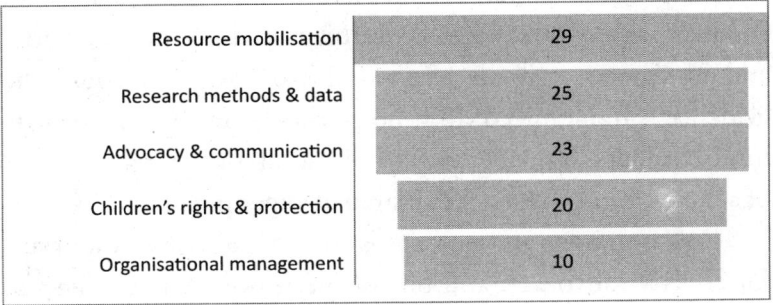

Resource mobilisation	29
Research methods & data	25
Advocacy & communication	23
Children's rights & protection	20
Organisational management	10

Figure 37: Areas for staff training by 'high priority' count

The only area to attract many 'low priority' designations (18 cases) was organisational management, and in two cases, it was said that this was not needed. The other areas were given 'low priority' in all cases where they were not 'high priority'. As a practical follow-up, informants were asked whether their staff members would be able to attend online training. Twenty-seven of the 30 confirmed that this would be possible. As a result of these findings, Uwezo Uganda is giving increased attention to training opportunities to partner CSOs.

5. Conclusion

This study provides a brief but meaningful appraisal of the civil society's role at the district level in Uganda's delivery of basic education. Although CSO representatives were likely to describe the CSO influence positively, the extent of this influence seems impressive. In some areas, CSOs splayed a similar role as 'citizen inspectorate' for primary schools, supplementing the work of official inspectors and advisers. Nevertheless, the influence of individual CSOs is likely to be constrained by their specific missions, religious denominations in some cases and their direct management of certain schools and centres.

The CSOs' appraisal of their own impact shows an encouraging degree of access to the district education authorities and to schools. On the effectiveness of the interaction, the evidence is more mixed. In general, they were able to advocate improvements in the delivery of education or the management of schools, but some of the desired changes proved elusive.

Collaboration among CSOs is seen as very important for effective advocacy, and one of the reasons for this may be that the larger CSOs, especially those coordinating networks, have more regular access to the district authorities. The specific collaboration with Uwezo Uganda, a national CSO that interacts with the central government and international organisations, is helpful for the CSOs in raising their profiles. Such collaboration also provides them with relevant findings from assessment and research and suggests issues for campaigning. These factors account for the positive attitudes of the informants to a continued and expanded collaboration with Uwezo Uganda.

The study provides evidence of a consensus (largely shared by Uwezo Uganda itself) that various specific educational issues deserve attention. It also highlights issues about which Uwezo Uganda could raise consciousness among the CSOs. The survey brings out staff training as one of the key areas of collaboration. Exploration is on for opportunities in the future so that Uwezo Uganda can provide the CSOs with the types of staff training to which they attach priority.

The ALiVE Project in East Africa
Can Collaborative Action Drive Learning Outcomes? A Critical Examination

Florence Nansubuga, Purity Ngina, Mauro Giacomazzi and John Mugo

1. Introduction

Collaboration as a means of addressing tenacious socio-economic concerns is now a global trend. Strategic efforts to address such concerns have promoted inter-organisational collaboration as a primary method for achieving short-term and long-term goals, which would be difficult to attain by a single entity working independently (Gajda, 2004). Various scholars have defined collaboration as a joint venture, an alliance, a partnership or network, and a means of pooling resources to achieve a common goal (Huxham, 2003). Across disciplines, collaboration has been adopted as a tool for interdisciplinary research, whereas for management scientists, collaboration is the ability to work together to improve an organisation's competitive advantage (Bedwell et al., 2012).

Despite these diverse conceptual definitions, it is still difficult in practice to understand the collaboration process and its complexities (Gajda, 2004; Bedwell et al., 2012). Gray and Wood (1991) noted that collaboration could be better understood if it is explained as a process that allows different parties to explore shared problems and search for solutions that go beyond each one's limited vision. Based on this idea, the Regional Educational Learning Initiative (RELI) in East Africa decided to adopt the collaboration lens to engage its partner organisations in implementing the ALiVE program. RELI Africa is a network of over 70 organisations across East Africa (Kenya, Tanzania, and Uganda). This network works towards advancing learning outcomes for all children by generating evidence on what works and amplifying the voices through collective action.

RELI's Assessment of Life Skills and Values in East Africa (ALiVE) is a three-year programme that targets adolescents aged 13 to 17 years, both in and out of school in Kenya, Tanzania, and Uganda. Specifically, the programme objectives are: to develop contextualised, open-source tools that can be used to measure four competencies in these adolescents, namely, 'self-awareness', 'collaboration', 'problem-solving' and 'respect'; to undertake an assessment of these competencies and to raise public awareness by informing policy decisions and by strengthening local capacities (Mugo et al., 2022).

The onset of the ALiVE program occurred when the COVID-19 pandemic was rampant across the globe in 2020. However, the adopted collaboration lens involved Global North-South stakeholders who were geographically spread and would require to travel to various East African countries to engage in workshop discussions. The fact that there were COVID-19 protocols established worldwide that enforced social distancing and, at times, lockdowns, travel exchanges and physical involvement of participants that was essential for the implementation of collaboration activities, was limited. This research examined the perceived motivation factors for collaboration, the ways of addressing associated challenges, including those that originated due to COVID-19, and the emergent resolutions that can aid the sustainability of inter-organisational collaboration and its capacities in solving complex problems.

2. The Nature of Inter-Organisational Collaboration

Dillenbourg (1999) postulated that collaboration is more likely to occur in symmetrical situations where a relatively similar level of expertise and power relations among collaborating agents/partners is assumed. Although collaboration may occur in asymmetrical situations, the hierarchical/vertical nature of interactions among partners in this situation is affected by the belief that the superior partner is an expert, resulting in other partners taking a weaker position of argument (Dillenbourg, 1999). It should be noted that whether the situation is symmetrical or asymmetrical, it is not possible for two or more individuals to share exactly the same level of knowledge and agree on the same course of action all the time, so symmetrical can eventually turn into asymmetrical. Nonetheless, some knowledge or action asymmetry among collaborating partners is considered appropriate, but a considerably high asymmetrical situation in terms of expertise or action may appear as one partner being the coach or a controller of the other.

Chrislip and Larson (1994) argued that among the collaborating parties, no single agent/party should impose its own views unilaterally since this can compromise the mutual engagement, interdependency and interactive facets of collaboration. However, there are often individuals among partners who tend to assume powerful leadership roles by fixing problems for the collaborating team or engaging in command

and control behaviour, rather than inspiring action or helping the team to create a shared vision and goals (Anslinger & Jenk, 2004). Mutual engagement and interdependency can only thrive if the participants share elaborate explanations of their ideas and, at the same time, have the will to listen and learn from the explanations of others (Lai, 2011; Chrislip and Larson, 1994).

3. Benefits of Inter-organisational Collaboration

Some of the benefits of inter-organisational collaboration are more explicit than others. For instance, collaboration can provide infrastructure for transmitting know-how and managing the distribution of responsibilities (Kosmutzky, 2018). Collaboration also offers social benefits such as friendships, professional networks and self-fulfilment by making individual participants feel they are contributing to the common goal (Ulnicane, 2015).

The nature of collaboration itself can have a crucial impact on the running of a project and its successful outcome. There are thus crucial benefits of working collaboratively for a common purpose. For example, Ulnicane (2015) noted that the administrative role of maintaining regular communication among partners is crucial since the outcomes of the project activities depend on the contributions and analysis of a group with a mix of expertise. Consequently, the quality of the final product becomes paramount, and this is a major indicator of collaboration success (Ulnicane, 2015). Selden et al. (2006) observed that the greater and more intense involvement of partners in the collaboration, the better the implementation of the services provided and the ownership of the project objectives by the target groups. Having a successful collaboration is not a matter of chance but an organised series of activities that focuses on interpersonal relationships as well as the constraining and enabling factors within the different operating systems of the partnering organisations (Leahey, 2016).

4. Challenges of Inter-organisational Collaboration

Joining efforts and finding synergies with a team of experts sometimes come with certain drawbacks, especially when non-committal participants fail to acknowledge the contributions of others (Kosmutzky, 2018). That is, the contributions of an individual participant may pass unnoticed because what is recognised are the mutual agreements of the whole team. Individuals who are motivated extrinsically through recognition may feel left out (Kosmutzky, 2018). Besides, inter-organisational collaboration processes tend to be time-consuming, requiring regular administration and coordination, as well as constant communication of events to team members across the board (Beaver, 2013). In this way, collaboration demands intercultural and interpersonal competencies, which may not be readily available within a diverse team (Dusdal & Powell, 2020).

Another concern is, when participants are working from different locations, advanced planning strategies and technological support are required to promote trust and sensitivity among the team (Livingston 2003). Spatially spread networks call for substantive coordination to effectively bring together ideas and expertise (Dusdal & Powell, 2020; Cummings & Kiesler, 2005). Chrislip (2002) argued that it is important for preliminary collaboration engagements to focus on creating an environment that allows participants to be a part of the process and also gives them a feeling of buy-in. This collaborative environment is characterised by three components: first is the step-by-step discussion of the collaboration goals and benefits, which may later result in comprehensive agreements; second is the clarification of information regarding rules and guidelines based on an open communication mode to obtain feedback from each party; and third is the anticipation of possible collaboration challenges so that they can be prevented (Chrislip, 2002).

Finally, while the goals of the collaboration may seem to be straightforward, the process of achieving them is quite difficult given the complexity of the operating contexts of each partner (Anslinger & Jenk, 2004). For instance, one may find that the socio-cultural, political and economic contexts within which the various partners operate differ; thus, their ability to provide resources to support the project is also varied. These differences limits the commitment of some partners to participate fully in the project activities. This challenge can only be addressed when the requirements and expectations of each partner are clearly defined and agreed upon during the planning stage (Anslinger & Jenk, 2004).

5. Review of Literature

This study explicitly highlights two important theories to explore the dynamics in the context and process of inter-organisational collaboration. These theories are McClelland's Theory of Needs (Angana & Chiroma, 2021) and Anselm Strauss's theory of Negotiated Order (Gray & Wood, 1991).

McClelland's Theory of Needs about collaboration states that participants' actions are driven by three motivators:

achievement, power and affiliation (Murray, 1938). These motivators are not innate but acquired through learning and life experiences. Individuals motivated by the need for power exhibit great work values, a high sense of control and influence over others, enjoyment of winning arguments and the status of recognition (Sinha, 2015). Their desire for power and influence tends to overshadow their ability to accommodate others' views as they keep defending their positions to win an argument. This type of character affects the collaboration relationship as it makes some participants feel less valuable or invisible (Chrislip & Larson, 1994).

Those motivated by the need for achievement tend to demonstrate a strong desire for mastery and goal accomplishment. They are self-driven and highly goal-oriented. Sometimes they prefer to work independently, pushing themselves to accomplish difficult goals rather than being delayed by others who are not similarly motivated by the need for achievement. Their desire to achieve overrides the process of mutual interactions and sharing of experiences that is essential in the collaboration process (Jaja, 2003). Lastly, those individuals who are motivated by the need for affiliation agree with the ideas of other participants because of their desire to be liked. Their high sense of belonging makes them vulnerable since they focus on pleasing others in any situation (Sinha, 2015).

It should be noted that having a team of participants with these different motives in a collaboration relationship may, at some point, cause conflict (Murray, 1938). Those seeking mastery and accomplishment of complex tasks feel compromised when working together with those who seek to control others by sticking to their arguments for the sake of winning a debate. Similarly, those who are motivated by the need for affiliation tend to agree with any position without an elaborate explanation, thus affecting mutual engagement, interactivity and interdependency facets of successful collaboration (Ang'ana & Chiroma, 2021).

In contrast to McClelland's motivational dimensions, there are other more positive explanations of why people are motivated to participate in inter-organisational collaborative alliances. Sonnenwald (2007) observed that partners are likely to be motivated to work with others who share a similar reputation, are highly visible and have access to funding opportunities. Developing new methods and sharing knowledge with a multidisciplinary team (including working with credible mentors) also motivates people to collaborate (Beaver, 2013). However, there are also personal reasons, apart from affiliation, for engaging in collaborations. These reasons could be the growth of one's professional network, or an intrinsic motivation or ambition for personal career growth (Conchi & Michels, 2014; Dusdal & Powell, 2021).

On the other hand, the Theory of Negotiated Order depicts the notion of a collaboration structure (i.e., approaches, guidelines and operations) as being in a continuous state of change (Strauss, 1993). The theory asserts that the capacity of partners to stick together in a relationship is not a result of structured responsibilities but because the participants consciously or unconsciously construct and reconstruct the order to continuously negotiate formal and informal arrangements among themselves (Maines, 1978; Strauss, 1993).

This theory underscores both the dynamic process-oriented elements of collaboration as well as the temporary and emergent nature of its working relationships. It describes the collaboration process as a vehicle through which parties with similar interests join efforts to address a problem. Collaboration as a negotiated order takes various forms/dimensions (Gray & Wood, 1991). First is the interdependence or symbiotic relationship, which is the emotional bond that partners share while maintaining self-worth (Laal, 2013; Rusbult & Van Lange, 2008; Wu, 2018). This kind of relationship brings partners together to accomplish tasks and achieve goals that are possibly not achievable by a single entity (Laal, 2013).

The second dimension is in the form of unlearning and relearning. During the collaboration process, partners tend to encounter new perspectives and approaches from each other. As they grapple with these diverse views, they find new interpretations of events, new ideas and new solutions (Ang'ana & Chiroma, 2021). The third dimension has to do with joint ownership of the process, which is crucial for the success of collaboration and occurs when partners agree on the direction of their goals. It involves sharing responsibility, agreement in all decisions, and adopting new patterns of behaviour (Gray & Wood 1991).

This flexibility helps the participants to feel that they are equally responsible for the collaboration process and its outcomes and that nothing can breakdown the relationship (Austin & Baldwin, 1991). The final dimension of collaboration, in line with the Theory of Negotiated Order, is the emergent process itself. This is demonstrated by the nature of decisions and goals that keep evolving as participants seek to understand the logic of the particular working approaches or rules and their relevance to the context (Austin & Baldwin, 1991).

Nzuve (2007) argues that since the motivation to collaborate is acquired through interactions and experiences, partners can be guided to appropriate their motives to positively support the contributions of others in a desired collaborative manner. In line with Nzuve's argument, the Theory of Negotiated Order is adopted in this study to explain how the participants' varied motives can be appropriated to enhance the collaboration process.

This study examines the effectiveness of the inter-organisational collaboration process and its contextual dynamism. Specifically, it interrogates theories that contribute to the understanding of how successful collaboration among various partners is achieved. The output of the study is a suggested inter-organisational collaboration framework. This framework could be used to inform policy and practice on applying collaborative alliances to improve learning in East Africa and beyond. Three key research questions (RQs) are posed here:

RQ1: What motivates members to remain committed to the collaboration process?

RQ2: What hinders the collaboration process, and how can this be resolved?

RQ3: What matters most to the success and sustainability of the collaboration process?

6. Method

6.1 Authors' Positionality Statement

The authors of this study are from different partner institutions/countries and represent both genders. While the lead author is an academic, the others are practitioners. The findings presented here are not completely unbiased, but the fact that the authors come from diverse backgrounds reduces the biases which could have crept into the work in the form of stereotypes.

6.2 Research Design

A phenomenological design was employed to tap into the experiences of the selected key informants and to explore their views on the collaboration process, which included the benefits gained and the challenges faced by the diverse collaborating partners. Phenomenological research was chosen due to its ability to illuminate insightful information about the participants' experiences while controlling the researcher's preconceived assumptions about the phenomenon. In addition, phenomenology has also been acknowledged for its production of lived experiences that provide deeper insights into how people understand a phenomenon (Husserl, 1970). This design has both philosophical and methodological stances, and therefore, while the research was guided by theory, interview discussions were used by the researchers to collect data (Giorgi & Giorgi, 2003).

6.3 Participants

This study initially targeted the group of 47 national technical experts of the ALiVE initiative who worked together collaboratively for over seven months while developing the assessment tools. This technical committee of experts comprised ALiVE leaders and managers from the five organisations leading the programme, representatives from other RELI member organisations, officials from the ministry of education of the three countries and representatives of the academia in East Africa. Among these, a sample of 29 key informants was purposely selected, based on their area of expertise. Of these, four were a part of the ALiVE leadership team.

6.4 Data Collection Methods and Tools

Two sets of online instruments consisting of structured open-ended interview guides were developed; one for the leadership team and another for the technical team. The guide for the leadership team had five questions, and that for the technical team had three questions. The first question for both teams focused on assessing the motivators that kept participants active in the collaboration process. The second focused on assessing the challenges associated with the collaboration process and how they could be resolved, while the third examined constructs that measured the sustainability of the collaboration process. The additional questions for the leadership team specifically asked what mattered for the collaboration to work; the process of building a coalition; the principles and shared values that drive working together; and what needed to be done to sustain the collaboration for the next three years. These two guides were administered using online forms to which the participants responded by writing short descriptions.

6.5 Coding System and Data Analysis

A coding system followed a thematic analysis, which is 'a method for identifying, analysing and reporting patterns (themes) within data' (Braun & Clarke, 2006), was established to analyse the data.

The coding system considered content variables related to (1) Motivation (MOT) to participate in the collaboration, (2) Challenges (CHAL) faced in the process and (3) Sustainability (SUS) of the collaborating process. The analysis was performed in qualitative terms as recommended by Gibbs (2018) by using the Atlas.ti programme (version 8.4.26.0). The process involved the identification of patterns of similar ideas, concepts or topics to establish the connection and integration with information with the theoretical foundation (Miles & Huberman, 1994). The codes were created following the criteria for qualitative evaluation: dependency, transferability, credibility and verifiability (Duffy, 1987).

7. Ethical Considerations

Ethical considerations in dealing with the participants included obtaining online informed consent, ensuring the confidentiality of information obtained from the participants, and ensuring voluntary participation. All data were collected and stored anonymously by changing the actual names of the participants.

8. Findings

The findings presented here are categorised into three sections according to the research questions of the study. Section one presents findings on the underlying factors that motivate partners to remain committed to the collaboration process. The second section presents findings on the challenges that leaders and participants face during the collaboration process and how they can be resolved. Finally, the third section presents findings on the sustainability of the collaborative process to allow the development of contextualised assessment tools.

RQ 1: Factors that motivate participants to remain active in the collaboration process

Our findings revealed six motivation factors that kept participants active in the collaboration process. Three of these factors (i.e., MOT1, MOT3, and MOT6) were closely associated with the need for achievement component of McClelland's motivational theory (Jaja, 2003; Chrislip, 2002; Murray, 1938); two other factors (i.e., MOT2 and MOT5) were associated with the need for affiliation while MOT4 was associated with the need for power and influence (Murray 1938). Table 44 illustrates the description and attributes of each motivation factor and the theory that explains it.

Table 44: Factors motivating participants to remain active in the collaboration :

Motivation Factor-code	Description	Attributes	Theoretical foundations
MOT1 - Clear Project Vision	Achieving desired outcomes with necessary resources in a specified time frame	• The need to support the children of East Africa • Developing contextualised life skills and value assessment tools • Finding ways of evaluating life skills to transform the education system in the region • Finding out how to effectively assess skills and values, and seeing their successful implementation • Being part of the collaboration process for tool development	Motivated by the need for achievement, self-driven, and goal-oriented (Jaja, 2003; Chrislip, 2002; Murray, 1938)
MOT2 – Teamwork	A synergetic effort to share responsibility aimed at a common goal	• The collaborative nature of the process • The pooling of resources, including cognitive resources and time • Having an equal chance to input expertise throughout the region • Building synergy as people learn from each other through discussions • Getting to know each other's strengths and weaknesses • Even when things get tough, participants are not ready to give up. • It is a community that you need to feel a part of. If you feel you do not belong, you may execute the duties, but you do not become creative	Motivated by the need for affiliation or a sense of belonging (Sinha, 2015; Murray, 1938)

Motivation Factor-code	Description	Attributes	Theoretical foundations
MOT3 - Learning/Understanding	Gaining knowledge through sharing experiences and abilities with others	• Developing a tool that provides meaningful feedback on gaps in life skills and values among adolescents • The knowledge gained through the process and its transferability • Allowance of diverse voices to be heard, creating space for capacity building, continued flexibility and learning through the process • Individual differences in experience and capacities strengthen learning • An initiative that provides a relevant context and originality of ideas • Learning and growing together amidst diverse opinions and approaches • A platform for learning, sharing knowledge, and networking • The opportunity to work with such energetic teams offers great learning • Members are willing to learn, unlearn and relearn	Motivated by the need for achievement, self-driven and goal-oriented (Jaja, 2003; Chrislip, 2002 & Murray, 1938)
MOT4 - Leadership	A process of influencing others to maximise efforts & achieve goals	• Many people remain part of the collaboration because of the leaders' character • Good leadership provided by the facilitator • Very interactive/proactive members and a good facilitator	Motivated by the need for power and influence (Murray, 1938)
MOT5 - Collective Decision-Making	Choosing from alternatives as a group	• Collective decisions where everyone feels accommodated • Involving members in group decisions is done in a more desirable way • Open lines of communication and participatory decision-making. • Listening to members and involving them in some decisions	Motivated by the need for affiliation or a sense of belonging (Sinha, 2015; Murray, 1938)
MOT6 - Commitment	Dedicating self to meet group obligations	• Working with a committed team • Dedication to the process • Committed participation in workshops, virtually or face to face • Commitment and innovativeness	Motivated by the need for achievement, self-driven and goal-oriented (Jaja, 2003; Chrislip, 2002; Murray, 1938)

The participants described the motivation factors by narrating real situations that occurred during the collaboration. For instance, a participant from the leadership team (LT2) had this to say:

> *The excitement of understanding the focused competencies day after day! The further the process, the deeper the understanding of competence! That is where my motivation comes from. I am also motivated by the fact that at the end of this process, we shall have a very meaningful tool that captures the real competencies to give us realistic feedback on where the adolescents are in terms of the focused competencies. I can say a lot, but lastly, I am motivated by all the knowledge I am gaining through this process and the fact that I can use the knowledge to come up with tools for measuring different competencies.*

The above statement clearly shows that knowing what one will achieve and how it will be achieved, and the actual learning that takes place are significant triggers for participation in collaboration. While some individuals are motivated by learning and goal achievement, others are motivated by affiliation. The following are quotes from a leadership team participant (LT1) and a technical team participant (TT14) who were motivated by affiliation:

> *I had the opportunity to be part of a locally developed and regional contextualised tool for life skills assessment among young people.*
>
> *I am motivated by teamwork, especially the pulling together of resources; the cognitive resources, if I may say. I learn from others and also contribute; that way, we build synergy and co-create tasks together within a reasonable time.*

In another scenario, one participant (LT4) expressed motivation that is associated with power and influence and said:

> *The leadership style matters a lot in collaboration. Many people remain part of the collaboration because of the leader's integrity, trust, openness, and knowing that others do care about their presence. However, the commitment, especially that of the technical team, was also attributed to their own career growth. Many are in spaces where the knowledge they acquire might be transferred to their own work.*

Similar motivating factors were expressed by other participants, which were mostly linked to the need for achievement. However, there was also a need for affiliation, and a few were motivated by the need for power. In summary, 83% participants indicated being motivated by the need for achievement, of which 58.6% were motivated by learning opportunity, 27.6% by clear project vision, and only 6.9% were motivated by commitment. Regarding the motivation by the need for affiliation, 34% were motivated by teamwork, and 6.9% were motivated by collective decision-making. Those motivated by the need for power and influence, i.e., leadership, were 13.4%. (Some participants indicated motivations across these factors, and therefore the percentages exceed 100%.)

RQ2: Challenges that affect the collaboration process and the proposed mitigating solutions

The participants expressed several challenges that were encountered during the collaboration process. Among them, three sets of challenges were identified: (1) Interdependence (ID), (2) Continuous unlearning and relearning (UR), and (3) Joint ownership of the collaboration processes, outputs, and outcomes (JO). Table 45 summarises the detailed challenges that were presented under each category.

Table 45: Challenges associated with the collaboration process

Collaboration Elements	Associated challenges	Emergent decisions/ resolutions
CHAL1 - Interdependence (ID)	ID1: There was limited time for performing certain exercises. ID2: It was difficult to draw activity schedules that favoured all team members from different locations ID3: Some members were not active or available during workshops ID4: Busy workplace schedules conflicted with workshop schedules ID5: Tremendous pressure of time; juggling between ALiVE demands and other commitments ID6: Covid-19 protocols limited physical interactions	• Preparation should be done in advance to enable effective time management • Try to schedule activities early in consultation with members • Virtual meetings should be held for members who cannot turn up physically • Formal reminders should be sent to members requesting full commitment
CHAL2 - Unlearning to relearn (UR)	UR1: Developing the criteria, the standards, and the scoring framework was a challenge UR2: The process of writing assessment tasks has been hectic and cumbersome UR3: The process of improving tasks keeps evolving with every meeting, and it wears one out UR4: Preparing tools from experiences and practices without much focus on the constructs/theories might limit replication UR5: Inadequate knowledge of online learning, specifically accessing work saved on Google drive	• Have time for self-criticism and re-evaluation of the goals and methods. • Become flexible to understand the ongoing process. • Become flexible to learn new things • Internally validate tools through peer-to-peer interviews before going to the field • Promoting diversity of ideas • Accommodating members with different experiences and capacities
CHAL3 - Joint ownership (JO)	JO1: National teams developed tools for specific competencies and missed out on others JO2: Missed important sessions due to unplanned virtual meetings outside the original workshops stated in the contract JO3: Documents were shared late, thus limiting the participants' preparation before the next event JO4: At times, there is a monopoly of knowledge, especially with more experienced team members	• All national teams concentrate on completing one task before moving to another • Letting workplace bosses know about your engagement with the ALiVE project • Make an effort to attend and contribute whenever you are invited • Consider diverse contributions

As much as 51.7% participants attributed the collaboration challenges to the concept of interdependence. This has been a result of the perceived nature of the collaboration arrangement that might have inhibited some individuals' full engagement. Some of the concerns justifying this perception are noted by participant TT9:

> *There is tremendous pressure on time, juggling between ALiVE activities with other commitments. I don't think I realised at the beginning, just how involved the activities could be. I try to contribute at key moments as there is no way I can fully be involved all the time.*

Another participant (TT24) identified challenges related to mutual understanding of the tasks assigned by the team. This is what the participant said.

> *The challenges started with developing the framework as a team. Understanding the criteria and standards to use in writing assessment tasks and determining scores has been painstakingly long and tedious. The tasks keep evolving with every meeting, and the improvement that is demanded could wear one out. To avoid getting stuck, every team member needs to contribute, and as the process continues, things become clearer.*

Regarding unlearn and relearn, the participant (TT9) expected learning to be simple and familiar. This participant defined the relearning challenge as:

> *Understanding between actors, common goals mediated by all the members, and a clear understanding of the task could be revisited from time to time. I feel that the process we are going through is getting more and more complicated, and I have lost some motivation since I expected to have something simpler, which could be used on a day-to-day basis.*

To improve the collaboration process, the participants also suggested ways of addressing the challenges accentuated above. They proposed the following: (1) Preparation and sharing of work documents in advance by the lead team; (2) Effective time management; (3) Scheduling follow-up meetings in consultation with technical team members; and (4) Sending reminders to absentees, requesting them to commit time to the project activities. In addition, both the leading team and the collaborating technical team were encouraged to be flexible to adopt the emerging new methods of learning and accommodate the diverse ideas that arise due to the varied experiences and capacities of the partners.

RQ 3: Ensuring success and sustainability of the collaboration process (what matters most)

Findings related to the success and sustainability of the collaboration process indicated that along with the motivating factors highlighted in Table 44, collaboration followed a three-step process. During the first step (defining the goal), the leadership team examined the educational curriculums of the three collaborating countries to identify competency gaps in terms of life skills and values. These gaps were strategically scrutinised and translated into clear project goals as well as personalised development goals. This preliminary arrangement served as a foundation to create an environment that allowed collaborating partners to gain trust and feel that they were owners of the project.

During the second step (defining how), the leading team designed and refined the methodological approaches for developing assessment tools for the identified life skills and values. They also recruited a team of experts from each of the collaborating countries and empowered them through induction to understand the project expectations and the various methods of analysis in use. Consecutive training sessions were offered to clarify the operational guidelines and the emerging work methods during the workshops that followed.

In step 3 (participation), four small teams, each comprising experts from different fields and countries, worked together to develop a contextualised assessment tool for a particular skill. This process involved plenaries where teams would give or receive feedback from other teams regarding the quality of the developed tool and suggestions on how to improve it. This mutual interaction among individual team members and between different teams promoted interdependence. It also helped participants to understand their tasks from different perspectives, thus amending the content of their assessment tools based on what had been agreed upon (unlearn and relearn). This process allowed all participants to contribute to the development of each assessment tool regardless of what their initial assignments were in their teams. The dynamism in the form of working relationships created a sense of joint ownership of the achieved goals as well as the entire collaboration process.

Another key aspect that counted in the collaboration journey was individual principles and values of partners. This included respecting others, exhibiting a passion for achieving the ultimate goals, personal accountability regarding their contributions, open-mindedness to accept divergent views, empathy, flexibility and cooperativeness. These principles were critical to the collaboration process since they influenced the three steps of collaboration.

Scaling and Role of Partnerships **287**

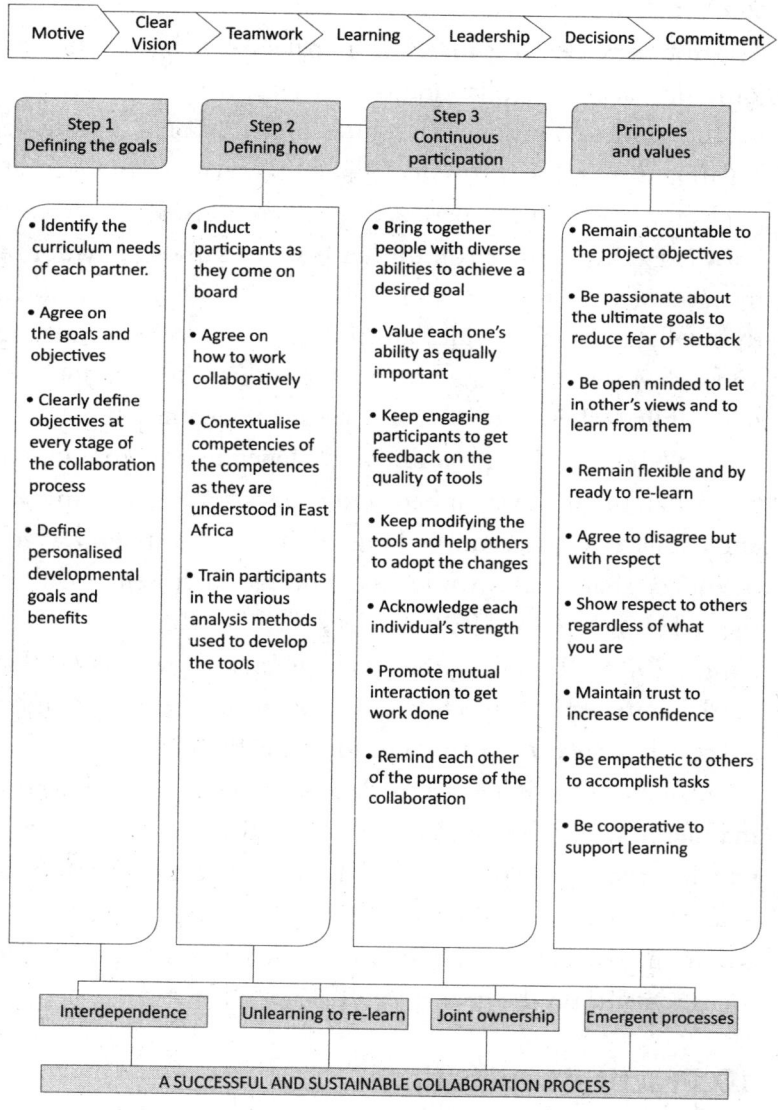

Figure 38: Framework for Developing a Sustainable Inter-organisational Collaboration Process

9. Discussion

The findings clearly show that partners can be inspired to join and stay in collaborations when they are interested in the project's vision. The inter-organisational nature of collaboration is a platform that allows partners to plan together, pool resources, share experiences and opinions, and gain new knowledge from other committed people. This explanation is in tandem with the views of Kosmutzky (2018), who noted that collaboration provides an infrastructure for transmitting know-how, and Ulnicane (2015), who argued that people feel self-fulfilled when they offer services for the common good.

Collaboration promotes interdependence (emotional bonds) among team members and creates space for teamwork and collective decision-making that is based on which members share ideas while maintaining their self-worth in the relationship (Wu, 2018; Laal, 2013; Rusbult & Van Lange, 2008). Regarding the above premise, it was found that participants aspired to collaborate on projects that provided an equal chance for members to share their expertise. This form of interdependency was demonstrated by the collective manner in which decisions are made and the level of teamwork, which makes participants feel that they are part of the project. The participants are thus united by their desire to achieve a common goal, and despite their individual contributions, their focus remains on the goal (Laal, 2013).

10. Practical implications

Collaboration challenges are process barriers that make it difficult for participants to achieve the desired goals (Kosmutzky, 2018). The participants in this research noted that unfavourable time schedules prevented them from working with others. Whenever there was an overlap between the project and workplace schedules, a section of the participants found it challenging to engage in the project activities. However, absence from project work itself was also perceived as a lack of commitment in the case of some individuals. This situation illustrates a challenge that affects the expected symbiotic relationship, a kind of relationship that brings people together to accomplish work in a cooperative manner (Gray & Wood 1991). To resolve the challenges, participants observed that preparation regarding meetings, particularly the follow-up meetings that emerged, needed to be done early and in consultation with the participants. This was accompanied by a set of reminders that urged total commitment from regular absentees. Additionally, documents containing guidelines for upcoming activities should be shared in advance to allow members to understand what would be expected of them. This intensive communication of reminders is important to encourage participants to stick to the project objectives and keep the collaboration going (Dusdal & Powell, 2020).

A section of participants reported that it was difficult for them to conceptualise certain aspects in the process of developing assessment tools because the team leaders assumed that everyone had the same level of knowledge. Gray and Wood (1991) observed that lack of continuous support in collaboration constrained participants and limited their capacity to learn new perspectives and approaches from their counterparts. However, these concerns fitted into the argument that extrinsically motivated people may feel left out once their ideas were not acknowledged (Kosmutzky, 2018). Suggestions for addressing these challenges included the flexibility to learn new things, accommodate people with diverse experiences and different capacities, and also internally validate tools before using them in the field. Generally, the whole emphasis was on encouraging participants to unlearn their old habits to learn new ways of doing things (Kosmutzky, 2018).

Furthermore, the idea of assigning a specific skill to be worked upon by the team of experts from three different countries was perceived a limitation. Participants expected that they would gain more knowledge if they were allowed to work on each target skill regardless of the assigned team. The challenge became more intense at the time of validation of tools when participants realised that they had no idea about the work done by different groups. Some participants also insinuated that there was an intended monopoly of knowledge by team members who identified themselves as more qualified/experienced. These experiences affected the spirit of joint ownership that was characterised by mutual agreement, advanced planning and functioning technological support and is necessary to promote trust and sensitivity among team members (Livingston, 2003). What transpired in these experiences could be a lack of understanding of the dynamics of the process or a lack of trust in the entire process (Ang'ana & Chiroma, 2021). Participants, however, resolved that to promote joint ownership, all teams should work on the same skill and then move to another. Chrislip (2002) observed that joint engagements need an environment that allows participants to feel that they are a part of the whole process. This can be realised by sharing the same information regarding rules, guidelines and operating procedures and by seeking continuous feedback from team members to prevent possible collaboration hiccups (Chrislip, 2002).

11. Theoretical Implications

Considering the theoretical assumption that people have motives that drive their actions (McClelland, 1985), the findings demonstrated that participants whose motivation in the collaboration was associated with achievement needs (83%) had a high degree of commitment. Their values were characterised by high levels of accountability for outputs, passion for ultimate goals, openness to others' opinions, and flexibility to learn. In addition, their actions were more coherent in situations that demanded solving problems. This aligns with Yamaguchi's (2003) observation that achievement needs are satisfied when individuals self-actualise their purpose and perform at a more advanced level than their peers.

On the other hand, participants who are motivated by affiliation needs were more emotionally attached to others and sought a greater sense of respect and cooperativeness in a team. This characteristic is further explained by Yamaguchi (2003), who contends that strong affiliation needs drive individuals to pursue team activities in which interdependency and cooperation with others are paramount.

The motivational aspects that are associated with power and influence in this study were only expressed in terms of leadership character. Participants strongly preferred working with leaders/facilitators who were empathetic, understanding and positively influential with good leadership competencies. Thus, participants emphasised interactive and proactive qualities as marks of good leaders. These qualities persuaded participants to remain part of the collaboration process. Collaboration researchers have stated that leadership with high levels of engagement and interactivity and less signs of power tend to inspire team members in a collaboration relationship (Anslinger & Jenk, 2004; Chrislip & Larson, 1994).

These results are fundamentally grounded on motivational theories and the Theory of Negotiated Order that facilitate continuity of collaboration among partners. However, the study is limited by the omission of other theories that could better explain the success and sustainability of inter-organisational collaboration. One such theory is the Theory of Cross-Boundary Collaboration (Black, 2002), which explains the collaboration patterns of partners in two completely different contexts. Therefore, this can be a potential area for further research.

12. Conclusion and Recommendations

Inter-organisational collaboration has proved to be a platform that offers opportunities for accessing multicultural and multidisciplinary expertise, gaining perspectives on topics of interest and building relationships with others who are interested in a common goal. The concern of this study is to examine the process of collaboration and its contextual dynamism to identify those aspects that contribute to its effectiveness, success and sustainability.

In general, we found that partners have personal motives for joining and staying in a collaboration. Partners are attracted to collaborations that have clear project visions; those with goals and objectives they can associate with; those that offer learning from different perspectives; those with empathetic leaders; those where decisions are collectively made; and, those in which participants demonstrate high levels of commitment to the planned goals. These motivators determine the level of mutual engagement, the quality of interaction, and the ability of the working methods to guide decision-making, feedback and overall achievement of goals.

The authors of this study urge collaborating partners to adopt collaborating approaches that offer participants the opportunity to contribute to the project objectives, alternate leading roles, share diverse experiences, and equally engage in decision-making.

Further, an environment in which members feel interdependent and highly committed should be nurtured, which induces a sense of belonging and ownership of the process and project outcomes in the short run. These factors, along with mutual respect, trust, passion for ultimate goals, accountability, openness to diverse views, flexibility, open communication, and cooperativeness, are critical for sustainable collaboration.

Finally, the success of inter-organisational collaboration and its sustainability depends on the partners' ability to synergistically address the potential collaboration process barriers. The following key issues need special attention: 1) Planning together to ensure that activity schedules are prepared in advance and that the agreed period is convenient for the majority of the participants that are committed to working with others; 2) Allowing the participants to contribute to various activities that exposes them to different knowledge experiences, enables them to appreciate the collaboration process and creates an opportunity for interacting with a large number of participants, resulting in social bonding.

REFERENCES

Abidogun, B. G., & Adebule, O. I. (2013). Contributions of Mother Tongue Education in Early Childhood Education. In 1st Annual International Interdisciplinary Conference, Portugal Proceedings (pp. 267-272).

Accountability: Faculty of Education. (2018). http://www.educ.cam.ac.uk/centres/real/researchthemes/teachingandlearning/accountability/

Acosta, F. (Ed.). (2021). Derecho a la educación y escolarización en América Latina. CLACSO.

Ahlqvist, G., Larsson, J. O., Rosen, T. V., Allodi, M. W., & Rydelius, P. A. (2019). The Sävsjö-school-project: a cluster-randomised trial aimed at improving the literacy of beginners—achievements, mental health, school satisfaction and reading capacity at the end of grade three using an alternative school curriculum. Child and Adolescent Psychiatry and Mental Health, 13(27), 1–15.

Ahluwalia, M. S., Carter, N. G., & Chenery, H. B. (1979). 'Growth and poverty in developing countries.' Journal of Development Economics, 6(3), 299-341.

Akmal, M., & Pritchett, L. (2019). Learning Equity Requires More than Equality: Learning Goals and Achievement Gaps between the Rich and the Poor in Five Developing Countries (RISE-WP-19/028; p. 49). RISE.

Akmal, M., Crawfurd, L., Hares, S., & Minardi, A. L. (2020, October). COVID-19 in Pakistan: A Phone Survey to Assess Education, Economic, and Health-Related Outcomes. Center for Global Development. https://www.cgdev.org/sites/default/files/COVID-19-pakistan-phone-survey-assess-education-economic-and-health-related-outcomes.pdf

Alcedo, Y., & Chacón, C. (2011). El enfoque lúdico como estrategia metodológica para promover el aprendizaje del inglés en niños de educación primaria. SABER. Revista Multidisciplinaria del Consejo de Investigación de la Universidad de Oriente, 23(1). https://www.redalyc.org/articulo.oa?id=427739445011

Alcott, B., Rose, P., Sabates, R., Alonso, M. L., Cherfils, M., (2018). Experience and lessons of learning intervention programmes across the PAL Network members. Policy Paper No. 18/4. REAL Centre, University of Cambridge.

Aldrin, E. (2016). Names and Identity. In C. Hough (ed.), The Oxford Handbook of Names and Naming. Oxford University Press. doi.org/10.1093/oxfordhb/9780199656431.013.24

Anderson, J. A. (2005). Accountability in education. IIEP; UNESCO. http://www.iaoed.org/files/Edpol1.pdf

Ang'ana, G. A., & Chiroma, J.A. (2021). Collaborative leadership and its influence in building and sustaining successful cross-functional relationships in organisations in Kenya. Journal of Business and Management, 23(8), 18–26, DOI: 10.9790/487X-2308061826

Annual Status of Education Report (ASER) 2018. New Delhi: ASER Centre.

Anslinger, P., & Jenk, J. (2004). Creating successful alliances. Journal of Business Strategy. 25(2), 18–22.

Archer, D., & Cameron, A. (2009). Collaborative leadership: How to succeed in an interconnected world. New York, NY: Taylor & Francis.

Arellano, S. (2020). El inmenso reto de frenar el abandono escolar. México Social [Versión web]. https://www.mexicosocial.org/el-inmenso-reto-de-frenar-el-abandono-escolar/

Arias-Gómez, J., Villasís-Keever, M., & Miranda-Novales, M. (2016). The research protocol III. Study population. Rev. Alerg. Mex., 63(2).

Arrow, A. W. (2010). Emergent Literacy Skills in New Zealand Kindergarten Children: Implications for Teaching and Learning in ECE Settings. He Kupu, 2(3), 57-69.

ASER Pakistan, Annual Status of Education Report National (2019)

ASER. (2014). Annual Status of Education Report. New Delhi. Retrieved from http://img.asercentre.org/docs/Publications/ASER%20Reports/ASER_2013/ASER2013_report%20sections/aser2013fullreportenglish.pdf

ASER. (2020). ASER 2020 Wave 1—ASER Centre. http://www.asercentre.org/Keywords/p/371.html

ASER. (2021). Status of learning during the pandemic: Evidence from three States in 2021. http://img.asercentre.org/docs/statusoflearning_22.04.pdf

Asia-Pacific Regional Network for Early Childhood. (2020, June). A survey on Perspectives on the impact of COVID-19 on young children and early childhood development in the Asia-Pacific region. https://arnec.net/publication/full-narrative-report-on-arnec-rapid-survey-:-perspectives-on-the-impact-of-COVID-19-on-young-children-and-ecd-in-the-asia-pacific-region

Atkinson, D. (1987). The Mother Tongue in The Classroom: A Neglected Resource? ELT Journal, 41(4), 241-247.

Ato, M., López, J., & Benavente, A. (2013). Un sistema de clasificación de los diseños de investigación en psicología. Anales de Psicología, 29(3).

Austin, A. E., & Baldwin, R. G. (1991). Faculty collaboration: Enhancing the quality of scholarship and teaching. School of Education and Human Development, The George Washington University.

Austin, C. (1994) The Process of Change: A Synthesis Study of Institutional Strengthening Projects and Experience (Evaluation Report EV559). London: Department for International Development.

Awopetu, A. V. (2016). Impact of Mother Tongue on Children's Learning Abilities in Early Childhood Classroom. Procedia-Social and Behavioral Sciences, 233, 58-63.

Azevedo, J. P. 2020. Learning Poverty: Measures and Simulations. Policy Research Working Paper; No. 9446. World Bank, Washington, DC. © World Bank. https://openknowledge.worldbank.org/handle/10986/34654License:CCBY3.0IGO.

Azevedo, P., Hasan, A., Goldemberg, D., Iqbal, S. A., & Geven, K. (2020). Simulating the Potential Impacts of COVID-19 School Closures on Schooling and Learning Outcomes: A Set of Global Estimates (Policy Research Working Paper Núm. 9284). The World Bank. https://doi.

org/10.1596/1813-9450-9284

Ball, J. (2010). Enhancing Learning Of Children From Diverse Language Backgrounds: Mother Tongue-Based Bilingual Or Multilingual Education In Early Childhood And Early Primary School Years. Victoria, Canada: Early Childhood Development Intercultural Partnerships, University of Victoria.

Ball, S. J. (2015). Education, governance, and the tyranny of numbers. Journal of Education Policy, 30(3), 299–301. https://doi.org/10.1080/02680939.2015.1013271

Banerjee, A. (2012). Teaching at the Right Level. Poverty Action Lab. https://www.povertyactionlab.org/sites/default/files/Teaching%20at%20the%20Right%20Level.pdf

Banerjee, A. V., Cole, S., Duflo, E., & Linden, L. (2007). Remedying education: Evidence from two randomised experiments in India. Quarterly Journal of Economics 122 (3), 1235–1264.

Banerjee, A., Banerji, R., Berry, J., Duflo, E., Kannan, H., Mukherji, S., Shotland, M., & Walton, M. (2016). Mainstreaming an Effective Intervention: Evidence from Randomised Evaluations of "Teaching at the Right Level" in India. National Bureau of Economic Research (NBER) Working paper. Accessible at: https://www.nber.org/papers/w22746[on26/09/21]

Banerjee, A., Banerji, R., Berry, J., Duflo, E., Kannan, H., Mukerji, S., Shotland, M., and Walton, M. (2017). From Proof of Concept to Scalable Policies: Challenges and Solutions, with an Application. The Journal of Economic Perspectives, 31(4):73-102.

Banerjee, A., Banerji, R., Berry, J., Duflo, E., Kannan, H., Mukherji, S., Shotland, M., & Walton, M. (2016). Mainstreaming an Effective Intervention: Evidence from Randomised Evaluations of "Teaching at the Right Level" in India. National Bureau of Economic Research.

Banerjee, A., Banerji, R., Berry, J., Duflo, E., Kannan, H., Mukherji, S., Shotland, M., Michael, W. (2016). Mainstreaming an Effective Intervention: Evidence from Randomised Evaluations of 'Teaching at the Right Level' in India. NBER Working Papers No. 22746.

Banerji, R. (2014, mayo 22). From Invisible to Visible: Being Able To "See" the Crisis in Learning. Brookings. https://www.brookings.edu/blog/

education-plus-development/2014/05/22/from-invisible-to-visible-being-able-to-see-the-crisis-in-learning/

Banerji, R. (2017). Teaching "Toppers" or Learning for All? In ASER Centre, Annual Status of Education Report (Rural) 2016 (pp. 12-15). New Delhi: ASER Centre.

Banerji, R. (2017). When Schooling Doesn't Mean Learning. Stanford Social Innovation, 4.

Banerji, R., & Chavan. M., (2016) "Improving literacy and math instruction at scale in India's primary schools: The case of Pratham's Read India program." Journal of Educational Change 17, no. 4: 453-475

Banerji, R., & Duflo, E. (2015). 'Teaching at the right level': Solutions for low learning levels in India. Retrieved from https://www.google.com/url?sa=i&rct=j&q=&esrc=s&source=web&cd=&cad=rja&uact=8&ved=0CAQQw7AJahcKEwjQ3J251478AhUAAAAAHQAAAAAQAw&url=https%3A%2F%2Funesdoc.unesco.org%2Fark%3A%2F48223%2Fpf0000373668&psig=AOvVaw3cY3WBQDzXkxoQA_fDd0vS&ust=1671848583217358

Banerji, R., Berry, J., & Shotland, M. (2015). The impact of mother literacy and participation programmes on child learning: Evidence from a randomised evaluation in India. International Initiative for Impact Evaluation. https://doi.org/10.23846/ow2153

Banerji, R., Bhattacharjea, S., & Wadhwa, W. (2013). The Annual Status of Education Report (ASER). Research in Comparative and International Education, 8(3), 387. https://doi.org/10.2304/rcie.2013.8.3.387

Barnett-Page, E., & Thomas, J. (2009). Methods for the Synthesis of Qualitative Research: A Critical Review. Bio-Medical Central Medical Research Methodology, 9(1):59.

Beaver, D. D. (2001). Reflections on scientific collaboration (and its study): Past, Present, and Future. Scientometrics, 52(3), 365–377.

Bedwell, W. L., Wildman, J. L., DiazGranados, D., Salazar, M., Kramer, W. S., & Salas, E. (2012). Collaboration At Work: An Integrative Multilevel Conceptualization. Human Resource Management Review, 22(2), 128–145.

Beeharry, G. (2021). The Pathway to Progress on SDG 4 Requires the

Global Education Architecture to Focus on Foundational Learning and to Hold Ourselves Accountable for Achieving It. International Journal of Educational Development, 82, 102375.

Benedetto, A. (2013). De la innovación al escalamiento. Reflexiones a partir de dos procesos de innovación local. Lima, Perú: IEP, IDRC-CRDI, FIDA.

Benner, A. D., & Mistry, R. S. (2007). Congruence of mother and teacher educational expectations and low-income youth's academic competence. Journal of Educational Psychology, 99(1), 140–153. https://doi.org/10.1037/0022-0663.99.1.140

Bernstein, B. (1971). Class, Codes and Control: Volume 1 – Theoretical Studies Towards A Sociology Of Language. London & New York: Routledge, Taylor & Francis Group.

Biddle, N. (2018). Location And Segregation: The Distribution of the Indigenous Population Across Australia's Urban Centres. Canberra, ACT: Centre for Aboriginal Economic Policy Research (CAEPR), The Australian National University.

Biddle, N., & Meehl, A. (2018). The Gendered Nature of Indigenous Education Participation and Attainment. Canberra, ACT: Centre for Aboriginal Economic Policy Research (CAEPR), The Australian National University.

Black L. 2002. Collaborating across boundaries: Theoretical, empirical, and simulated explorations. PhD. Dissertation, Sloan School of Management. MIT. Cambridge, MA.

Blaxter, L., Hughes, C., & Tight, M. (2011). Cómo se investiga. España: Graó.

Blimpo, M., P., Evans, D., & Lahire. N., (2015). Parental human capital and effective school management: evidence from The Gambia. Policy Research working paper; no. WPS 7238

Bloom, N., Renata L., Raffaella S., and John V. R., (2015). "Does Management Matter in Schools?" Economic Journal 125 (584): 647–74.

BMJ Publishing Group Limited, n.d. Best Practice. What is GRADE? https://bestpractice.bmj.com/info/toolkit/learn-ebm/what-is-grade/

Bold, T., Deon F., Gayle M., Ezequiel M., Brian S., Christophe R., Jakob

S., (2017). "What Do Teachers Know and Do? Does It Matter? Evidence from Primary Schools in Africa." Policy Research Working Paper 7956, World Bank, Washington, DC

Bozkurt, A. (2019). From Distance Education to Open and Distance Learning: A Holistic Evaluation of History, Definitions, and Theories. In Handbook of Research on Learning in the Age of Transhumanism (pp. 252-273). IGI Global.

Braun, V., & Clarke, V. (2006). Using thematic analysis in psychology. Qualitative Research in Psychology, 3(2), 77–101. https://doi.org/10.1191/1478088706qp063oa

Brownson, R. C., Fielding, J. E. & Green, L. W. (2018). Building Capacity for Evidence-Based Public Health: Reconciling the Pulls of Practice and the Push of Research. Annual Review of Public Health, 39(1):27-53. http:// www.annualreviews.org/doi/10.1146/annurev-publhealth-040617-014746

Bulsari, S., Siddiqui, N., Saeed, S., & Sarfraz, H. (2020, July 15). Adapting to the new normal in survey research. British Educational Research Association (BERA)

Caballero, G. (2021). Las actividades lúdicas para el aprendizaje. Polo del Conocimiento, 6(4). https://dialnet.unirioja.es/descarga/articulo/7926973.pdf

Cairns, B., Harris, M., & Young, P. (2005). Building the capacity of the voluntary non-profit sector: challenges of theory and practice. International Journal of Public Administration, 28, 869-885. DOI: 10.1081/PAD-200067377

Camacho-Thompson, D. E., Gillen-O'Neel, C., Gonzales, N. A., & Fuligni, A. J. (2016). Financial Strain, Major Family Life Events, and Parental Academic Involvement During Adolescence. Journal of Youth and Adolescence, 45(6), 1065–1074. https://doi.org/10.1007/s10964-016-0443-0

Cárdenas, C., Farías, G., & Méndez, G. (2017). ¿Existe Relación entre la Gestión Administrativa y la Innovación Educativa? Un Estudio de Caso en Educación Superior. REICE. Revista Iberoamericana sobre Calidad, Eficacia y Cambio en Educación, 15(1). https://repositorio.uam.es/handle/10486/676774

Carneiro, P., Meghir, C., & Parey, M. (2013). Maternal Education, Home Environments, and the Development of Children and Adolescents. Journal of the European Economic Association, 11(suppl_1), 123–160. https://doi.org/10.1111/j.1542-4774.2012.01096.x

Carreón, G. P., Drake, C., & Barton, A. C. (2005). The Importance of Presence: Immigrant Parents' School Engagement Experiences. American Educational Research Journal, 42(3), 465–498. https://doi.org/10.3102/00028312042003465

Casas, J. R., Repullo, J. R., & Campos, D. (2002). La encuesta como técnica de investigación. Elaboración de cuestionarios y tratamiento estadístico de los datos. Aten Primaria, 31(8). https://core.ac.uk/download/pdf/82245762.pdf

Cashman, L., Sabates, R., & Alcott, B. (2021). Parental involvement in low-achieving children's learning: The role of household wealth in rural India. International Journal of Educational Research, 105, 101701. https://doi.org/10.1016/j.ijer.2020.101701

Cea, M. A. (1998). Metodología cuantitativa. Estrategias y técnicas de investigación social. Madrid: Síntesis.

CEPAL, & UNESCO. (2020). La educación en tiempos de la pandemia de COVID-19 (p. 21). CEPAL; UNESCO.

Challenger, B.R., & Ferraro, J. (2020). 6 Practical Ways to Increase Diversity in Clinical Trials. https://www.clinicalleader.com/doc/practical-ways-to-increase-diversity-in-clinical-trials-0001.

Chalmers H. (2022). Can Education Learn from Evidence-Based Medicine? https://ebmlive.org/can-education-learn-from-evidence-based-medicine/

Chavan, M. (2013). Who needs classrooms? In C. Chandler, & A. Zainulbhai eds. Reimaging India: Unlocking the potential of Asia's next superpower (pp. 221 – 226). New York: Simon and Schuster.

Cheesman, N., & Fisher, J. (2020). Authoritarian Africa: Repression, Resistance, and the Power of Ideas. Oxford: Oxford University Press.

Chen, I. J. (2005). Using games to promote communicative skills in language learning. The Internet TESL Journal, XI (2).

Chrislip, D. D (2002). The collaborative leadership fieldbook. San Francisco: Jossey-Bass.

Chrislip, D. D., & Larson, C. (1994). Collaborative Leadership: How Citizens and Civic Leaders Can Make a Difference. San Francisco: Jossey-Bass.

Chuck, A. (2009). Disparities in the System: The Effects of Free Primary Education (FPE) on the Quality of Education in Nairobi's Public Schools.

Cochrane (2019). Embracing Diversity. 2019 Annual Review. https://www.cochrane.org/sites/default/files/public/uploads/2019_annual_review_-june_2020-final_1.pdf.

Cohen, L., Manion, L., & Morrison, K. (2017). Research Methods in Education. Routledge.

Collins, K. M. T., Onwuegbuzie, A. J., & Jiao, Q. G. (2006). Prevalence of Mixed-methods Sampling Designs in Social Science Research. Evaluation & Research in Education, 19(2), 83–101. https://doi.org/10.2167/eri421.0

Conchi, S., & Michels, C. (2014) Scientific mobility: An analysis of Germany, Austria, France and Great Britain. Fraunhofer ISI Discussion Papers Innovation Systems and Policy Analysis, No. 41. Karlsruhe: Fraunhofer ISI.

Cooley, L., & Linn, J. (2014). Taking Innovations to Scale: Methods, Applications and Lessons. Washington, DC: Results for Development Institute.

Cooper, H., Charlton, K., Valentine, J. C., & Muhlenbruck, L. (2000). Making the Most of Summer School: A Meta-Analytic and Narrative Review. Monographs of the Society for Research in Child Development, 65(1).

Córdoba, E. F., Lara, F. & García, A. (2017). El juego como estrategia lúdica para la educación inclusiva del buen vivir. ENSAYOS, Revista de la Facultad de Educación de Albacete, 32(1).

Creswell, J. W., & Creswell, D. (2018). Research design Qualitative, Quantitative and Mixed Methods Approaches. USA: Sage Publications.

Creswell, J. W., & Plano-Clark, V. L. (2017). Designing and conducting Mixed Method Research. Thousand Oaks CA, EE.UU.: Sage.

Crouch, L. (2020). Systems Implications for Core Instructional Support Lessons from Sobral (Brazil), Puebla (Mexico), and Kenya. Research on Improving Systems of Education (RISE). https://riseprogramme.org/publications/systemsimplications-core-instructional-support-lessons-sobral-brazil-puebla-mexico

Crozier, G. (1999). Is it a case of 'We know when we're not wanted'? The parents' perspective on parent-teacher roles and relationships. Educational Research, 41(3), 315-328.

Cummings, J. N., & Kiesler, S. (2005). Collaborative research across disciplinary and organisational boundaries. Social Studies of Science, 35(5), 703–722. https://doi.org/10.1177/03063127050555

Dados, N., & Connell, R. (2012). The Global South. Contexts, 11(1), 12–13. https://doi.org/10.1177/1536504212436479

David, M. K., Ostler, N., & Dealwis, C. (2007). Working Together for Endangered Languages: Research Challenges and Social Impacts. FEL XI: Foundation for Endangered Languages, University Malaya. –Kuala Lumpur, Malaysia, 26–28.

Davidson, M., Ralaingita, W., Marsden, E., and Long, E. (2022). Science of Teaching for Foundational Literacy and Numeracy. In https://scienceofteaching.site/assets/docs/Remediation%20Strategies%20and%20Approaches/REM_Remediation%20Literature%20Review.pdf

Dietz, G., & Cortés, L. S. M. (2019). Las universidades interculturales en México, logros y retos de un nuevo subsistema de educación superior. Estudios sobre las culturas contemporáneas, 25(49), 163-190.

Dillenbourg P. (1999). What do you mean by collaborative learning? In P. Dillenbourg (Ed.) Collaborative-learning: Cognitive and computational approaches (pp.1–19). Oxford, UK: Elsevier.

Dixon, Kerryn. (2018). 'Seven reasons for teachers to welcome home languages in education.' Voices Magazine, British Council. Retrieved from https://www.google.com/url?sa=i&rct=j&q=&esrc=s&source=web&cd=&cad=rja&uact=8&ved=0CAQQw7AJahcKEwioyZu61Y78AhUAAAAAHQAAAAAQAw&url=https%3A%2F%2Fwww.britishcouncil.org%2Fvoices-magazine%2Freasons-for-teachers-to-prioritise-home-languages-in-education&psig=AOvVaw3y7f64cGcRtu4hnwEnpp0K&ust=1671848048208698

Donovan, M. S., Snow, C., & Daro, P (2013). The SERP Approach to Problem-Solving Research, Development, and Implementation. Yearbook of the National Society for the Study of Education, 112(2):400-425.

Duckworth, K., Akerman, R., MacGregor, A., Salter, E., & Vorhaus, J. (2009). Self-regulated learning: a literature review. The University of London, Institute of Education, Centre for Research on the Wider Benefits of Learning. London: Institute of Education, University of London.

Duffy, M. E. (1987). Methodological triangulation: A vehicle for merging quantitative and qualitative research methods. The Journal of Nursing Scholarship, 19 (3), 130–133.

Duflo, A. and Kiessel, J. (2012). Every Child Can, Every Child Counts An evaluation of the Teacher Community Assistant Initiative (TCAI) Pilot Programme in Ghana. [online] Innovations for Poverty Action (IPA). Available at: https://www.theigc.org/wp-content/uploads/2014/10/Duflo-Kiessel2012-Working-Paper.pdf

Duflo, E., Dupas P., and Kremer, M. (2011). "Peer Effects, Teacher Incentives, and the Impact of Tracking: Evidence from a Randomised Evaluation in Kenya." American Economic Review 101(5): 1739-74.

Duncan, G. J., & Magnuson, K. A. (2003). Off with Hollingshead: Socio-economic resources,
parenting, and child development. Socio-economic status, parenting, and child development, 287, 83-106.

Dusdal, J., & Powell, J. W. (2021). Benefits, motivations, and challenges of international collaborative research: A sociology of science case study. Science and Public Policy, 48(2), 235–245. https://doi.org/10.1093/scipol/scab010

Eade, D. (2007) Capacity building: who builds whose capacity? Development in Practice, 17, 630-639. DOI: 10.1080/09614520701469807

Eberhard, David M., Gary F. Simons, and Charles D. Fennig (eds.). 2022. Ethnologue: Languages of the World, 25th edn. Dallas, Texas.

Education Endowment Foundation (2017). Teaching & Learning Toolkit. https://educationendowmentfoundation.org.uk/resources/teaching-learning-toolkit/.

Education Partnerships Group (2020). Systems-Level Analysis of Education Service Delivery in Sierra Leone. https://mbsse.gov.sl/reports/.

Education, UNESCO (2020). From disruption to recovery. https://en.unesco.org/covid19/educationresponse

Education.org (2021a). Covid-19 and School Responses: Tracking and Analysis. https://education.org/covid-19

Education.org (2021b) Calling for an Education Knowledge Bridge. A White Paper to Advance Evidence Use in Education. https://education.org/white-paper

El- Shamy, S. (2001). Training Games: Everything You Need to Know About Using Games to Reinforce Learning. Virginia : Stylus Publishing.

Elsamadony, M., Fujii, M., Ryo, M., Nerini, F. F., Kakinuma, K., & Kanae, S. (2022). Preliminary Quantitative Assessment of The Multidimensional Impact of The COVID-19 Pandemic on Sustainable Development Goals. Journal of cleaner production, 372, 133812.

Epstein, J. L. (1987). Parent Involvement: What Research Says to Administrators. Education and Urban Society, 19(2), 119–136. https://doi.org/10.1177/0013124587019002002

Epstein, J. L. (1990). School and Family Connections: Theory, Research, and Implications for Integrating Sociologies of Education and Family. Marriage & Family Review, 15(1–2), 99–126. https://doi.org/10.1300/J002v15n01_06

Epstein, J. L., & Becker, H. J. (1982). Teachers' Reported Practices of Parent Involvement: Problems and Possibilities. The Elementary School Journal, 83(2), 103–113. https://doi.org/10.1086/461298

Executive Summary: Teaching at the Right Level Pilot, (2018), Building tomorrow) file:///C:/Users/USER/Downloads/TaRL-Literacy-Pilot-Executive-Summary.pdf

Family Lives (2021) https://www.familylives.org.uk/advice/early-years-development/learning-and-play/why-play-matters/

Fan X. & Chen, M. J. (2001). Parental Involvement and Students' Academic Achievement: A Meta-Analysis. Educational Psychology Review, 22.

Fan, W., & Williams, C. M. (2010). The effects of parental involvement on students' academic self-efficacy, engagement, and intrinsic motivation. Educational Psychology, 30(1), 53–74. https://doi.org/10.1080/01443410903353302

Fidalgo, A. (2014). Innovación educativa en la sociedad del conocimiento. Teoría de la Educación. Educación y Cultura en la Sociedad de la Información, 15(3).

Fine, G. A. (2012). Tiny Publics: A Theory of Group Action and Culture. Russell Sage Foundation.

Finn, J. D. (1998). Parental Engagement That Makes a Difference. Educational Leadership, 55(8), 20–24.

Flotts, P., Manzi, J., Jiménez, D., Abarzúa, A., Cayuman, C., & García, M. J. (2016). Informe de resultados TERCE. Tercer estudio regional comparativo y explicativo. Logros de aprendizaje. Laboratorio Latinoamericano de evaluación de la calidad de la educación. Chile: UNESCO.

Fox, J. A. (2015). Social Accountability: What Does the Evidence Really Say? World Development, 72, 346 – 361.

French, R., & Kingdon, G. (2010). The relative effectiveness of private and government schools in Rural India: Evidence from ASER data. Dept. of Quantitative Social Science Working paper -10-03. Institute of Education, University of London, DoQSS Working Papers.

Fricke, S., Bowyer-Crane, C., Haley, A. J., Hulme, C., & Snowling, M. J. (2012). Efficacy of language intervention in the early years. Journal of Child Psychology and Psychiatry, 54(3), 280–290. https://doi.org/10.1111/jcpp.12010

Gajda, R. (2004). Utilising Collaboration Theory to Evaluate Strategic Alliances. American Journal of Evaluation, 25(1), 65–77.

Galindo, D., García, L., García, R., González, P., Hernández, P. C., López, M., Luna, V., & Moreno, C. I. (2020). Recomendaciones didácticas para adaptarse a la enseñanza remota de emergencia. Revista Digital Universitaria RDU, 21(5). http://doi.org/10.22201/cuaieed.16076079e.2020.21.5.15

Galla, C. K. (2016). Indigenous Language Revitalisation, Promotion, and Education: Function of Digital Technology. Computer Assisted Language

Learning, 29(7), 1137–1151. https://doi.org/10.1080/09588221.2016.1166137

García-Alix, L. (2003). Foro permanente para las cuestiones indígenas. IWGIA.

Geven, K., & Hasan, A. (2020, October). Learning Losses in Pakistan Due to COVID-19 School Closures: A Technical Note on Simulation Results. World Bank. https://openknowledge.worldbank.org/handle/10986/34659?locale-attribute=en

Giallo, R., Treyvaud, K., Cooklin, A., & Wade, C. (2013). Mothers' and fathers' involvement in home activities with their children: Psychosocial factors and the role of parental self-efficacy. Early Child Development and Care, 183(3–4), 343–359. https://doi.org/10.1080/03004430.2012.711587

Gibbs, G. R. (2018). Analysing Qualitative Data. London: SAGE Publications.

Giganti, P. (2014). Matemáticas en la casa: Ayudando a sus Niños a Disfrutar de las Matemáticas [versión web]. Oficina de Educación del Condado de Sonoma.

Gil, J. D., Ewerling, F., Ferreira, L. Z., & Barros, A. J. (2020). Early childhood suspected developmental delay in 63 low- and middle-income countries: Large within- and between-country inequalities documented using national health surveys. Journal of Global Health, 10(1). https://doi.org/10.7189/jogh.10.010427

Giorgi, A. P., & Giorgi, B. M. (2003). The descriptive phenomenological psychological method. In P. Camic, J. Rhodes, & L. Yardley (Eds.) Qualitative research in psychology: Expanding perspectives in methodology and design (pp. 243–273). Washington, DC: American Psychological Association. https://doi.org/10.1037/10595-013

Glewwe, P. W., Hanushek, E. A., Humpage, S. D., & Ravina, R. (2011). School Resources and Educational Outcomes in Developing Countries: A Review of the Literature from 1990 to 2010. National Bureau of Economic Research, Inc.

Glewwe, P., Kremer, M., and Moulin, S., (2009). "Many Children Left Behind? Textbooks and Test Scores in Kenya." American Economic Journal: Applied Economics 1(1): 112-35.

Glewwe, P., Kremer, M., Moulin, S., & Zitzewitz, E. (2004). "Retrospective vs Prospective Analyses of School Inputs: The Case of Flip Charts in Kenya." Journal of Development Economics 74(2004): 251-68.

Goldmann, G., & Racine, A. (2021). "Show Me the Money": The Returns to Education for Indigenous Canadians. Canadian Studies in Population, 1-21.

Goulet, L. M., & Goulet, K. N. (2014). Teaching Each Other: Nehinuw Concepts and Indigenous Pedagogies. UBC Press.

Gove, A, & Cvelich, P. (2011). "Early Reading, Igniting Education for All: A Report by the Early Grade Learning Community of Practice." Rev. ed. Research Triangle Park, NC: Research Triangle Institute

Government of Pakistan, "Chapter 2: Key Features and Implementation Strategies of the Education Sector Reforms", Pakistan Education Sector Reforms: Action Plan (2001 – 2005).

Government of Pakistan, National Curriculum: Early Childhood Education (2002)

Government of Pakistan, National Education Policy (2009)

Government of Pakistan, National Plan of Action (2001-2015)

Government of the Punjab (Bureau of Statistics Punjab) and UNICEF, Multiple Indicator Cluster Survey (2014)

Government of the Punjab, Punjab Early Childhood Education Policy (2017)

Government of the Punjab, Punjab School Education Sector Plan (2013-17)

Government of the Punjab, Punjab School Education Sector Plan (2019-24)

Government of the Punjab, The New Deal 2018-2023 (2019)

Government of the Punjab, The Punjab Free and Compulsory Education Act (2014)

Government of Uganda (2016). The Non-Governmental Organisations Act (Acts Supplement No. 4 to the Uganda Gazette, No. 14, Vol. CIX). Entebbe: Government Printer.

Government of Uganda (2017) The Non-Governmental Organisations

Regulations (Statutory Instruments Supplement No. 13 to the Uganda Gazette, No. 25, Vol. CX). Entebbe: Government Printer.

Govinda, R. (2020). 'Learning in the Margin: Reflections on Indian Policies and Programmes for Education of the Disadvantaged. Lecture at LBOP2: Applying Research to Policy and Practice, Virtual Invitational Conference, 7-8 December; Country Case Studies, IIEP-UNESCO. Doi:10.11647/obp.0256.09

GPE KIX (2020). Retrieved from https://www.gpekix.org

Granada Preparatory School, (2018), Top 5 Benefits of Learning Through Play, 10400 Zelzah Avenue, Northridge, CA 91326

Gray, A. (2018). The Explosion of Aboriginality: Components of Indigenous Population Growth 1991-1996. Canberra, ACT: Centre for Aboriginal Economic Policy Research (CAEPR), The Australian National University.

Gray, B. & Wood, D. J. (1991). Collaborative alliances: Moving from practice to theory. Journal of Applied Behavioural Science, 27(1), 3–22. https://doi.org/10.1177/0021886391271001

Gray, K., & Gills, B. K. (2016) South–South cooperation and the rise of the Global South. Third World Quarterly, 37(4), 557–574. https://doi.org/10.1080/01436597.2015.1128817

Green, C. L., Walker, J. M. T., Hoover-Dempsey, K. V., & Sandler, H. M. (2007). Parents' motivations for involvement in children's education: An empirical test of a theoretical model of parental involvement. Journal of Educational Psychology, 99(3), 532–544. https://doi.org/10.1037/0022-0663.99.3.532

Grek, S. (2009). Governing by numbers: The PISA 'effect' in Europe. Journal of Education Policy, 24(1), 23–37. https://doi.org/10.1080/02680930802412669

Guach, J., & Peña, R. L. (2001). El método de seguimiento y monitoreo. Una experiencia en la formación reflexivo-creativa del Programa PRYCREA. Revista Crecemos, 5(2). http://biblioteca.clacso.edu.ar/ar/libros/cuba/cips/caudales05/Caudales/ARTICULOS/ArticulosPDF/0524GP052.pdf

Haezrahi, P. (1949). 'The Desired and the Desirable.' Analysis 10.2 (Dec Issue): 40-49. Oxford University Press. https://doi.org/10.2307/3326904

Hale, C. (2004). Rethinking Indigenous Politics in the Era of the "indio permitido". NACLA Report on the Americas, 38(2), pp.16-21.

Hale, C. (2006). Más que un indio: racial ambivalence and the paradox of neoliberal multiculturalism in Guatemala. Santa Fe, NM: School of American Research Press.

Hall, G., & Gandolfo, A. (2016). Poverty and Exclusion Among Indigenous Peoples: the Global Evidence. World Bank Blogs.

Hammett, D., & Jackson, L. (2017). Developing a 'civil' society in partial democracies: in/civility and a critical public sphere in Uganda and Singapore. Political Geography, 67, 145-155. DOI: 10.1016/j.polgeo.2017.08.004

Hang, S. (2017). Using games to teach young children English language. Vrije Universiteit Brussel.

Hanushek, E. A., & Raymond, M. (2004). Does School Accountability Lead to Improved Student Performance? (Núm. 10591; National Bureau of Economic Research Working Paper). National Bureau of Economic Research. http://www.nber.org/papers/w10591.pdf?new_window=1

Hanushek, E. A., & Woessmann, L. (2007). The Role of Education Quality for Economic Growth. Policy Research Working Paper; No. 4122.

Hanushek, E.A, (1995). "Interpreting Recent Research on Schooling in Developing Countries." World Bank Research Observer 10 (2): 227–46.

Haugen, E.I. (1974). The ecology of language. In The ecology of languages: Essays by Einar Haugen, ed. by Anwar Dil, pp. 325-339. Stanford: Stanford University Press.

Hevia, F. J., & Vergara-Lope, S. (2019). Educational Accountability or Social Accountability in Education? Similarities, Tensions, and Differences (Working Paper Núm. 5; p. 64). Medición Independiente de Aprendizajes; Accountability Research Center. https://accountabilityresearch.org/publication/educational-accountability-or-social-accountability-in-education-similarities-tensions-and-differences/

Hevia, F. J., Vergara-Lope, S., & Velásquez-Durán, A. (2019). Prácticas basadas en evidencia: Efectos en lectura y escritura de intervenciones que enseñan en el nivel adecuado en Veracruz. XV Congreso Nacional de Investigación Educativa, Acapulco.

Hevia, F. J., Vergara-Lope, S., & Velásquez-Durán, A. (2020). ¿Qué hacer para convertir el regreso a clases en una oportunidad para abatir el rezago de aprendizajes básicos?: Una propuesta en tres pasos. Faro Educativo, Apunte de política N°14. México: INIDE-UIA.

Hevia, F. J., Vergara-Lope, S., & Velásquez-Durán, A. (2021). Evidence-based Practices: Effects on Literacy and Numeracy using Teaching at the Right Level Approach in Mexico. En Ishmael I. Munene (Ed.), Ensuring all Children Learn: Lessons on Inclusion and Equity from the South (pp. 201-212). Lexington Books. ISBN: 978-1793636270

Hidalgo, H., Tenorio, G. & Ramírez, M. (2016). Atributos de innovación en el desarrollo de competencias digitales en educación básica usando recursos educativos abiertos en una comunidad rural de Colombia. CPU-e Revista de Investigación Educativa, 22.

Hodges, C., Moore, S., Lockee, B., Trust, T., & Bond, A. (2020). The difference between emergency remote teaching and online learning. EDUCAUSE Review. https://er.educause.edu/articles/2020/3/the-difference-between-emergency-remote-teaching-and-online-learning

Honig, M. I., & Rainey, L. R. (2012). Autonomy and School Improvement What Do We Know and Where Do We Go From Here? Educational Policy, 26(3), 465–495. https://doi.org/10.1177/0895904811417590

Hoover-Dempsey, K. V., & Sandler, H. M. (1997). Why Do Parents Become Involved in Their Children's Education? Review of Educational Research, 67(1), 3–42. https://doi.org/10.3102/00346543067001003

http://www.yourarticlelibrary.com/entreprene

https://blogs.worldbank.org/voices/poverty-and-exclusion-among-indigenous-peoples-global-evidence (accessed on May 31, 2020)

https://doi.org/10.3768/rtipress.2011.bk.0007.1109.

https://www.bera.ac.uk/blog/adapting-to-the-new-normal-in-survey-research

https://www.ucpress.edu/ebook.php?isbn=9780520949904

Hueso, A., & Cascant, M. J. (2012). Metodología y Técnicas Cuantitativas de Investigación [versión web]. https://riunet.upv.es/handle/10251/17004

Husserl, E. (1970). Logical investigations (D. Carr, Trans.). New York, Humanities Press.

Huxham, C. (2003). Theorising Collaboration Practice. Public Management Review, 5(3), 401–423. Doi: 10.1080/1471903032000146964

Hwa, Y., Kaffenberger, M. and Silberstein, J (2020). Aligning Levels of Instruction with Goals and the Needs of Students (ALIGNS): Varied Approaches, Common Principles. RISE Programme, RISE Insight Series, 2020/022. https://doi.org/10.35489/BSGRISE-RI_2020/022

IIEP. (2015). OVERVIEW. Incorporating safety, resilience, and social cohesion in education sector planning. UNESCO.

IIEP-UNESCO (n.d.). Planning Education, Building the Future. http://www.iiep.unesco.org/en .

Independent Measurement of Learning (MIA). (2020), MIAventura de verano. México: CIESAS y Universidad Veracruzana. https://www.medicionmia.org.mx/laradioesmia

Institute for the Study of Knowledge Management in Education. https://www.iskme.org/about-us

Institute of University and Education Research. (2020). Educación y pandemia. Una visión académica. México: UNAM. http://www.iisue.unam.iisue/covid/educacion-y-pandemia

International Step by Step Association (ISSA) (n.d.). About us. https://www.issa.nl/about_us

Jackson, S., & Martin, P. Y. (1998). Surviving the care system: education and resilience. Journal of Adolescence, 21(5), 569-83.

Jacob, W. J., Cheng, S. Y., & Porter, M. K. (2015). Global Review of Indigenous Education: Issues of Identity, Culture, and Language. Indigenous education, 1-35.

Jaja, S. A. (2003). Praxis of Work Behaviour. Lagos: Pinnacle Publishers.

James J. Heckman. (2008). Schools, Skills, and Synapses. Social Science Research Network.

JanMohamed, A., & Lloyd, D. (2014). Toward a Theory of Minority Discourse: What is to be Done? In Postcolonial criticism (pp. 234-247). Routledge.

Jeynes, W. H. (2007). The Relationship Between Parental Involvement and Urban Secondary School Student Academic Achievement: A Meta-Analysis. Urban Education, 42(1), 82–110. https://doi.org/10.1177/0042085906293818

Joint Learning Network (n.d.). What We Do. https://www.jointlearningnetwork.org/what-we-do/ .

Jones, T. L., & Prinz, R. J. (2005). Potential roles of parental self-efficacy in parent and child adjustment: A review. Clinical Psychology Review, 25(3), 341–363. https://doi.org/10.1016/j.cpr.2004.12.004

Jukes, M. C. H., Sitabkhan, Y., and Tibenda, J. J. (2021). Adapting Pedagogy to Cultural Context. RTI Press Publication No. OP-0070-2109. Research Triangle Park, NC: RTI Press.

Kaffenberger, M. (2021). Modelling the long-run learning impact of the Covid-19 learning shock: Actions to (more than) mitigate loss. International Journal of Educational Development, 81.

Kaffenberger, M., and Spivack, M. (2022). System Coherence for Learning: Applications of the RISE Education Systems Framework. RISE Working Paper Series 22/086, January. https://doi.org/10.35489/BSG-RISEWP_2022/086.

Kalinaki, D. K. (2014). Kizza Besigye and Uganda's Unfinished Revolution. Kampala: Dominant Seven.

Kam, M., Mathur, A., Kumar, A., & Canny, J. (2009). Designing digital games for rural children: a study of traditional village games in India. Proceedings of the SIGCHI Conference on Human Factors in Computing Systems (pp. 31– 40). New York, NY, USA: Association for Computing Machinery.

Kam, M., Mathur, A., Kumar, A., & Canny, J. (2009). Designing Digital Games for Rural Children: A Study of Traditional Village Games in India. Conference: Proceedings of the SIGCHI International Conference on Human Factors in Computing Systems. 31–40. Boston, MA, USA. https://doi.org/10.1145/1518701.1518707

Kana' iaupuni, S. M., Ledward, B., & Malone, N. (2017). Mohala i ka wai: Cultural Advantage as a Framework for Indigenous Culture-Based Education and Student Outcomes. American Educational Research Journal, 54(1_suppl), 311S-339S.

Kaplan, A. (2000). Capacity building: shifting the paradigm of practice. Development in Practice, 10, 517-526.

Khanna, S. (n.d.). Indian toys and toy makers. Retrieved from http://www.arvindguptatoys.com/arvindgupta/sudarshan.pdf

Kingdon, G. (2017, March). The Private Schooling Phenomenon in India: A Review. The Journal of Development Studies, 56, 1–23. https://doi.org/10.1080/00220388.2020.1715943

Komba, A. and Shukia, R. (2021). Accountability Relationships in 3Rs Curriculum Reform Implementation: Implication for Pupils' Acquisition of Literacy and Numeracy Skills in Tanzania's Primary Schools. RISE Working Paper Series. 21/065. https://doi.org/10.35489/BSG-RISE-WP_2021/065

Kosmutzky, A. (2018) Tracing the development of international branch campuses: From local founding waves to global diffusion? Globalisation, Societies and Education, 16(4), 453–477. Doi: 10.1080/14767724.2018.1512044

Krithika, R. (2019, June 21). Let children learn by doing. The Hindu. https://www.thehindu.com/education/schools/a-conversation-with-renowned-scientist-and-educator-arvind-gupta/article28098701.ece.

Kuhfeld, M. (2019). Surprising New Evidence on Summer Learning Loss. Phi Delta Kappan, 101(1). doi: 10.1177/0031721719871560

Kuhfeld, M., & Tarasawa, B. (2020). The COVID-19 slide: What Summer Learning Loss Can Tell us about the Potential Impact of School Closures on Student Academic Achievement, NWEA. https://www.nwea.org/content/uploads/2020/05/Collaborative-Brief_Covid19-Slide-APR20.pdf

Kwan, J. & Sandercock, P (2003). In-Hospital Care Pathways for Stroke: A Cochrane Systematic Review [Abstract]. Stroke, 34(2):587-588.

Laal, M. (2013). Positive interdependence in collaborative learning. Social and Behavioural Sciences, 93, 1433–1437.

Lai, E. R. (2011). Collaboration: A Literature Review. Pearson. http://images.pearsonassessments.com/images/tmrs/Collaboration-Review.pdf

Lakhsman, S. (2019). Improving reading and arithmetic outcomes at scale: Teaching at the Right Level (TaRL), Pratham's approach to teaching and learning. Revue Internationale d'éducation de Sèvres.(Online)

Lareau, A. (1987, April). Social Class Differences in Family-School Relationships: The Importance of Cultural Capital. Sociology of Education, 60(2), 73–85.

Lavinas, L., & Veiga, A., (20130. "Brazil's One Laptop Per Child Program: Impact Evaluation and Implementation Assessment." Cadernos de Pesquisa 43 (149).

Leahey, E. (2016). From sole investigator to team scientist: Trends in the practice and study of research collaboration. Annual Review of Sociology, 42, 81–100. https://doi.org/10.1146/annurev-soc-081715-074219

Lee, T. S. (2007). Connecting Academics, Indigenous Knowledge, and Commitment to Community: High School Students' Perceptions of a Community-Based Education. Canadian Journal of Native Education, 30(2), 196.

Lenaiyasa, S. K. (2004). Toys and Learning Materials Made by Parents for Children in Kenya. Nairobi: Christian Children's Fund Kenya.

Lewin, S., Booth, A., Glenton, C., Munthe-Kaas, H., Rashidian, A., Wainwright, M., Bohren, M.A., Tunçalp, O., Colvin, C.J., Garside, R., Carlsen, B., Langlois, E.V. & Noyes, J. (2018). Applying GRADE-CERQual to Qualitative Evidence Synthesis Findings. Implementation Science, 13(Supplement 1):1-10.

Livingston, S. (2003) On the challenges of cross-national comparative media research. European Journal of Communication, 18(4), 477–500. https://doi.org/10.1177/0267323103184003

Loreman, T., Forlin, C., & Sharma, U. (2014). Measuring Indicators of Inclusive Education: A Systematic Review of the Literature. Measuring Inclusive Education (International Perspectives on Inclusive Education, Vol. 3), pp. 165–187.

Loureiro, A. and Cruz, L. (2020). Achieving World-Class Education in Adverse Socioeconomic Conditions: The Case of Sobral in Brazil. World Bank.

Lynch, G., & Crawford, G. (2011). Democratisation in Africa 1990-2010, Democratisation, 18, 275-310. DOI: 10.1080/13510347.2011.554175

Machida, S., Taylor, A. R., & Kim, J. (2002). The Role of Maternal Beliefs in Predicting Home Learning Activities in Head Start Families*. Family Relations, 51(2), 176–184. https://doi.org/10.1111/j.1741-3729.2002.00176

Maines, D. R. (1978). Structural parameters and negotiated orders: Comment on Benson, and Day and Day. The Sociological Quarterly, 19(3), 491–496.

Mandillah, L. (2019). Kenyan Curriculum Reforms and Mother Tongue Education: Issues, Challenges and Implementation Strategies. Education as Change, 23, 18. https://doi.org/10.25159/1947-9417/3379

Martinez Novo, C. (2006). Who Defines Indigenous? Identities, Development, Intellectuals, and the State in Northern Mexico. New Brunswick, NJ: Rutgers University Press.

Martínez, H. (2018). Metodología de la investigación. México: Cengage Learning.

May, S. (Ed.). (1999). Indigenous Community-Based Education. Multilingual Matters.

Mayhew, L. B. (1990). The quest for quality: The challenge for undergraduate education in the 1990s (1st ed.). Jossey-Bass.

Maynes, M. J. (1985). Schooling in Western Europe: A social history. State University of New York Press.

McClelland, D. C. (1985). Human motivation. Glenview, IL: Scott Foresman.

McConville, K. (2019) 'Language barriers in the classroom: From Mother-tongue to National Language.' Retrieved from https://www.google.com/url?sa=t&rct=j&q=&esrc=s&source=web&cd=&ved=2ahUKEwiF1bOH4oz8AhUhaGwGHXrXAtgQFnoECBQQAQ&url=https%3A%2F%2Fwww.concernusa.org%2Fstory%2Flanguage-barriers-in-classroom%2F&usg=AOvVaw1jy9CAlRP4chcrqSsXSs6F

McCoy, D. C., Evan D. P., Majid E, Goodarz D., Black, M. M., (2016). "Early Childhood Developmental Status in Low- and Middle-Income

Countries: National, Regional, and Global Prevalence Estimates Using Predictive Modeling." PLOS Medicine 13 (6): e1002034

McDonald, S. K., Keesler, V. A., Kauffman, N. J., & Schneider, B. (2006). Scaling-Up Exemplary Interventions. Educational Researcher, 35(3). https://doi.org/10.3102/0013189X035003015

Miks, J., & McIlwaine, J. (2020, April 20). Keeping the world's children learning through COVID-19. UNICEF. https://www.unicef.org/coronavirus/keeping-worlds-children-learning-through-COVID-19

Miles, M. B., & Huberman, A. M. (1994). An expanded sourcebook: Qualitative data, 2nd edition. London: SAGE Publications.

Ministry of Federal Education and Professional Training, Pakistan National Education Response and Resilience Plan (K-12) for COVID-19 (2020)

Miranda-Novales, M. G., Rendón-Macías, M. E., & Villasís-Keeve, M. A. (2016). Estadística descriptiva. Revista Alergia México, 63(4), 397-407

Mmasa, M., & Anney, V. N. (2016). Exploring Literacy and Numeracy Teaching in Tanzanian Classrooms: Insights from Teachers' Classroom Practices. Journal of Education and Practice, 7(9), 137-154.

Moir, T. (2018). Why Is Implementation Science Important for Intervention Design and Evaluation within Educational Settings? Frontiers in Education, 3:61.

Montoya, S. (2018, August 27). There's a global learning crisis and it's leaving millions without basic skills. World Economic Forum. https://www.weforum.org/agenda/2018/08/global-learning-crisis-millions-without-basic-skills-unesco/

Morgan, D. et al., eds. (1967) (eds) Biological science. The web of life. Canberra: Australian Academy of Science. Committee on Biological Education.

Morrison, G., WOIKA, M. J., & BREFFNI, L. (2009). Early Childhood Education. Ohio: Charles Merrill.

Mufwene, S. S. (2017). Language Evolution from an Ecological Perspective 1. In The Routledge handbook of ecolinguistics (pp. 73-88). Oxfordshire, England: Routledge.

Mugo, J., Mauro, G., Ngina, P., & Khadija, S. (2022). The ALiVE Way: Contextualising the Measurement of Life Skills and Values in Kenya, Tanzania, and Uganda. Regional Education Learning Initiative, East Africa.

Mühlhäusler, P. (1992). Preserving Languages or Language Ecologies? A Top-down Approach to Language Survival. Oceanic Linguistics, 31(2), 163-180. https://doi.org/10.2307/3623012

Mujica J., A. S. (2012). Estrategias para estimular el dibujo en los estudiantes de educación inicial. Revista de Investigación, (77), 36, 147- 164.

Mulimani P., 2019. Publication Bias towards Western Populations Harms Humanity. Natural Human Behaviour, 3(10):1026-1027.

Munene, I. I. (Ed.). (2021). Ensuring All Children Learn: Lessons from the South on What Works in Equity and Inclusion. Lexington Books.

Murray, M. (2003). 'A Catalogue of Mistaken Interests: Reflections on the Desired and the Desirable.' International Journal of Philosophical Studies 11(1),1-23. https://doi.org/10.1080/0967255032000050411

Murry, H. A. (1938). Explorations in personality. New York: Oxford University Press.

Naik, N. (2014). A comparative evaluation of games-based learning: Digital or non-digital games? Proceedings of the European Conference on Games-based Learning, 1(2).

Nakabugo, M.G., Barrett, E., McEvoy, P. & Munck, R. (2020). Best Practice in North-South research relationships in higher education: The Irish African partnership model, Policy & Practice: A Development Education Review, PP 89-98.

Nambissan, G. B. (1994). 'Language and schooling of tribal children: Issues related to medium of instruction.' Economic and Political Weekly 29.42 (Oct 15 issue): 2747 & 2751-54.

Naranjo, Y. J. (2011). Exclusión, asimilación, integración, pluralismo cultural y "modernización" en el sistema educativo mexicano: un acercamiento histórico a las escuelas de educación pública para indígenas. CPU-e, Revista de Investigación Educativa, (12), 1-24.

National Education Policy (2020). Ministry of Education, Government of India. Accessed at https://www.education.gov.in/sites/upload_files/mhrd/

files/NEP_Final_English_0.pdf

National Institute for the Evaluation of Education. (2016). Resultados Nacionales del Tercer Estudio Regional Comparativo y Explicativo TERCE 2013. México: INEE.

Ndamba, G. T. (2008). Mother Tongue Usage in Learning: an Examination of Language Preferences in Zimbabwe. Journal of Pan African Studies, 2(4).

Neill, J. T., & Dias, K. L. (2001). Adventure Education and Resilience: The Double-Edged Sword. Journal of Adventure Education and Outdoor Learning, 1(2), 35– 42. doi:10.1080/14729670185200061

Nelson, C. A., (2016) "Brain Imaging as a Measure of Future Cognitive Outcomes: A Study of Children in Bangladesh Exposed to Multiple Levels of Adversity." Presentation, CMU Department of Psychology Colloquium, Department of Psychology, College of Humanities and Social Sciences, Carnegie Mellon University, Pittsburgh, September 29.

Nishanthi, R. (2020). Understanding of the Importance of Mother Tongue Learning. International Journal of Trend in Scientific Research and Development, 5(1), 77-80.

Nkwatsibwe, C. (2019). Winning and Sustaining Space for Civil Society in Semi-authoritarian Settings: What Works and What Doesn't Work, the Case of Uganda (Master's Dissertation Series No. 9). Cape Town: Nelson Mandela School of Public Governance, University of Cape Town.

Northern Care Alliance (n.d.) Why is Research Important? https://www.pat.nhs.uk/education-and-research/why-is-research-important.htm.

Nunes. P. (1994). Educación Lúdica. Bogotá: Ediciones San Pablo.

Nzuve, S. (2007). Elements of Organisational Behaviour. Nairobi, Kenya: University of Nairobi Press.

OECD (2017). The Funding of School Education: Connecting Resources and Learning. https://www.oecd.org/governance/the-funding-of- school-education-9789264276147-en.htm.

Oketch, M., Ngware, M., Mutisya, M., Kassahun, A., Abuya, B., & Musyoka, P. (2014). When to Randomise: Lessons From Independent Impact Evaluation of Reading to Learn (RtL) Programme to Improve

Literacy and Numeracy in Kenya and Uganda. Peabody Journal of Education, 89(1), 17–42.

Omair, A.A. (2015). Selecting the appropriate study design for your research: Descriptive study designs. Journal of Health Specialties, 3, 153 - 156.

Organisation for Economic Cooperation and Development. (2019). Programa para la evaluación internacional de alumnos PISA 2018 - Resultados. https://www.oecd.org/pisa/publications/PISA2018_CN_MEX_Spanish.pdf

Pansiri, O. Nkobi and Gabatshwane T. Tsayang. (2017). "A Situational Analysis of Basic Literacy and Numeracy levels at early grade levels in Botswana." Background Report.

Park, R. (2014). Play, games and cognitive development: Late-nineteenth century and early-twentieth century medical, neurologists, psychologists and others already knew what they proclaim today. International Journal of the History of the Sport, 31(9). doi: 10.1080 / 09523367.2013.877448

Park, S., & Holloway, S. D. (2013). No Parent Left Behind: Predicting Parental Involvement in Adolescents' Education Within a Sociodemographically Diverse Population. The Journal of Educational Research, 106(2), 105–119. https://doi.org/10.1080/00220671.2012.667012

Payton, J., Weissberg, R.P., Durlak, J.A., Dymnicki, A.B., Taylor, R.D., Schellinger, K.B., & Pachan, M. (2008). The positive impact of social and emotional learning for kindergarten to eighth-grade students: Findings from three scientific reviews. Chicago, IL: Collaborative for Academic, Social, and Emotional Learning.

Peters, D.H., Adam, T., Alonge, O., Agyepong, I.A. & Tran, N. (2013). Implementation Research: What It Is and How To Do It. British Medical Journal, 48(8):731-736.

Pihama, L., Lee-Morgan, J., Smith, L.T., Tiakiwai, S.J. And Seed-Pihama, J. (2019). MAI Te Kupenga: Supporting Māori and Indigenous Doctoral Scholars within Higher Education. AlterNative: An International Journal of Indigenous Peoples, vol. 15, no. 1, pp. 52-61. Available from: https://doi.org/10.1177/1177180119828065 ISSN 1177-1801. DOI 10.1177/1177180119828065.

Piper, B., Destefano, J., Kinyanjui, E. M., & Ong'ele, S. (2018). Scaling up successfully: Lessons from Kenya's Tusome national literacy program. Journal of Educational Change, 19(3), 293–321. https://doi.org/10.1007/s10833-018-9325-4

Plato, & Cornford, F. M. (1945). The Republic of Plato. London: Oxford University Press.

Portillo, S., Castellanos, L., Reynoso, O., & Gavotto, O. (2020). Enseñanza remota de emergencia ante la pandemia Covid-19 en Educación Media Superior y Educación Superior. Propósitos y Representaciones, 8, 1-27.doi:10.20511/pyr2020.v8nSPE3.589

Portillo, S., Reynoso, O., & Castellanos, L. I. (2020). El inicio de un nuevo ciclo escolar en México ante el Covid-19. Comparativo entre contextos rural y urbano. Conrado, 16(77). http://scielo.sld.cu/scielo.php?script=sci_arttext&pid=S1990-86442020000600218&lng=es&tlng=es

Postero, N.G. (2007). Now We are Citizens: Indigenous Politics in Postmulticultural Bolivia. Stanford, CA: Stanford University Press.

Potter, H., Cooper, L. (2016). Project Whitestreaming: a Report on the Generalising of Māori Specialist Staff Positions in the Tertiary Education Sector. Wellington: Tertiary Education Union.

Power, T., Wilson, D., Best, O., Brockie, T., Bearskin, L. B., Millender, E., & Lowe, J. (2020). COVID-19 and Indigenous Peoples: an Imperative for Action. Journal of clinical nursing.

Pratham Education Foundation [Pratham], & Abdul Latif Jameel Poverty Action Lab. (2019). Teaching at the Right Level: Evidence [versión web]. https://www.teachingattherightlevel.org/evidence/

Pratham Education Foundation. (2016). Concept Note – Combined Activities for Maximized Learning (CAMaL). http://img.asercentre.org/docs/Capacity%20building/Kamaal%20ke%20Shikshak/camalconceptnote.pdf

Pratham Education Foundation. (2017). Pratham. Every child in school & learning well [versión web]. http://www.pratham.org

Pratham Education Foundation. (2018). Quién, qué y cómo. [Blog]. http://www.pratham.org/about-us/about-pratham

Presidency of the Republic of Mexico. (2019). Plan Nacional de Desarrollo 2019-2024 [versión web]. Recuperado de https://lopezobrador. org.mx/wp-content/uploads/2019/05/PLAN-NACIONAL-DE-DESARROLLO-2019-2024.pdf

Prince, M., Tenorio, G. & Ramírez, M. (2016). Educational innovation and digital competencies: the case of OER in a private Venezuelan university. International Journal of Educational Technology, 13 (10).

Pritchett, L. (2013). The Rebirth of Education: Schooling Ain't Learning. Center for Global Development.

Pritchett, L. (2015). Creating Education Systems Coherent for Learning Outcomes. RISE Working Paper Series.15/005. https://doi.org/10.35489/BSG-RISE-WP_2015/005

Programme d'analyse des systèmes éducatifs de la confemen (PASEC). (2014). "PASEC2014 Education System Performance in Francophone Sub-Saharan Africa – competencies and learning factors in primary education." Accessed January 11, 2019. http://www.pasec.confemen.org/wp-content/uploads/2015/12/Rapport_Pasec2014_GB_webv2.pdf

Quam D. J.K., 2016. The Publication Gap: Western Bias in Educational Psychology Journals. Medium.

Radner, J. M., Ferrer, M. J. S., Mcmahon, D., Black, F. D. B., Shankar, A. H., & Silver, K. L. (2018). Practical Considerations for Transitioning Early Childhood Development Interventions to Scale: A Saving Brains Portfolio Analysis. Annals of the New York Academy of Sciences. https://nyaspubs.onlinelibrary.wiley.com/doi/10.1111/nyas.13684
Raikes, Yoshikawa, Rebello Britto, & Iruka. (2017). Children, Youth and Developmental Science in the 2015–2030 Global Sustainable Development Goals. In Social Policy Report.

Ramey, C. T., & Ramey, S. L. (2004). Early Learning and School Readiness: Can Early Intervention Make a Difference? Merrill-Palmer Quarterly, 50(4), 471–491. https://doi.org/10.1353/mpq.2004.0034

Ramírez-Sánchez, N. A., Díaz-Murillo, M. P., Reyes, P., & Cueca-González, O. (2011). Educación lúdica: una opción dentro de la educación ambiental en salud. Seguimiento de una experiencia rural colombiana sobre las geohelmintiasis. Revista Med, 19(1).

Reimers, F., & Schleicher, A. (2020). Aprendiendo durante la pandemia: De la disrupción a la innovación. Chipre: OECD. https://globaled.gse.harvard.edu/files/geii/files/aprendiendo_durante_la_pandemia_v2-2.pdf

Reininger, T., & Santana López, A. (2017). Parental involvement in municipal schools in Chile: Why do parents choose to get involved? School Psychology International, 38(4), 363–379. https://doi.org/10.1177/0143034317695378

Renganathan, S., & Kral, I. (2018). Exploring Language and Education Policies for the Indigenous Minorities in Australia and Malaysia. International Journal of Multicultural Education, 20(1), 138-156.

Reynolds, A. J. (1992). Comparing measures of parental involvement and their effects on academic achievement. Early Childhood Research Quarterly, 7(3), 441–462. https://doi.org/10.1016/0885-2006(92)90031-S

Richter, L., Black, M., Britto, P., Daelmans, B., Desmond, C., Devercelli, A., Dua, T., Fink, G., Heymann, J., Lombardi, J., Lu, C., Naicker, S., & Vargas-Barón, E. (2019). Early childhood development: an imperative for action and measurement at scale. BMJ Global Health, 4(Suppl 4), e001302. https://doi.org/10.1136/bmjgh-2018-001302

Right fit evidence unit (innovations for poverty Action). Teaching at the Right Level (PEC) Company Partner/J-Pal. Evaluation report. Prepared by Innovation for Poverty Action's Right-Fit Evidence Unit

Robinson, J. P., Winthrop, R., & McGivney, E. (2016). Millions Learning: Scaling up Quality Education in Developing Countries. Washington: Center for Universal Education at The Brookings Institution.

Robinson, J. P. & Winthrop, R (2016). Millions Learning; Scaling up Quality Education in Developing Countries. SSRN Electronic Journal. https://www.br.ookings.edu/wp-content/uploads/2016/04/FINAL-Millions-Learning-Report-1.pdf.

Rockoff, J. E. (2004). "The Impact of Individual Teachers on Student Achievement: Evidence from Panel Data." American Economic Review 94 (2): 247–52.

Rodriguez-Segura, D. and Mbiti, I. (2022). Back to the Basics: Curriculum Reform and Student Learning in Tanzania. RISE Working

Paper Series. 22/099. https://doi.org/10.35489/BSG-RISE-WP_2022/099

Rodriguez-Segura, D. and Mbiti, I. 2022. Back to the Basics: Curriculum Reform and Student Learning in Tanzania. RISE Working Paper Series. 22/099. https://doi.org/10.35489/BSG-RISE-WP_2022/099

Rose, P. (2020, April 7). Rethinking education in the time of COVID-19: What can we contribute as researchers? Retrieved from UKFIET: https://www.ukfiet.org/2020/rethinking-education-in-the-time-of-covid-19-what-can-we-contribute-as-researchers/#comments

Rose, P. (2020, April 7). Rethinking Education in the time of COVID-19: What Can We Contribute as Researchers? The Education and Development Forum (UKFIET). https://www.ukfiet.org/2020/rethinking-education-in-the-time-of-covid-19-what-can-we-contribute-as-researchers/

Roser, M., & Ortiz-Ospina, E. (2013). Primary and Secondary Education. Our World in Data. https://ourworldindata.org/primary-and-secondary-education

Rusbult, C. E. and Van Lange, P. A. M (2008). Why we need interdependence theory. Social and Personality Psychology Compass, 2(5), 2049–2070. Doi: 10.1111/j.1751-9004.2008.00147.

Sabarwal, S., Evans, D. K., & Marshak, A. (2014). The Permanent Input Hypothesis: The Case of Textbooks and (no) Student Learning in Sierra Leone. The World Bank. https://doi.org/10.1596/1813-9450-7021

Sabates, R., & Carter, E. (2020). Estimating learning loss by looking at time away from school during grade transition in Ghana | The Education and Development Forum.

Sabates, R., Carter, E., & Stern, J. M. B. (2021). Using educational transitions to estimate learning loss due to COVID-19 school closures: The case of Complementary Basic Education in Ghana. International Journal of Educational Development, 82, 102377. https://doi.org/10.1016/j.ijedudev.2021.102377

Saldaña, J. (2009). The coding manual for qualitative researchers (2nd ed). SAGE.

Sampson, R., Johnson, D., Somanchi, A., Barton, H., Joshi, R., Seth, M., & Shotland, M. (2019). The EdTech Lab Series: Insights from rapid evaluations of EdTech products. IDinsight and Central Square Foundation.

Saran, A., Albright, K., Adona, J.& White, H (2020). Mega-Map of Studies Shows Large but Unevenly Distributed Research Base on Child Well-Being in Low- and Middle-Income Countries. Campbell Systematic Review. Saving Brains Learning Platform (2019). Government Partnerships. https://www.savingbrainslearning.com/scaling-government-partnerships

Savitz, D. A., Wellenius, G. A., & Trikalinos, T. A. (2019). The Problem with Mechanistic Risk of Bias Assessments in Evidence Synthesis of Observational Studies and a Practical Alternative: Assessing the Impact of Specific Sources of Potential Bias. American Journal of Epidemiology, 188(9):1581-5.

Sayer, L. C., Bianchi, S. M., & Robinson, J. P. (2004). Are Parents Investing Less in Children? Trends in Mothers' and Fathers' Time with Children. American Journal of Sociology, 110(1), 1–43. https://doi.org/10.1086/386270

Secretariat of Public Education. (2019). La Nueva Escuela Mexicana: principios y orientaciones pedagógicas [versión web]. https://dfa.edomex.gob.mx/sites/dfa.edomex.gob.mx/files/files/NEM%20principios%20y%20orientacio%C3%ADn%20pedago%C3%ADgica.pdf

Secretariat of Public Education. (2020). Aprende en Casa II [versión web]. https://aprendeencasa.sep.gob.mx/

Secretariat of Public Education. (2021). Visión y Misión de la SEP [versión web]. https://www.gob.mx/sep/acciones-y-programas/vision-y-mision-de-la-sep?state=published

Selden, S. C., Sowa, J. E., & Sandfort, J. (2006). The impact of non-profit collaboration in early childcare and education on management and program outcomes. Public Administration Review, 66(3), 412–425.

Shah, R. (2019). Transforming Systems in Times of Adversity: Education and Resilience. Office of Education. USAID.

Sharma S. (2010). How to Become a Competent Medical Writer. Perspective in Clinical Research, 1:33-37.

Shumow, L., & Lomax, R. (2002). Parental Efficacy: Predictor of Parenting Behavior and Adolescent Outcomes. Parenting, 2(2), 127–150. https://doi.org/10.1207/S15327922PAR0202_03

Siddiqui, N. (2020, July 15). Adapting to the new normal in survey research. BERA. https://www.bera.ac.uk/blog/adapting-to-the-new-normal-in-survey-research

Sigsgaard, M. (2011). On the road to resilience: capacity development with the Ministry of Education in Afghanistan.

Siliezar J., 2020. Joseph Henrich Explores WEIRD societies. Harvard Gazette.

Singh, R., Sharma, N., & Verma, K. (2017). Learning and Evolving in Hybrid Learning: A PAR Perspective. In: Kidwai, H., Iyengar, R., Witenstein, M., Byker, E., Setty, R. (eds) Participatory Action Research and Educational Development (pp. 161-183). Palgrave Macmillan, Cham. https://doi.org/10.1007/978-3-319-48905-6_7

Singh, U. N., Singh, R. & Banerjee, P. (2020). 'Learning challenges for the marginalised: Opportunities within the heterogeneous landscape of India.' Lecture at LBOP2: Applying Research to Policy and Practice, Virtual Invitational Conference, 7-8 December; Country Case Studies, IIEP-UNESCO.

Sinha, D. K, (2015) McClelland's Need for Achievement Theory.

Sinha, D. K., (2015) McClelland's Need for Achievement Theory. Retrieved on September 15, 2017.

Sonn, C., Bishop, B., & Humphries, R. (2000). Encounters with the Dominant Culture: Voices of Indigenous Students in Mainstream Higher Education. Australian psychologist, 35(2), 128-135.

Sonnenwald, D. H. (2007). Scientific collaboration. Annual Review of Information Science and Technology, 41(1): 643–681.

Southern and Eastern Africa Consortium for Monitoring Educational Quality (SACMEQ) (2010)."What are the levels and trends in grade repetition?" SACMEQ Policy Issue Series available from www.sacmeq.org, 2010.

Sparapani, E. F., Perez, D. C., Gould, J., Hillman, S., & Clark, L. (2014, April- June). A Global Curriculum? Understanding Teaching and Learning in the United States, Taiwan, India, and Mexico. SAGE Open, 1– 15.

Spivack, M. (2021). Applying Systems Thinking to Education: The RISE Systems Framework. https://riseprogramme.org/publications/applying-systems-thinking-education-risesystems-framework

Stefani, G. Andrés, L., & Oanes, E. (2014). Transformaciones lúdicas. Un estudio preliminar sobre tipos de juego y espacios lúdicos. Interdisciplinaria, 31(1), 39-55

Strauss, A. L. (1993). Continual Permutations of Action. New York: Aldine de Gruyter.

Suárez, J., Maiz, F., & Meza, M. (2010). Inteligencias múltiples: una innovación pedagógica para potenciar el proceso enseñanza aprendizaje. Investigación y Posgrado, 25(1), 81-94. https://www.redalyc.org/pdf/658/65822264005.pdf

Sui-Chu, E. H., & Willms, J. D. (1996). Effects of Parental Involvement on Eighth-Grade Achievement. Sociology of Education, 69(2), 126. https://doi.org/10.2307/2112802

Sutherland, W. J. & Wordley, C. F. R. (2018). A Fresh Approach to Evidence Synthesis. Nature, 558.

Tan, C. Y., Lyu, M., & Peng, B. (2020). Academic Benefits from Parental Involvement are Stratified by Parental Socio-economic Status: A Meta-analysis. Parenting, 20(4), 241–287. https://doi.org/10.1080/15295192.2019.1694836

TaRLAfrica (2023) https://www.teachingattherightlevel.org/research-and-learning/evidence/

Taylor, J. (2018). Short-Term Indigenous Population Mobility and Service Delivery.

Taylor, J., & Bell, M. (2018). Changing Places: Indigenous Population Movement in the 1990s. Canberra, ACT: Centre for Aboriginal Economic Policy Research (CAEPR), The Australian National University.

Taylor, J., Gray, M., Yap, M., Lahn, J., & Hunter, B. (2018). Higher Education and the Growth of Indigenous Participation in Professional and Managerial Occupations.

Tazouti, Y., & Jarlégan, A. (2019). The mediating effects of parental self-efficacy and parental involvement on the link between family socio-economic status and children's academic achievement. Journal of Family Studies, 25(3), 250–266. https://doi.org/10.1080/13229400.2016.1241185

The Lego Foundation, in Support of UNICEF (2018) Learning Through play

The Royal Society, Academy of Medical Sciences 2018). Evidence Synthesis for Policy: A Statement of Principles. https://royalsociety.org/-/media/policy/projects/evidence-synthesis/evidence-synthesis-statement-principles.pdf.

The World Bank. Global Education Evidence Advisory Panel (2020). Cost-Effective Approaches to Improve Global Learning: What Does Recent Evidence Tell Us Are "Smart Buys" for Improving Learning in Low-and Middle-Income Countries? https://www.worldbank.org/en/topic/teachingandlearning/publication/cost-effective-approaches-to-improve-global-learning.

The World Bank. Global Education Evidence Advisory Panel (n.d.). https://www.worldbank.org/en/topic/teachingandlearning/brief/global-education-evidence-advisory-paneltheory/40683/urship/motivation

Tröhler, D., Popkewitz, T. S., & Labaree, D. F. (2011). Schooling and the making of citizens in the long nineteenth century: Comparative visions (Vol. 57). Routledge. https://doi.org/10.4324/9780203818053

Uganda National NGO Forum (UNNGOF) (2018). State of Civil Society Report 2018. Kampala: UNNGOF.

UIS. (2017). Fact Sheet No. 46 (UIS/FS/2017/ED/46): More Than One-Half of Children and Adolescents Are Not Learning Worldwide. UNESCO Institute for Statistics.

Ulnicane, I. (2015). Why do international research collaborations last? Virtuous circle of feedback loops, continuity, and renewal. Science and Public Policy, 42(4): 433–447. https://doi.org/10.1093/scipol/scu060

UNESCO IIEP. (2015). Overview: incorporating safety, resilience, and social cohesion in education sector planning. UNESCO IIEP, UNESCO International Bureau of Education, Education Above All (Qatar).

UNESCO Institute for Statistics (UIS). (2006). Teachers and Educational Quality: Monitoring Global Needs for 2015. Montreal: UIS

UNESCO Institute for Statistics (UIS). (2017). More Than One-Half of Children and Adolescents are Not Learning Worldwide. UIS Fact Sheet No. 46. Montreal: UIS

UNESCO Institute for Statistics (UIS). (2018). Data to Nurture Learning. SDG 4 Data Digest 2018. Montreal: UIS.

UNESCO Institute for Statistics. (2019). SDG 4 Data Digest. How to Produce and Use the Global and Thematic Education Indicators (UIS/2019/ED/SD/2) [versión web]. http://uis.unesco.org/sites/default/files/documents/sdg4-data-digest-2019-en_0.pdf

UNESCO International Bureau of Education (Geneva), "Pakistan: Early childhood care and education (ECCE) programmes," Education for All Global Monitoring Report 2007, 2006.

UNESCO. (2015). DME WIDE • World Inequality Database on Education. http://www.education-inequalities.org/

UNESCO. (2018). SDG4 Data Digest. Data to Nurture Learning. UNESCO Institute for Statistics. UNESCO. (2020). COVID-19 Impact on Education. Retrieved from https://en.unesco.org/covid19/educationresponse/

UNESCO. (2022a). Declarations. UNESCO. https://en.unesco.org/about-us/legal-affairs/instruments/declarations

UNESCO. (2022b). Global Monitoring of School Closures caused by COVID-19 Pandemic – Dashboards – Covid-19 Response. https://covid19.uis.unesco.org/global-monitoring-school-closures-covid19/

UNICEF (2020). Data Must Speak: Country Initiatives. https://www.unicef.org/education/data-must-speak-country-initiatives

United Nations (2015). The Millenium Development Goals Report. Cited in https://www.un.org/millenniumgoals/2015_MDG_Report/pdf/backgrounders/MDG%202015%20PR%20Bg%20SSA.pdf

United Nations Children's Fund (2019), Guidelines for Adapting the Foundational Learning Module to Non-Multiple Indicator Cluster Household Surveys, UNICEF, New York, August 2019.

United Nations Children's Fund. (2018). Aprendizaje a través del juego. Nueva York, USA: UNICEF.

United Nations Educational, Scientific and Cultural Organization. (2014). Innovación. Educativa. Serie Herramientas de apoyo para el trabajo docente. http://www.cne.gob.pe/images/stories/cnepublicaciones/AvancesPEN.pdf.

United Nations. (2020), Policy Brief: Education during COVID-19 and beyond. https://www.un.org/development/desa/dspd/wp-content/uploads/sites/22/2020/08/sg_policy_brief_covid-19_and_education_august_2020.pdf

United Nations. (2022). SDG 4.1.1 Measurement Tools—Applications in the Wake of COVID-19 | Education within the 2030 Agenda for Sustainable Development. https://www.sdg4education2030.org/sdg-411-measurement-tools-applications-wake-covid-19

URT, Ministry of Education and Vocational Training (2014). Education and Training Policy 2014. Dar es Salaam: MoEVT.

USAID, UKAID, and the Zambian Government (2015), "Proposing Benchmarks and Targets for Early Grade Reading and Mathematics in Zambia."

Uwezo (2014): Are Our Children Learning? Literacy and Numeracy in Uganda 2014. Kampala: Twaweza East Africa.

Uwezo (2016) "Are Our Children Learning?" Uwezo Kenya Sixth Learning Assessment Report. Twaweza East Africa. Accessed October 24, 2018.

Uwezo (2017): Are Our Children Learning? Uwezo Tanzania Sixth Learning Assessment Report. Dar es Salaam: Twaweza East Africa.

Uwezo (2019) "Are Our Children Learning?" Uwezo Tanzania Learning Assessment Report. Dar es Salaam: Twaweza East Africa.

Uwezo (2019) Are Our Children Learning? Uwezo Uganda Eighth Learning Assessment Report. Kampala: Twaweza East Africa.

Uwezo (2021): Are All Our Children Learning? Uwezo 7th Learning Assessment Report. Nairobi: Usawa Agenda.

Uwezo Uganda (2020) Promoting Equitable Quality Education in East Africa: Uwezo Uganda Adapted Strategy (2020-23). Kampala: Uwezo Uganda.

Velásquez-Durán, A., Hevia, F. J. & Vergara-Lope, S. (2021). Improvement in Basic Learning through the Scaling Up of Educational Innovations. En Ishamel I. Munene (Ed.), Ensuring all Children Learn: Lessons on Inclusion and Equity from the South (pp.183-200). Lexington Books. ISBN: 978-1793636270.

Velásquez-Durán, A., Hevia, F. J., & Vergara-Lope, S. (2020). Innovaciones educativas para mejorar aprendizajes básicos. Reporte de investigación. México: CIESAS.

Vergara-Lope, S. (2018). Aprendizajes básicos y factores asociados en niños y niñas de Veracruz: Primeros resultados de la Medición Independiente de Aprendizajes (MIA). Revista Interaméricana de Educación de Adultos, 40(2), 43-78.

Vergara-Lope, S., & Hevia, F. J. (2018). Rezago en aprendizajes básicos: El elefante en la sala de la reforma educativa. En A. Martínez & A. Navarro Arredondo (Eds.), Qué podemos reformar de la Reforma educativa: Una mirada sobre sus principales alcances y retos (pp. 45–66). Instituto Belisario Domínguez. Senado de la República.

Vergara-Lope, S., & Hevia, F. J. (2018). Rezago en aprendizajes básicos: El elefante en la sala de la reforma educativa. En A. Martínez & A. Navarro Arredondo (Eds.), Qué podemos reformar de la Reforma educativa: Una mirada sobre sus principales alcances y retos. México: Instituto Belisario Domínguez. Senado de la República.

Veriava, F., Thom, A., & Fish, H. T. (2017). Basic education rights handbook: Education rights in South Africa.

Waanders, C., Mendez, J. L., & Downer, J. T. (2007). Parent characteristics, economic stress, and neighborhood context as predictors of parent involvement in preschool children's education. Journal of School Psychology, 45(6), 619–636. https://doi.org/10.1016/j.jsp.2007.07.003

Wadhwa, W. (2020, June 11). Foundational learning a vital need, in India and worldwide. Deccan Chronicle(https://www.deccanchronicle.com/opinion/columnists/110720/wilima-wadhwa-foundational-learning-a-vital-need-in-india-and-world.html).

Wadhwa, W. (2021, January 27). Children from economically weaker backgrounds have fallen behind as classes shifted to the digital mode. Retrieved from indianexpress.com: https://indianexpress.com/article/opinion/columns/coronavirus-pandemic-schools-shut-india-online-classes-7162807/

Wagner, D. A., & Castillo, N. M. (2014). Learning at the bottom of the pyramid: Constraints, comparability, and policy in developing countries. Prospects, (44), 627–638.

Walker, J. and Baboo, N. (2020). Global report - Leave No Child Behind: Invest in the early years. Light for the world.

Walpole, R. E., & Myers, R. H. (1996). Probabilidad y Estadística. México: McGraw-Hill.

Wangia, J. I., Bunyi, G. W., Magoma, C. M., & Limboro, C. M. (2013). Learning to Teach Reading and Mathematics and Influences on Practice: A Study of Teacher Education in Kenya. Brighton, UK: University of Sussex, Centre for International Education.

Waxman, H. C., Gray, J. P., & Padron, Y. N. (2003). Review of Research on Educational Resilience. UC Berkeley: Center for Research on Education, Diversity and Excellence.

Wetterberg, A., & Gove, A. (2011). The Early Grade Reading Assessment: Applications and Interventions to Improve Basic Literacy.

White H. (2018) Must Try Harder: Policy Influence from Campbell Reviews. https://campbellcollaboration.org/blog/must-try-harder-policy-influence-from-campbell-reviews.html

White, H., Albers, B., Gaarder M, Kornør, H., Littell, J., Marshall, Z., Mathew, C., Pigott, T., Snilstveit, B., Waddington, H. & Welch, V (2020). Guidance for Producing a Campbell Evidence and Gap Map. Campbell Systematic Review, 16.

Winthrop, R. and McGivney, E. (2015). Why wait 100 years? Bridging the gap in Global Education. The Brookings Institution, June 2015. Retrieved from https://www.google.com/url?sa=i&rct=j&q=&esrc=s&source=web&cd=&cad=rja&uact=8&ved=0CAQQw7AJahcKEwigwoCS04z8AhUAAAAAHQAAAAAQAw&url=https%3A%2F%2Fwww.brookings.edu%2Fresearch%2Fwhy-wait-100-years-bridging-the-gap-in-global-education%2F&psig=AOvVaw0bPJ8sv1uie6kSt7woCR5X&ust=1671778707123416

World Bank, UNESCO, & UNICEF. (2021). The State of the Global Education Crisis: A Path to Recovery. The World Bank; UNESCO; UNICEF.

World Bank. (2018). Learning to realise education's promise (p. 239) [World Development Report 2018]. The World Bank.

World Bank. (2019). Ending Learning Poverty: What Will it Take? World Bank. (2019). Mexico. Learning Poverty Brief. World Bank. https://www.

worldbank.org/en/topic/education/brief/learning-poverty

World Bank. (2019, November 8). Ending Learning Poverty: A Target to Galvanise Action on Literacy. Retrieved from https://www.worldbank.org/en/news/immersive-story/2019/11/06/a-learning-target-for-a-learning-revolution

World Bank. (2019, October 15). Learning Poverty. Retrieved from worldbank.org: https://www.worldbank.org/en/topic/education/brief/learning-poverty (Link does not take to the intended page.)

World Bank. (2019a). Ending Learning Poverty: What will it take? World Bank. World Bank. (2019b). Learning Poverty [Text/HTML]. World Bank. https://www.worldbank.org/en/topic/education/brief/learning-poverty

World Bank. (2020). The COVID-19 Pandemic : Shocks to Education and Policy Responses. Washington, DC: World Bank.

World Bank. (2021). Realising the Future of Learning. From Learning Poverty to Learning for Everyone, Everywhere. World Bank.

World Bank. (2022). The State of Global Learning Poverty: 2022 Update.

World Economic Forum. (2020). Schools of the Future: Defining New Models of Education for the Fourth Industrial Revolution. World Economic Forum.

Writer, L. M. H. S. (2022, May 5). Remote learning likely widened racial, economic achievement gap. https://news.harvard.edu/gazette/story/2022/05/remote-learning-likely-widened-racial-economic-achievement-gap/

Wu, Y. (2018). Behavioural interdependence in project team collaboration: A study of engineering students' collaborative behaviours in high levels of interdependent task settings (Dissertations – ALL 883) [Doctoral dissertation, Syracuse University]

Yadav, M. K. (2014). Role of Mother Tongue in Second Language Learning. International Journal of Research, 1(11), 572-582.

Yamaguchi, I. (2003). The relations among individual differences, needs, and equity sensitivity. Journal of Managerial Psychology, 18(4), 324–344

Zubairi, M., & Rose, M. (2017). Bright and Early: How Financing Pre-Primary Education Gives Every Child a Fair Start in Life. In Theirworld (UK).

ABBREVIATIONS

COVID-19	Corona Virus Disease 2019
PAL	People's Action for Learning Network
SDGs	Sustainable Development Goals
ASER	Annual Status of Education Report
ICAN	Instrument for Classification and Assessment Needs
ELTU	Every Language Teaches Us
UNESCO	The United Nations Educational, Scientific and Cultural Organization
UNICEF	United Nations Children's Fund
CAMaL	Combined Activities for Maximized Learning
CIESAS	Centro de Investigaciones y Estudios Superiores en Antropología Social
MIA	Medición Independente de Aprendizajes
MDGs	Millennium Development Goals
UN	United Nations
UIS	UNESCO Institute for Statistics
WDR	World Development Report
FPE	Free Primary Education
ECDE	Early Childhood Development and Education
TaRL	Teaching at the Right Level
TCAI	Teacher Community Assistants Initiative
STARS	Strengthening Teaching- Learning and Results for States

NEM	Nueva Escuela Mexicana
PISA	Programme for International Student Assessment
OECD	Organisation for Economic Co-operation and Development
PLANEA	Plan Nacional para la Evaluación de los Aprendizajes
INEE	Inter-agency Network for Education in Emergencies
SES	Socio-economic status
REAL Centre	Research for Equitable Access and Learning Centre
DISE	District Information System for Education
SMC	School Management Committee
OLS	Ordinary Least Squares
MELQO	Measuring Early Learning and Quality Outcomes
ARNEC	Asia-Pacific Regional Network for Early Childhood
ELP	Early Learning Partnership
ECCE	Early Childhood Care and Education
SED	Special Education Department
MODEL	Measure of Development and Early Learning
PPS	Probability Proposal to Size
DEA	District Education Authority
CFM	Child Functioning Module
PMIU	Programme Monitoring and Implementation Unit
CEO	Chief Executive Officer
AEOs	Assistant Education Officers
FGD	Focus Group Discussion
PEC	Programme d'Enseignement Ciblé
QAED	Quaid-e-Azam Academy for Educational Development
PRIMR	Primary Math and Reading
EGRA	Early Grade Reading Assessment

EGMA	Early Grade Mathematics Assessment
PISA	OECD's Programme for International Student Assessment
CSEA	Centre for the Study of the Economies of Africa
SMERU	Social Monitoring and Early Response Unit
INOVASI	Innovation for Indonesia's School Children
RTI	Research Triangle Institute
CIASES	Centro de Investigación y Acción Educativa Social
ADEA	Association for the Development of Education in Africa
GDP	Gross Domestic Product
OTT	Over the Top
NCERT	National Council of Educational Research and Training
EAA	Education Above All
SSA	Sarva Shiksha Abhiyan
NEP 2020	National Education Policy 2020
LMICs	Low- and Middle-Income Countries
HICs	High-Income Countries
CREFAL	Center for Regional Cooperation for Adult Education in Latin America and the Caribbean
CLAs	Citizen-led Assessments
PraDigi	Pratham Digital
CERQual	Confidence in the Evidence from Reviews of Qualitative Research
NNA	In the Spanish language, the acronym NNA is an inclusive term to refer to children and adolescents. NNA is used to refer to children in Mexico
ISKME	Institute for the Study of Knowledge Management in Education
OERs	Open Educational Resources
IIEP	International Institute for Education Planning
DMS	Data Must Speak

MBSSE	Ministry of Basic and Senior Secondary Education
JLN	Joint Learning Network for Universal Health Coverage
AfECN	Africa Early Childhood Network
ECD	Early Childhood Development
ARNEC	Asia-Pacific Regional Network for Early Childhood
ANECD	Arab Network for Early Childhood
ISSA	International Step by Step Association
NGO	Non-governmental Orgnaisation
CSOs	Civil Society Organisations
OVC	Orphans and Vulnerable Children
VAC	Violence Against Children
PTA	Parent-Teacher Association
SMC	School Management Committee
CHAL	This is coding used in the paper for Challenge
MOT	This is coding used in the paper for Motivation
SUS	This is coding used in the paper for Sustainability
ID	This is coding used in the paper for Interdependence
UR	This is just coding used in the paper for continuous unlearning and relearning
JO	This is coding used in the paper for joint ownership of the collaboration processes, outputs, and outcomes
TT24	Coded name of a participant who was quoted
TT9	Coded name of a different participant who was quoted

ANNEXURES

Annexure I: Interview Schedule for Representatives of District-Level CSOs

Name of CSO:_____Name of interviewer:_____
District:_____Date of interview:_____

Name of informant:_____

[The interview has been arranged in advance by telephone or email, and it has been explained that the personal identities of informants will not be used in the reporting. Organisations would only be named with permission in the reporting.]

Introductory statement
Good Morning / Afternoon. Thank you for agreeing to take part in this interview. My name is ….. and I am a member of staff of Uwezo Uganda, based in Kampala. We are conducting this small research project so as to be better informed about the civil society organisations that work with us at district level, especially in our assessments. By learning from you, we hope to improve the way we collaborate with you. This interview will probably take 30-40 minutes. May we begin?

Questions

1. Please tell me a little about [name of the organisation]. When was it established and for what purposes? [Prompt as necessary to find out whether the CSO provides any services as well as doing advocacy.]
2. How does the work of your organisation relate to education? [Prompt if necessary to see how it relates to primary education.]
3. What educational problems do you see as being important for the advocacy that you do and [if applicable] the services you provide? [Prompt if necessary on issues such as children's access to education, conditions in schools and the results of education]
4. What kinds of advocacy do you engage in within the district? [Specify the name of the district: the one in which they have helped with Uwezo assessments.]
5. How is your organisation managed? Please describe the structure.
6. Does the organisation have a formal membership? [If so] Are the members individuals or groups and how does one become a member?
7. How are your activities funded? How continuous is the funding?
8. Have you and other representatives been able to discuss educational problems with the district educational authorities? [If so] Have the discussions produced the results that you hoped for?
9. Has your organisation been able to influence the management and work of particular schools in the district? How do you interact with schools? [Prompt as necessary on whether they are represented on SMCs and/or work through PTAs.]

10. Does your district have an NGO Monitoring Committee? [If so] Is your organisation represented and active in, the Committee?
11. Does your organisation collaborate with other NGOs or CSOs (other than Uwezo) on educational issues within the district? [If so] How effective is the collaboration?
12. Has the link with Uwezo been helpful for your advocacy and research? (Please refer especially to the past five years.)
13. Have you been able to use the results of the 2018 Assessment for your advocacy within the district? And those of previous assessments [if applicable]? [If necessary probe for more details on how they were used]
14. Your organisation provided volunteers for Uwezo's national assessment in 2018. Has that experience of the assessment process been helpful for your work?
15. Are there any ways in which you would like the link with Uwezo to be improved or developed?
16. Does your staff have specific training needs that Uwezo may be able to help with? [If so] During the restrictions due to Covid-19, would they be able to take part in online training?
17. After we have completed these interviews, we plan to construct a questionnaire on the issues and send it to CSO representatives. Are you willing to receive and complete the questionnaire on behalf of your organisation? [If so] Please provide an alternative email address at which you can be contacted.

Annexure II: Questionnaire for Representatives of District-Level CSOs CSO details (These will not be used in reporting.)

Name of your organisation:_____

District in which you assisted Uwezo in the 2018 Assessment:_____

Section A. Organisational Characteristics

What are the main functions of your CSO? Please put X in the boxes on the right to show ALL items that apply.	
Provision of welfare services to families and communities.	
Managing schools and/or early childhood (ECD) centres.	
Advocacy on various social issues, some being educational.	
Advocacy on educational issues only.	
Coordination with a group of CSOs.	
Other (specify)	
In how many districts does your CSO work? (Put the number in the box.)	
How many full-time employees does your CSO have? (Put the number in the box.)	
What types of source of funding does the CSO have? Please put X in the boxes to show ALL items that apply.	
Grants from within Uganda.	
Grants from outside Uganda.	
Consultancy fees.	
Membership fees.	
Donations.	
Sales of goods or produce.	
Provision of services	
Renting of property.	
Other (specify)	
What types of membership does the CSO have? Please put X in the boxes to show ALL that apply.	
Individual membership.	
Organisational membership.	
No membership.	

Section B. Interaction on Educational Issues

1. The list below represents educational issues or concerns on which your CSO may have reported or intervened recently (within the past three years). Please put X in the boxes to show ALL items on which it has reported or intervened.

a.	School physical facilities.	
b.	School feeding.	
c.	Effectiveness of school management committees (SMCs).	
d.	Effectiveness of parent-teacher associations (PTAs).	
e.	School inspections/monitoring of schools.	
f.	Poor learning outcomes.	
g.	Disparities between schools.	
h.	Teacher appointments and transfers.	
i.	Teacher absenteeism.	
j.	Other teacher misconduct.	
k.	Pupil absenteeism and/or dropout.	
l.	Provision of learning materials.	
m.	Provision for children with disabilities and other special needs.	
n.	Support for the education of orphans and other vulnerable children.	
o.	Violence against children in school.	
p.	Molestation of female pupils.	
q.	Girls' menstrual hygiene.	
r.	Bursaries/costs of schooling to families.	
s.	Other (specify)	

2. Please indicate how far you agree with each of the following statements by putting X in the box for ONE alternative in the columns on the right, where SA = Strongly agree, A = Agree, N = Neutral, D = Disagree and SD = Strongly disagree.

Statement		SA	A	N	D	SD
a.	My CSO is able to interact with the District Education Officer on educational issues.					
b.	The district education authorities have taken action as a result of advocacy or reports by our CSO.					
c.	Insufficient funding has prevented the district authorities from making educational improvements that we have requested.					
d.	Our CSO has been able to interact with head teachers and school management committees (SMCs) on important issues.					
e.	Our CSO has been able to interact with parent-teacher associations (PTAs) on important issues.					
f.	Our attempts to influence head teachers, SMCs and/or PTAs have not resulted in the improvements we wanted.					

Section C. Collaboration with Other Organisations

3. Please put X in the boxes to show whether you agree or disagree with each of the following statements about collaboration by your CSO.

Statement		Agree	Disagree
a.	Our CSO collaborates with other CSOs in the district for advocacy purposes.		
b.	Collaboration with other CSOs makes our advocacy more effective.		
c.	We are member of a regional advocacy network.		
d.	We coordinate regional advocacy network.		
e.	We are members of a district advocacy network		
f.	We coordinate district advocacy network		

4. We wish to ask about your experience with Uwezo. Please indicate how far you agree with each of the following statements by putting X in the box for ONE alternative in the columns on the right, where SA = Strongly agree, A = Agree, N = Neutral, D = Disagree and SD = Strongly disagree.

Statement		SA	A	N	D	SD
a.	The findings of the Uwezo assessment of children's literacy and numeracy in 2018 and other years only told us things that we already knew.					
b.	The findings of the Uwezo assessment of children's literacy and numeracy in 2018 and other years have been useful for our advocacy in the district.					
c.	Our volunteers who assisted in the 2018 Uwezo assessment have continued to be useful for our work.					
d.	For financial reasons we have not made further use of the volunteers that we provided for the 2018 Uwezo assessment.					
e.	From the 2018 Uwezo assessment, we have made more use of the district findings than of the national findings.					

Section D. Views on Further Collaboration with Uwezo Uganda

5. Possible areas of collaboration are listed below. In each case, please put X in the box under 'Yes' or 'No' to show whether you think that collaboration between your CSO and Uwezo Uganda in that area would be useful in the future. (N.B. We cannot make any promise that such collaboration will be possible, but we would like to know your views.)

Area		Yes	No
a.	Further national assessments of children's literacy and numeracy.		
b.	Educational research in the district.		
c.	Research on cross-cutting social issues* in the district.		
d.	Educational advocacy in the district.		
e.	Advocacy on cross-cutting social issues in the district.		

* Examples of cross-cutting social issues are child welfare, family poverty, disability, gender issues, livelihood improvement and youth issues.

6. Please indicate the areas of further training for your staff to which you give priority by putting X in the box for 'high priority', 'low priority' or 'not needed' for each area listed. (Again, we cannot promise that Uwezo could assist.)

Area for training	High priority	Low priority	Not needed
a. Advocacy/communication methods			
b. Organisational management			
c. Research methods & data management			
d. Resource mobilisation			
e. Rights & protection of children			
f. Training on adopting online training			
g. Other (specify) …			

7. Would your staff members be able to attend training online? (Put X in the box for 'yes' or 'no'.)

Yes	No

Thank you for your time. We wish you success in your work.

If you have any additional comments, please use the space below.

EPILOGUE

By: Armando Ali, Chief Executive Officer (CEO), PAL Network

By bringing together different stories and reflections in the same work, PAL has become like itself: a space for sharing and building the voice of the Global South. This work is neither the beginning nor the end. It's one more step in raising the contributions of citizens, women and men, in solving the problem of poor learning in our children.

When in 2005 a group of mothers and fathers in India began to question whether our children are learning, we never thought it would take so long for us to be heard. That citizens' movement later spread to Africa and the Americas won many admirers and placed the issue of learning at the top of the world's priorities. In 2022, the United Nations adopted the Call for Action to Transform Education, which clearly recognises that millions of children in the world attend school but are not learning. This is an opportunity to thank the many people who have carried this cause, in particular, two women: Rukmini Banerji and Sara Ruto.

The story of this citizen's movement started in the late nineties when Rukmini had moved to Mumbai and wanted to work with children from the schools of the Mumbai municipal corporation. That did not work out perhaps because she was destined to "blend in" with Pratham, which was then a fledgling NGO started by Dr Madhav Chavan and Mrs Farida Lambay.

As Pratham worked to set up children's centres (balwadis in Hindi) in Mumbai, the team noticed that getting children to school was just part of the problem. The large enrolment in school was not translating into learning. Thus started the ASER exercise in 2005, a citizen-led assessment to find out how much children were actually learning in schools. With Rukmini at the helm, this first-of-its-kind exercise covered more than 600 rural districts in India that year.

The assessments not only brought into light the glaring lack of learning but also gave an opportunity to citizens and local actors and provided them with a role to do something about it. More than two decades later the exercise is covering more than 1 million children in India. The ASER surveys have now become important reference points that guide policies in education.

However, the assessments were only highlighting the problem, but an approach was needed to alleviate the situation. The answer was a simple and innovative approach - Teaching at the Right Level - pioneered by Rukmini at Pratham. Like all elegant solutions, it was brilliant in its simplicity —grouping children according to their learning levels and reinforcing foundational skills before they left primary school.

TaRL required nothing else but to use a different lens to see the problem. It is an approach that is now adopted in many countries across the world. And, if there is one person that this could be attributed to it is Sara Ruto.

Sara's journey in education started with academics. A teacher at Kenyatta University for fifteen years, her research work focused on primary education and school reform. Four years after the CLAs were started in India, Sara took up the initiative in Africa.

Her aim was to make sure that schooling meant that there were actual learning outcomes. Sara realised that hard evidence was needed to focus attention of the policymakers from enrolment to learning. This was the start of the citizen-led assessments in 2009 in Kenya, Tanzania and Uganda. A few years later, in 2016, the first TaRL programme took place in Africa. It was Sara's vision that led to the adapting of the TaRL programme to the African context. TaRL Africa is now an independent organisation working with the governments in Côte d'Ivoire, Kenya, Nigeria and Zambia.

She is the mother of the Uwezo and PAL Network which has taken south-south partnerships to innovations at the global scale, whether it is CLAs, Common Assessments, or Accelerated Learning Approaches.

It is the leadership and global vision of these two women that made possible the creation of this great family that is today called PAL Network. But, there is perhaps another secret ingredient that led them to successfully create initiatives of such a large scale, their empathy for children and a deep understanding of what learners really need.

These two are joined by many others such as Baela Jamil, Zaida Mgalla, Abdou Salam Fall, Emmanuel Manyasa, Mary Goretti Nakabugo and Felipe Hevia, who systematically questioned whether our children were learning. As we celebrate the global consensus on the current learning crisis, it is worth saying "thank you" to them for bringing to light a latent problem in the education system in the Global South.

I am pleased to note that this book talks more about possible avenues for resolving the current learning crisis. It talks about adapting innovative methodologies, involving mothers in education, preschool learning, the role that technology can play in learning and the need to change systems. This focus on solutions reflects the current concern of the PAL Network to find the best ways to make more children in the Global South to be able to read and do basic arithmetic, as a condition for them to learn more in life.

We are grateful to all those who contributed to this work by sharing their life lessons with the world. We are grateful to all the anonymous citizens who in various villages around the world have helped to assess children's learning and to teach others to read and do basic arithmetic. We are grateful to everyone who sat under the trees to agree with what to do to improve the learning of children in their village, province, or country. While we wait for further steps, let's celebrate the ones we've taken together.

We count on you for new battles on this long journey to make all children learn and prosper.

BOOK EDITORS

Baela Raza Jamil
Baela Raza Jamil is the CEO of Idara-e-Taleem-o-Aagahi (ITA), a centre for education and consciousness, as well as the founder of the Children's and Teacher's Literature Festivals in Pakistan. Baela has worked with provincial and federal governments as a technical advisor in the education sector, focusing on reforms, public-private partnerships, innovations, and financing. She leads the citizen-led assessment and accountability initiative, the Annual Status of Education Report (ASER) Pakistan, which triggered the creation of the CLF in 2011 due to the low learning outcomes of children. Baela aims to mobilize multiple allies to transform the Pakistan Learning Festival into a social movement that promotes reading, expression, and creativity as an equalizer. She serves as a Commissioner to the Education Commission and is associated with various global, regional, national, and provincial boards.

Felipe José Hevia de la Jara
Dr Felipe Hevia is a Professor at the 'Centro de Investigaciones y Estudios Superiores en Antropología Social' (CIESAS) in Mexico. He is involved in Mexico's citizen-led assessment – MIA. His research interests include the relationship between society and the state, citizen participation, accountability, social policy, and education in

Mexico and Latin America. Felipe's research has received awards and recognition from the governments of Mexico and Brazil, UNDP, the Latin American Council for Development, the International Network for Social Cohesion, and the University of Luxembourg.

Indrani Roy
Linguist by training, Indrani Roy is an independent consultant who has worked in diverse fields like software, education and electronic media. Her work has involved applying Linguistics to various domains such as education, software development, user experience and localisation.

Ishmael Irungu Munene
Prof Ishmael I. Munene's expertise is in African higher education, education in Africa, higher education (governance, globalisation, and marketisation), education research methods, and the general field of African Studies. His university teaching experience includes New York, Florida, and Kenya. He has been a Carnegie African Diaspora Scholar at universities in Africa and has served as the Executive Secretary of the African Studies and Research Forum.

Pauline Rose
Prof Pauline Rose joined Cambridge University in February 2014 as a Professor of International Education, where she is the Director of Research for Equitable Access and Learning (REAL) Centre in the Faculty of Education. She is also a Senior Research Fellow at the UK Department for International Development. Prior to joining Cambridge, Pauline was Director of the EFA Global Monitoring Report (since August 2011) during which time she directed two reports on youth, skills, and work, and on teaching and learning. Before becoming Director, she worked as a Senior Policy Analyst

with the team for three years, leading the research for three reports on the themes of governance, marginalisation, and conflict. Before joining the EFA Global Monitoring Report, Pauline was a Reader in international education and development at the University of Sussex.

Ricardo Sabates

Development Economist with 15 years of experience working in areas of educational inequalities mostly in the context of international development. An academic since 2002, started at the Institute of Education London as a research fellow (then senior research fellow) at the Centre for Research on the Wider Benefits of Learning. In 2008 moved to the Department of Education, University of Sussex as a Senior Lecturer (later Reader) where he led the MA programme in Education and International Development (2010-2012). During 2012 to 2014 lived in Rwanda and continued to undertake research in educational inequalities for the Centre for International Education, University of Sussex.

He is currently Deputy Director of Research at the Faculty of Education.

ACKNOWLEDGEMENT

We would like to express our sincere gratitude to all the authors for taking the time to present their abstracts during the 2021 PAL Network conference and sharing their complete papers with us. This publication would not be a success without your invaluable contribution. We would also like to acknowledge all reviewers who went through each paper and shared feedback with the authors for consideration. Your insights and feedback were instrumental in shaping this work.